# CHRISTOPHER LLOYD'S
# GARDENING YEAR

# CHRISTOPHER LLOYD'S
# GARDENING YEAR

Photographs by Jonathan Buckley

FRANCES LINCOLN

Frances Lincoln Limited
4 Torriano Mews
Torriano Avenue
London NW5 2RZ

British Library Cataloguing in Publication Data
A catalogue record for this book is available
from the British Library.
ISBN 0 7112 1533 2
1 3 5 7 9 8 6 4 2

Printed and bound by Conti Tipocolor srl, Italy

HALF TITLE The front entrance path at Great Dixter, with
*Camassia cusickii*

TITLE Topiary peoples the garden and creates its own
atmosphere

RIGHT, CLOCKWISE FROM TOP LEFT Helichrysum drying in the
porch for winter decoration; winter-flowering *Mahonia japonica*
with winter-ripening *Aucuba japonica* f. *longifolia*; 'Emperor'
daffodils and spring blossom in the orchard; *Dahlia* 'David
Howard' and *Canna* 'Wyoming'

# Contents

# Introduction

Before launching into my gardening year, month by month, I have a clear duty to explain who I am, where I live and why I should be writing about my garden at all. In fact, I have been writing about it for many years, since it has been my main quarry for innumerable gardening articles, started in 1952. I have been writing in every issue of the weekly magazine *Country Life* since 1963, am currently doing a weekly piece for the *Guardian*, and also contribute frequently to America's *Horticulture* magazine and to the Royal Horticultural Society's journal, *The Garden*. And there are other occasional commitments. In fact it's hard to get away from me, my trouble being that I like writing. I don't know how many books I have clocked up – quite a large number, of which I consider *The Well-Tempered Garden* to be seminal.

My mother was a tremendous reader of the classics and reading aloud was an experience I was brought up with, first she to me; later I to her. When we were away at boarding school, it was insisted that each of us wrote home weekly and she did quite as much or more by us. I was also lucky, between the ages of ten and thirteen, to have an excellent English teacher at school, Morgan Shelby, who gave me a thorough grounding in grammar (sadly lacking in most teaching) and in the writing of essays. Reading and writing became second nature.

I am one of those once common, now rare, people who still, near the end of his long life (seventy-eight years, to date) lives in the house where he was born – it wasn't normal to be born in hospital, in those days.

My parents bought Dixter, as it was then called and as I always think of it (they added the Great to distinguish it more certainly from neighbouring Little Dixter, which they also bought), in 1910. My father engaged Edwin Lutyens to make the restorations and additions and to design the garden.

Dixter, a manor house, is a large timber-framed building constructed around 1460 and situated in the high weald. The weald of Kent and Sussex lies between the chalk of the North and South Downs, in south-east England, and the high weald is the centre part of this area. Luckily for us, Dixter was

LEFT Spring in the sunk garden
ABOVE RIGHT The sunk garden in 1922

sited on a south-west-facing slope 55m/180ft above sea level (the sea being some ten miles distant), and although not very high it is near the top of its hill and commands all-round views (once you have stepped outside the garden) in every direction except east. The land slopes down to the Rother valley; the River Rother itself, which here forms the boundary between Sussex and Kent (we being in Sussex) was tidal as I first remember it. The valley, as is the way of valleys, attracts frost and fog. It is marvellous to be perched above all that. On the other hand we are, or were, exposed to wind from most directions. Wind is a great enemy to gardening, and we have blithely planted out our views with trees and hedges so that wind damage has been considerably mitigated. I even planted a few Leyland cypresses on our south-west boundary, from which the fiercest winds blow, as a bulwark to defend our nursery area, where there is much glass. Yet we are still close enough to the sea to experience a markedly milder climate than, say, Sissinghurst Castle, which also stands on a hill and is only eleven miles distant by road, but is just that much further inland to register a palpable climatic difference.

The whole of the weald (German: *Wald*, a wood, has the same stem) was once covered by oak forest (it is still well wooded and the woods are crammed with primroses, anemones and bluebells in the spring). There is little suitable building stone just where we are, so nearly all the houses were built of oak, infilled with lath and plaster. Those of any size, belonging to our period, were hall houses. Our great hall is a large room made for communal living, open from floor to roof and from outside wall to outside wall. The large oak beam tying these walls is 10m/35ft long. But when, in Tudor times, the fashion changed to smaller rooms and greater privacy, our hall (with all others like it) was filled in with extra floors and numerous partitions.

Other rooms were similarly treated. Lutyens restored the building to the *status quo ante* as far as was reasonable for a more comfortable and modern style of living and without resorting to too much guesswork where the evidence was no longer extant. This lost the building much floor space, so two principal additions were made. Another, smaller, hall house, dated about 1500, was to be destroyed by its owner at Benenden, nine miles distant. My father bought it for £75; its beams were all numbered, it was taken down stick by stick, moved to Dixter and re-erected. The other new wing built on was entirely of Lutyens's design, but working in the vernacular so as to marry discreetly with the original.

There was virtually no garden at Dixter in 1910. The property had in any case been on the agent's books for the past ten years – as 'an agricultural property with farmhouse attached' – and was occupied only by a summer tenant during that period. There were two mixed orchards – the trees planted along ridges which show that the land had been ploughed in medieval times – and a few odd trees besides. A bay laurel, a wild pear and a fig survive. But there were farm buildings – a barn (possibly as old as Dixter itself) and oast house alongside (dating from around 1890), a thatched (now shingled) stable unit, and cow houses, locally known as hovels. Also two round and two rectangular brick cattle drinking tanks. These were ornamental; Lutyens saw how valuable they would be as framework to and ingredients in a new garden, so they were all worked into his design.

The gardens lie around the house, which is roughly in their centre, so that you have only to walk around the building to have made the garden circuit. It is a satisfyingly intimate arrangement. If you want to dash out to pick some *Iris unguicularis* buds or some sprigs of witch hazel or a bunch of lilies-of-the-valley or a last-minute lettuce or bowl of raspberries, you can choose an exit so that nothing is far from your starting point.

Lutyens designed the garden walls and how the hedges should run, which is not in the least stodgy or predictable. My father had a great interest in topiary and he oversaw the planting, training and care of the yew and box hedges and of the many topiary pieces. Based on his experiences, mainly gained at Dixter, he wrote and illustrated a book that has lately been republished, with some extra photographs: *Garden Craftsmanship in Yew and Box*. It first came out in 1923, but is still a most useful practical guide. In later editions of *The English Flower Garden*, William Robinson, who loathed topiary, made a snide reference to its use in Northiam (our village), for it was also notable at Brickwall, a house at the other end of the village.

My father was originally a colour printer and founded his business, Nathaniel Lloyd and Co., in Blackfriars. But he gave this up on coming to live at Dixter (he was forty-four in 1910) and trained himself to be an architect (in a small way) and, more importantly, an architectural historian and also a photographer of buildings. Two of his major works are still in print.

Apart from the topiary, his main contribution to the gardens was the sunk garden, made in 1923. It has an octagonal pool (two opposite sides are longer than the other six, which makes it look relaxed) surrounded by flagstone paving; then dry walling up to grass slopes (beasts to mow), and so to the garden's main level, the framework being barns on two sides, a Lutyens wall on the third and a yew hedge on the fourth.

Typical Lutyens work at Dixter

Originally there was just a farm track across this area. It is a scene of great repose: wherever you stand there is a pleasing prospect across to the other side. The area is not vast and visitors relate easily to it. 'If I could have just one piece of your garden it would be this,' they tell me, forgetting that there has to be a considerable back-up area to serve it. The gardens throughout consist of mixed borders where annuals and bedding plants are worked in (rather than given beds to themselves) among shrubs and perennials. These plants need to be raised behind the scenes.

With his architect's eye for strong design, my father originally planted the four corners of the quadrangular barn garden (above and surrounding the sunk garden) with *Yucca gloriosa*. And the corner bed surrounding each yucca was planted with bearded irises. The theme was of spear and sword leaves. My mother, who was my great gardening influence and inspiration, was a plantswoman. She loved plants for their own sake. She did not love the yuccas, because of the danger to her children (six of us) and to everyone else from those sharp points. After my father died in 1933, the yuccas went. She replaced them with four *Malus sargentii*, having fallen for them at a Chelsea Flower Show. This is seldom a sound basis for an important choice. The shrubs grew very large. They had no particular shape, their fruits were minute, and so they gave only a week of pleasure in the year and made no kind of unifying impact in their important positions.

She didn't like me for replacing them, in 1950, with *Osmanthus delavayi* (from Marchant's, in Dorset), but she did come to like the replacements very much indeed. Apart from their April flowering, they are comely evergreen shrubs (clipped annually) with neat little leaves, but I have to admit that, year-round, *Yucca gloriosa*, properly looked after with its dead leaves pulled off, would look better. I would not reinstate the irises. The bearded kinds look sordid for too much of the year, and there is no way to disguise them, as their rhizomes require a summer baking. My mother doted on irises and used to accept gifts of bearded varieties which, in bloom, swept her off her feet. This made me cross, and I made her grow them in spare corners where they did not interfere with the garden proper. (Your own children can become dictators, when power comes their way.)

When you have two strong-willed people working in the same garden (my mother died in 1972 and was active till the last ten days of her ninety-one years) there are sure

ABOVE LEFT  My mother and me by the aubretia wall
RIGHT  The sunk garden with my father's octagonal pool

to be many clashes, and there were. But, as we loved each other, our shared pleasures in the garden were by far the strongest element in this partnership.

Gertrude Jekyll never had anything to do with the planting of the garden although my parents did visit her at Munstead Wood on at least two occasions, and I, as a small boy, very much impressed, was there on one of them. Miss Jekyll blessed me and hoped that I would grow up to be a great gardener. The original planting of our borders was planned by Sir George Thorold, a member of the old Lincolnshire family. Clearly he was under the Jekyll influence – witness large corner blocks of *Bergenia* (at that time *Megasea*) *cordifolia*. However, my mother's gardening bible was *The English Flower Garden*, and never mind what Robinson thought about topiary. Our battered, back-broken edition, with 'N. Lloyd' inscribed on the first page in my father's hand, was published in 1906 (my parents were married in 1905) and it is larded with bookmarks.

My mother's taste for wild gardening in rough grass was probably derived from Robinson, and also the manner of planting that he recommended. Our orchard, adjoining the long border (I love that conjunction of highly organized border and tall meadow grasses with just a path and a strip of mown grass dividing them), was planted with such daffodils and narcissi as were fashionable at that time (other gardens including the same varieties can be dated as of the same period). Robinson wrote proudly of his own plantings that they throve and that 'the flowers are large and

Red valerian in the upper terrace wall above the upper moat meadow

handsome, and in most cases have not diminished in size'. By modern standards, the flowers were of modest proportions (perhaps he would have disliked the modern monsters as much as I do), and so they are at Dixter in the orchard. What is so pleasing here is that perhaps only one third of the area is planted up with daffodils. The rest is left as fine turf, wherein earlier-flowering snowdrops and crocuses also find a place. So there is no feeling of overcrowding or showing off.

But the main fun my mother had with meadow gardening was elsewhere. The upper moat, drained on our arrival to form a piece of turf in the shape of a bath, was her principal scene of action in the early days. Here she started growing snakeshead fritillaries, *Fritillaria meleagris*, which she used to raise from seed sown in boxes, pricked out into more boxes and then planted out with a bulb planter (a marvellous implement still going strong) and a trugful of potting soil. She also established, here, polyanthus that had previously been used for spring bedding. They have lasted so well that they form an interesting record of the appearance of these florists' flowers eighty and more years ago. I remember her adding *Anemone apennina* to her tapestry, and many more things, including *Orchis mascula*. There were no narcissi here at all. Nor any of the coarse hybrids in the meadow garden front of the house, but here is the main concentration of Lent lilies, *Narcissus pseudonarcissus*, of which she was originally given stock from Beckley or Peasmarsh, only a few miles distant from Northiam, where they grow wild. I suspect that they came from the garden of a close friend, Molly Liddell, at Place House, Peasmarsh. From small beginnings my mother increased them from seed and after that they sowed themselves. We subsequently started North American camassias, with racemes of blue stars, and have had particular success with *Camassia quamash*, a deep blue one of moderate height, which both self-sows and clumps up. This is what naturalizing is all about. This meadow flanks the front path on either side as you approach the porch and many visitors, since it is surrounded by trim yew hedges, think that lawns must have become neglected from shortage of labour, whereas actually wild gardening was intended here from the first.

There is another small meadow area, similarly puzzling to the public, which goes right up to the south-east end of the house. Planted with lilacs, it is notable chiefly for its display of goldilocks, *Ranunculus auricomus* – which is a small, early-flowering buttercup – lady's smock and wood anemones. No one wittingly introduced them but they could hardly be improved upon. We call this the cats' garden, because in the old days the kitchen cats had their stronghold in the boiler house, here.

The area round the horse pond, including the pond itself, was originally iron ore workings made when the local iron industry flourished. The excavations terminated at a steep bank, on which my brother Oliver planted birch and aspen saplings collected from one of our woods in the 1930s. Between this and the approach drive, called the forstal, are a few sixty-year-old oaks which were seedlings self-sown at a time when, following my father's death, this area was neglected and filled with brambles, broom and rabbits. We subsequently cleaned it up and I have planted rhododendrons (they are none too happy), as well as smaller things that enjoy some shade.

The horse pond is so called because the farm horses used to be led into it to drink and wallow at the end of their working day. It is a water garden now, and the grassy banks overlooking it are a particularly pleasant place of relaxation where I and my less formal friends (the majority) like to bring our coffee after lunch and enjoy the busy life that is conducted in and around a pond by birds, fish, snakes, frogs, toads, insects and other forms of life. Unfortunately, of late, with so many visitors surging into the gardens when we open at 2 p.m., the horse pond has become a rather too populous area to relax by (I like to doze). There are a few relic heathers, *Calluna vulgaris*, here, improbably reaching out over the pond. My father planted two large patches of them and of gorse, which he called whins, from habit. His mother was a Scot and he was brought up in Scotland.

My own interest in gardening goes back as far as I can remember, and it was encouraged by both my parents. In 1947, after demobilization, I studied horticulture at Wye College (University of London) in Kent and took a degree. Then I spent the next four years teaching there, after Miss Page, the lecturer in decorative (now called 'amenity', of all horrible words) horticulture, fell seriously ill. Those seven years gave me just the scientific and practical training I needed to make me feel at home in my subject. Wye is only twenty-five miles from Dixter, so I was able to spend one or two days a week in my garden through this period, while leaving my mother a list of instructions for the days when I was away. In the meantime my brother Quentin, whose home was Little Dixter, looked after the estate and all matters pertaining to

opening to the public. He died in 1995 and I now have a business manager.

In 1954 I returned home for good and started a nursery devoted to the kinds of plants, many of them unusual, which I like to grow in the garden. Most sales are to visitors on the spot, but mail orders account for a small part of the business. I never intended it to become the tail that wags the dog, because enjoyment of a business of this kind arises

from being able to handle much of it yourself, with all the personal contacts with like-minded people that this entails. Many of my friends have been made in this way or from talking to visitors in the garden and it has been a rewarding life. However, in my old age, I have relinquished the handling of the nursery business side, and that is quite a relief.

An all-important change and improvement in the fortunes of Dixter came about when Fergus Garrett became head gardener. Till then, many areas in our labour-intensive garden were semi-neglected. I could see what needed doing to them and did what I could myself, but there was insufficient dynamism − or staff − to do the job really thoroughly.

I first met Fergus in 1988 when, aged twenty-two, he was one of a party of visiting second-year students from Wye College, where he had switched from agriculture to horticulture. We soon became firm friends and he visited often. After achieving a good honours degree, he worked here and there − at Beth Chatto's, then in the south of France and in Switzerland, always preferring the practical side of our subject, although an excellent organizer, too. He didn't want to live permanently abroad and returned to England in 1992. His mother is Turkish and Turkish is his first language as his early years

Looking through the gothic framework of the porch

were spent in Turkey, but his and his elder brother's schooling was in Brighton, where he still has dear friends.

After he'd been happily casting around a while, I rather belatedly had the bright idea of asking him to be my head gardener – I'd done without one for a number of years. Fergus hesitated but at last became enthusiastic and started with me just before his twenty-seventh birthday in February 1993.

He is ready to undertake anything and my earliest wish was to transform the rose garden – first by getting rid of the roses. The noise of tearing old rose roots as they were being exhumed was music to my ears. Lutyens designed this area as a rose garden on the site of an old cattle yard, and it had remained basically unchanged for nearly eighty years – surely long enough.

Because of replant disease, you cannot replace rose bushes that have weakened or that you've got tired of with other roses, unless you first change the soil they'll be growing in. Otherwise the replants will either falter or fail. This requirement is a great imposition. There is no replacement soil handy. In any case I do not like monocultures. Not only do they encourage the pests and diseases of that plant to move in and have a field day, but a lot of roses together don't seem to me to add up, even at their best. They are blobby and without style and for much of the year the bushes themselves are undisguisably ugly. Vicious too; I always pruned them myself. Besides which, this is the hottest spot in the garden, in summer, and roses wilt in the heat.

It seemed to me ideal, however, for luxuriant plants that would, for two or three months each summer, give a tropical feel (some, in fact, are perfectly hardy, but still look exotic). It has become the exotic garden (though I habitually refer to it, to Fergus, as the old rose garden). From 1994 on, we've had the whale of a time there and most visitors love it (some, of course, disapprove and some think I'm mad). It is a wonderful opportunity for experimenting. There are so many tender plants, assumed to be year-round conservatory inmates, which no one has experimented with on a summer outing, so that's what we're up to and have built two extra bits of greenhouse to house the plants in winter.

The principal change in the nursery and sales area is that it is now used far more intensively and economically, in terms of space and that a wider range of plants is grown in larger pots. Both Kathleen Leighton and Michael Morphy work here full-time and Brenda Common attends to sales for much of the time from spring to autumn.

I am constantly being asked (additionally to 'How many do you have working for you?') what's new this year. My mind goes blank. I never think in terms of novelty but of course I enjoy working out fresh ideas or approaches and so does Fergus. He, for instance, looking at stock beds in the garden where plants were in rows, queried our growing them like that. After all, we didn't use machinery in the rows, so why not arrange the plantings informally, so that they looked nice? So we've been doing that, first to one plot, then to another, and that's been great, like having the bonus of a new area of garden to play with. It has enabled us to have large groupings and to try out different combinations.

Some areas, where the clay (we are on Wadhurst clay) is near the surface, he has taken in hand in a big way, draining, where necessary, and adding masses of grit and organic compost, with deep cultivations – by hand! The change in plant performance needs to be seen to be believed.

Both of us are keen that the garden should continue to be lively and full of interest and colour long after the middle of August, when there is a perceptible falling off unless you're watching out for it. So we plan to have the garden looking beautiful in the golden light of autumn and right up to the end of October, when we finally close to the public. This means two things. We are still making new plantings for the current season right into September and we cannot begin to house tender plants or make preparations for the spring (we are both passionate about tulips) until late autumn, which puts considerable pressures on us as the days shorten and the weather deteriorates. Never mind; we do it.

As staunch a member of my staff as Fergus is Perry Rodriguez, who started at Dixter a couple of months before Fergus. If anything goes wrong, indoors or out, Perry is the man to turn to. The growing of vegetables was assigned to him, although he had no previous experience in this. But he took to it at once, reading up what he didn't know, and I have never had better vegetables and salads, in a wide range. Perry makes notes of sowing dates, which is so useful for comparison from year to year and also helps me when I want to write on the subject. There are three other permanent members of staff and we do have quite a few extras, from time to time – volunteers, mainly. Fergus is excellent at both picking and managing them and we are a remarkably happy team.

A novelty in 1998 was the mosaic and paving installed in the wall garden, to replace a boring central rectangle of lawn. The mosaic was designed, off the cuff, by a friend, Miles Johnson, when he was spending the weekend here. He thought of a design relevant to Dixter and portrayed my two dachshunds, Dahlia and Canna, lying end to end on their backs, looking very relaxed. We found the right people to install this – Maggie Howarth from Lancashire and her assistant Mark Davidson from New Zealand. They've done a splendid job. The borders round it have doubled in personality. I really enjoy going into that garden, now, instead of thinking of it mainly as a passage.

The number of paying visitors has increased with the years, which helps us financially but imposes its own pressures. Like others in our position, we wish they spread themselves more evenly over the open season. We can only marginally bring that about by ensuring that the gardens are worth visiting in spring and autumn, as much as in the popular summer period. But that is a challenge that we enjoy meeting and we love the demands and rewards of a high-maintenance garden, which this

With Fergus in the long border

certainly is. We are plantsmen, loving plants for their own sake as well as thinking out effective ways to use them.

As to changes to the garden's overall design, I am not tempted to make any; the original bones were so sound and satisfying. My great good fortune is in having been able to make my home into a going business concern. I have never had to commute to work. What happens after me is something I refuse to worry about. If I have done what I can for Dixter in my lifetime, that is enough for me. I only want to concern myself about the future to the extent of making it easier for my niece, Olivia, who will inherit, to take over. Since she lives abroad, it seems unlikely that she will want or be able to live at Dixter. She must make provisions for it as she sees fit. What the public currently appreciate about it most, perhaps, is that it is so evidently a home, not an institution. I am asked if I don't rattle about on my own, here. Not in the least. I fill the house perfectly, taking up more or less space and changing which rooms I occupy according to the season, summer or winter, open to the public or closed. And I am visited by plenty of friends and relations, for whom I enjoy cooking.

I think of this book as the record of an oasis – a particularly happy period in its long existence. If readers can identify with that, I shall have achieved my aim.

January

This is, or should be, the coldest month. Everyone expects to see snow pictures and when we do have snow, the sound from a nearby field of children enjoying the slide (often on plastic fertilizer sacks, sometimes on toboggans) down a steep slope continues all day long. At the first hint of snow, the school shuts down, in case a teacher cannot reach it, so the children are gloriously free.

Dixter is rich in topiary and that always looks extra-comical when the dark figures, especially the 'peacocks', are snow-capped. Caps of snow also suit the sere remains of perennials that we deliberately refrain from cutting down in autumn: lofty cardoons are the most prominent, but there are also such as sedums and yarrows. All the dark evergreens come into their own, by way of contrast to the dazzling white, and not least among these are the self-sown ivies clambering up our more or less threadbare deciduous trees, in particular the ashes. Ash trees' branches are thick right to the black bud tips of their smallest twigs. The wind soughs in them to a hollow tune, but they are never dense. Much light filters through, even at midsummer, so they are the wild ivies' favourite hosts.

Hoar frost brings out the photographers. It may accumulate through days of freezing fog. When the fog clears and the sun shines through, there is a rush to seize the moment on film. It is good to have the record, because an hour or two of sunshine ruins everything – if that is the way you look at thaw. Personally, I love a thaw if it is sudden and thorough and follows a long period of frost by day as well as night. Snow is exciting when it first falls, but soon tarnishes. My dogs seek out areas, especially under the bay, where it is thin on the ground and they can perform their usual functions.

Unless the paths are quickly cleared, snow soon packs down and freezes, becoming slithery. It weighs down the looser evergreens, like my soft cones of *Chamaecyparis thyoides* 'Ericoides'. They are easily and irremediably opened out, never quite returning to normal. One should be out there, beating their branches with a stick, while the snow is falling, even in a blizzard, even in the night, to prevent this weight from accumulating. No one is keen on this job. The need will probably arise at the weekend, anyway, when most crises beset us and there's only myself to cope. Skip it. The older I get, the more I enjoy home comforts (I'll return to them).

A slow thaw is better than nothing, though disappointing. Patches of snow that have drifted and are deeper than elsewhere refuse to depart. 'Waiting for more' is the old saying, and it is often true. There is a return of the cold, with more snow. Those persistent anticyclones that take up their positions over Scandinavia or south of Greenland are the culprits and they have a way of continually renewing themselves. However, a full-throated thaw, with all the drains gurgling, is a great event. It is usually accompanied by chilling fog, as warm air meets frozen ground, but in time the warm air wins and there is a general mood of relaxation.

PAGES 18–19 *Miscanthus sinensis* 'Silver Feather' in the high garden

The reality of January, in east Sussex, most often has nothing to do with frost or snow. There are days and days of heavy, overcast weather – Beth Chatto's 'dustbin lid' – that just broods over you and weighs down your spirits. Or there is a seemingly endless succession of gales and driving rain. Now and again, there is a day's interlude, when the wind drops, the sun shines and you can feel it on your back, through your clothes. That is bliss and everyone cheers up.

In a wet winter and on our clay soil, the persistent garden problem is drainage. Whatever we do, we're never on top of it for long. It keeps recurring, usually in the same problem places. Luckily we're on a slope; even so, drain piping can never be laid deep, as the surface water simply will not reach it but will swim about near the surface.

This quickly becomes alarming, because many tree and shrub roots will die of asphyxiation, if the normal soil air spaces, kept open by earthworms, are clogged up. Yews are particularly sensitive. I have not forgotten losing a considerable stretch of yew hedging, in the ultra-wet winter of 1960. My father knew of the danger and laid 5cm/2in tile drains along the length and down the centre of every hedge, before it was planted. But they soon clogged up. All drains do, even the modern perforated plastic pipes which we are currently using. We surround them, above, below and at the sides, with a good layer of sea shingle or coarser pebbles, to delay the penetration of sludge to the pipe.

In meadow areas or beneath paths, the pipes are laid a mere 20cm/8in deep, but on cultivated ground, where a spade needs to be able to delve a good way down without fouling anything, the depth is 30cm/1ft or more.

In some places, badger excavations foil our drainage plans. There's a principal ditch between us and our neighbours, but badgers will dig bypasses so that the water is diverted into the long border instead of continuing along its official channel. I know that badgers are fascinating animals, but there are so many of them, these days. The results of their daily nocturnal excavations are everywhere apparent. They have areas where they regularly dig holes in which to defecate. Most of these are in meadow areas and instead of fine turf these are turned into coarse, second-rate vegetation largely invaded by hogweed. The badgers have a regular track across the long border and they like to dig near it, probably for worms or beetles, but they turn up plants (especially achilleas) with monotonous regularity. We try to deflect them with a row of mini-hurdles. In the summer, they are death to underground wasps' nests and totally oblivious to their stings. Perhaps that is the reason for the wasps' increasing tendency to nest in roofs, walls and straw stacks.

## Evergreens

Gardening literature will always emphasize the importance of evergreens, in a garden, as something to look at in the winter. True, but there are evergreens and evergreens. Some of them look pretty battered or threadbare by January – *Eucryphia* x *nymansensis* 'Nymansay', for instance. It is a reluctant evergreen anyway, losing half its leaves in autumn. There are others like this, usually of hybrid origin, with one evergreen parent, one deciduous. *Viburnum* x *burkwoodii* is another example. The June- to autumn-flowering honeysuckle *Lonicera japonica* 'Halliana' often has its evergreenery quoted on its behalf as a reason for planting it, but it looks so shabby in winter that one wishes it would lose its leaves.

Bamboos are technically all evergreen, but the one bamboo genus that is truly handsome through to spring is *Phyllostachys*, and I have a lot of that (its bad moment comes in early summer when, however, there are plenty of distractions). Too many evergreens in a garden make it look heavy in the summer and I possibly need fewer of them as background material because of our extensive yew hedging. But phyllostachys are feathery in growth and a light shade of green so, in fact, they contrast admirably with yews, and I have placed a specimen of *P. nigra* (offshoot from an old colony in Sheffield Park gardens) as foreground to a big architectural arrangement of yew, where two curved hedges and a yew archway join up with the big yew (colloquially known among us as Big Dick) which was the free-standing tree already at Dixter on the Lloyd family's arrival. My father cut it back and trained it into a topiary specimen. Behind these heavyweights, the architecture of the house makes another bold statement, so the bamboo acts as light relief. All this can best be viewed from the steps that rise from the orchard garden to the high garden.

In the high garden itself, straight paths form a cross and there is a square, paved area which provides a resting point (while you decide which way to turn) where they meet. It was originally planted around with wishy-washy (neither pink nor blue) bun-headed hydrangeas – 'Madame R. Riverain' – watered every day from cans by a garden boy, in summer, his task also including the many tub-grown hydrangeas (Lutyens-designed oak tubs; they were lovely).

I have made this a fairly important centrepiece with a preponderance of evergreens. Not all the same evergreen; that makes you a hostage to fortune, when one of them fails and unity is destroyed. Besides, the very concept of strict unity seems out of tune with the free-and-easy atmosphere of Dixter. But there is a feeling of solidity using different units, largely conifers. In fact, I (unofficially) call it conifer corner. One of the 'conifers' is *Hebe cupressoides* 'Boughton Dome', a witch's broom sport from the species which Valerie Finnis spotted in a Scottish garden. She named it after the shape of the dome at Boughton House (in the Dower House of which she lives) in Northamptonshire. It looks like a conifer and, curiously, has an aroma of cedar that you catch in passing. Unfortunately (or fortunately) nothing is for ever and my plant, which was the largest specimen I have seen, has developed a die-back, which afflicts first one branch, then a neighbouring couple *und so wieder*. These afflictions are caused by a soil-borne fungus and they are not uncommon. I lost a prostrate juniper in the sunk garden, this way (another remains). We seem to be able to arrest the disease's progress by drenching the soil with systemic fungicide from time to time, but the hebe's days are clearly numbered. Nothing will grow in the hole that has been opened up, but we can jump into it and treat it as a pulpit when addressing a large party of visitors, fitting tightly into the square arena.

The high garden, I tell them, is of a design commonly in use in Edwardian times where it was an ornamental part of the kitchen garden. Narrow flower borders lined the sides of the paths. Behind them were espalier and cordon fruit ('Doyenné du Comice' pears in our case), then the mundane vegetables, whose presence was concealed in so far as possible.

Another feature in this square is a large, thick-pencil-shaped *Chamaecyparis lawsoniana* 'Ellwood's Gold' – only noticeably golden on its young shoots in spring. It was given me as a baby by Tom Wright, when he was teaching at Pershore College in the West Midlands. It seemed a ridiculous pygmy, at that time, but how it has grown. I should like it to last me out but am not the sort to indulge in prolonged grief if replacement becomes necessary.

Then the two 1.8m/6ft cones, now growing into each other but still individuals, of *Chamaecyparis thyoides* 'Ericoides', whose soft texture I mentioned in connection with snow damage. And on that account, this is the second pair I have grown in this position and we have taken cuttings with a view to having further replacements in the probably not-too-distant future. The softness of these and many other man-selected conifers is on account of all their foliage being of the juvenile type, retained in

The bamboo *Phyllostachys nigra* softens the architectural outlines of house and hedge and Big Dick

these cases right through their lives. It gives them an attractive featheriness. The normal summer colouring is sea green, but this changes to rich purple in autumn. By now, however (and, I always feel, prematurely, but nothing can reverse the reaction), the colour has changed most of the way back to green.

In front of this pair is a planting of the inestimable *Helichrysum splendidum*, which is one of the few ever-grey shrubs that does not look depressed beneath grey winter's skies. Its stiffly upright shoots terminate in a loose rosette of small leaves. The success or failure of this little shrub (I never let it exceed a height of 60cm/2ft) depends entirely on its being regularly hard-pruned back each spring. The result looks crude at the time but comeliness is soon restored and no flowering occurs. The mingy little yellow flower heads could attract nobody. And a no-pruning treatment results in a scraggy shrub.

Next to this group is the contrasting *Thuja occidentalis* 'Rheingold', which is a 1.8m/6ft cone of burnished golden yellow in winter. This is its best season, but it never lets you down. I have a dark background for it in the almost too widely planted *Prunus laurocerasus* 'Otto Luyken' – described as motorway stuff, by one friend. But you should never allow snobbishness to deter you from growing a good plant. This is a compact cherry laurel of rather upright habit, with rich green, highly glossy and sharply pointed oval leaves. In a border setting, its growth needs to be controlled, from time to time, but not so frequently as to make it look a characterless dumpling. A hard cut-back once in seven years or so will do the trick. The white flowers are borne on loose spikes, both in spring and again in autumn, after which you can give just an annual tidying, by removing the flowered shoots.

On the next corner, a deciduous shrub makes a change: it is the lime-green-leaved form of a native currant, *Ribes alpinum* 'Aureum'. A dense and exceedingly twiggy 1.5m/5ft shrub, it has great character, especially in winter. Never believe that it is only the evergreens among shrubs that provide winter interest.

On the 'Boughton Dome' corner, the back-up feature is a silver fir, *Abies koreana* – my second of this species, because I am liable to grow a tree where there is no space for it in maturity. I enjoy it as a juvenile and then cast it out, wasting no sentiment over the loss. The reason for this fir's being so popular is that its dwarf form cones, or is expected to cone, as quite a baby. The cones are tubby upright candles borne on the upper side of horizontal lateral branches and on quite minuscule specimens. They vary in colour, sometimes dove mauve, sometimes (if you are lucky) navy blue. All *A. koreana* are seedlings, so there is a good deal of variation.

I had not appreciated a snag. The dwarf form of *A. koreana* comes from an island separate from the Korean mainland. On the latter, this species assumes the stature of a normal, fast-growing tree. You might easily, without knowing, purchase a seedling of the vigorous type, which is just what happened to me. My tree has shot up and coned very little. In its way, I like the shapeliness a lot, though the pleasure given is of quite a different order from that planned. Oh well. I suppose it will have to go soon and I can try again.

## The bay laurel

The most important evergreen on this property is the bay laurel, *Laurus nobilis*, alongside the front path as you approach the house on foot. I don't know its age. It was there before 1910 and you cannot cut it down and count the rings as it is, basically, a multi-stemmed shrub, though of tree-like proportions and some 6m/20ft high. Bay green is descriptive of a colour – a singularly warm shade without any hint of blue, but, rather, of yellow. This is emphasized in winter sunlight, when we appreciate the bay most.

Its branches are highly flexible and get weighed to the ground if there is a heavy fall of snow. It always reminds me of Ernest Shepard's drawings of Eeyore getting snowed under, in the first chapter of *The House at Pooh Corner*. But the branches bounce back. Prolonged, hard frost can be a problem. At the end of a really hard winter, the tree will turn brown and look dead. The temptation is to cut it right down, and to wait for re-growth from the base. This will surely come, but it will be so soft and sappy that the hazards to it in the next winter will be greatly increased. Don't be in a hurry, but do make a start, in the spring, by cutting branches cleanly back to quite thick wood. Then wait, patiently, and by early July (no sooner) you will see tiny sprouts of young growth buds appearing out of the old wood.

The bay tree flowers, briefly but beautifully, most years in early May – an abundance of pale yellow blossom lining the young shoots, and wafting an etherealized bay fragrance if the air is warm and damp. In our case, almost the entire display is created by stamens, as we have a male tree. Our neighbours have females and these ripen fruit, which is black and looks rather like a small damson. It must be agreeable to birds as we often find bird-sown seedlings in this garden. Otherwise we propagate from cuttings.

The leaves are highly aromatic and useful (though in moderation) for flavouring stocks and stews and a delicious dish made with morello cherries (see Jane Grigson's *Fruit Book*). When branches snap off, they are joyfully put on my fire. The smell from bay-leaf smoke is intense and satisfying. The leaves being large, the blisters that form on them as they heat are large and resound, as they burst, in a loud cannonade (which Canna loathes and Dahlia hardly notices). Yew leaves, being small, make much less noise and pine needles more of a hissing than explosions.

A bay tree's branches would normally reach to the ground, but my mother had the lowest, up to a height of 90cm/3ft or so, removed, so that she could garden this extra space, and it is the focus of her principal planting of *Cyclamen hederifolium*. Its foliage is a feature from autumn to spring, and the fact that it is excessively dry, here, in summer, matters not at all, as the tubers are dormant then. It is also a good site, I find, for crocuses, especially the autumn-flowering *Crocus speciosus*. That is dormant in summer, too, and its flowering may be delayed if the autumn is dry, but who cares? If I want to accelerate it, I can irrigate the bay, and quite often do.

## Evergreen perennials

This is where I should wax lyrical on winter colour in bergenia foliage, their beautiful shades of beetroot and red and the proud carriage and outlines of the best varieties. Alas, they hate me. I don't mean that I cannot grow them – it would be almost impossible to kill one – but that their sombre, slug-hole-riddled, leather leaves are very far from making a joyful winter contribution. The only one that achieves a hint of self-respect is *Bergenia purpurascens*. I like its cheeky, prick-eared habit and its abundant May flowering on good long stems.

Phormiums border on tenderness but *Phormium cookianum* 'Tricolor' is flatteringly foolproof. Its arching leaves have narrow purple margins and are striped alternately in green and cream, at different widths, within. It looks as great at winter's end as at the start and will become quite exciting in early summer when it puts up flowering stems, which it regularly does. It then rises from 1 metre to nearly 2 (3ft to 6ft).

My other phormium is the 1.5m/5ft 'Sundowner', in which bands of pink are the notable feature, along with cream and green, the margins purple, again. That is far less hardy, but may survive a mild winter without any damage. In spring, it'll want tidying up. When phormiums become large and thick and difficult to keep looking pristine, they really need replanting, but this is a mammoth task. I don't blame anyone for shirking it. Furthermore, they always sulk for a year, even following a spring disturbance, which is the safest.

Some of the evergreen ferns remain great allies through the dark months, notably the rather lacy-leaved form of *Polypodium interjectum* called 'Cornubiense'. Only 23cm/9in or so tall, its slowly creeping habit becomes a mat and its vivid green colouring is especially welcome just now. I have moved some of this alongside my hermaphrodite form of butcher's broom, *Ruscus aculeatus*, which is covered all winter (some years better than others) with large, bright red berries, these set off by the gloomiest green foliage conceivable. With a touch of sunlight on them they certainly transform a winter's day.

Hartstongue ferns, *Asplenium scolopendrium*, are a standby now. They self-sow in particular in the cracks and along the foot of brick walls cemented with lime-rich mortar. The ferns make bouquets of strap leaves and they show up well now that deciduous plants and shrubs around them have virtually disappeared. Another good'un is *Polystichum setiferum* 'Pulcherrimum Bevis'

Unfurling fronds of *Asplenium ceterach* in the terrace wall

('Bevis' is the bit to remember) – a large clump-maker with elegant bipinnate fronds that draw to a fishtail point. That is a feature for most of the year and associates handsomely with contrasting foliage like ivies, fatsia, fatshedera and, in summer, *Clerodendrum bungei*, all of them shade-tolerant, so there be plenty of nourishment and moisture available.

As there may not be space for it at another season and anyway it is at its best when there is moisture around, I must squeeze a mention in of the rusty-back fern, till recently *Ceterach officinarum*, now considered a spleenwort, *Asplenium ceterach*. It is abundant in the cracks of shady old stone walls in the west country but less common my way and I have no doubt my mother introduced it to one of our stone retaining walls. It is an inspiring little plant, with crenately lobed foliage, rusty on the back. It very gradually spreads by running along the cracks. In time of drought the leaves wither entirely, but return as by magic as soon as rain returns.

## Deciduous shrubs and trees

As I remarked of *Ribes alpinum*, deciduous shrubs and trees, as well as the evergreens, may often be pleasing in their skeleton winter framework. We cannot accommodate many trees, as they don't really tally with a garden consisting so prominently of yew hedges and topiary. Among the best are pears, which grow into a wholly characteristic shape whose essence I am unable to describe. They are usually fairly upright but with drooping branches. As fruit trees go, they are long-lived; we still have three specimens that were here before 1910, whereas all the old apples have gone.

Mulberries make a handsome head of lacy branches. Our remaining tree suffered seriously in the 1987 storm, so its winter appearance is still rather unbalanced, with a thicker trunk than the branches seem to warrant. I doubt it will last many more years; I should be starting a youngster. Mulberries are not long-lived and legends of ancient specimens are spurious. One hundred and fifty years at the outside, I should say.

Magnolias can make beautiful old bones, especially those of twiggy rather than coarse habit (like *Magnolia campbellii*). I loved my *M. denudata*, with its domed, mushroom-cap crown, but it died and I've not replaced it as its flowering season is desperately short – one week – all the buds opening simultaneously. *M. stellata* is good, and among more recent plantings I am greatly enamoured of *M.* x *loebneri* 'Leonard Messel'. It has a dense arrangement of twiggy branches, each twig tipped by a furry grey flower bud. Magnolias bud up in autumn and give you plenty of opportunity for gloating anticipation. Pride comes before a fall, but then we all know that and allow for it and gloat just the same. *My* buds on *my* magnolia; yummy, yummy, yummy.

One of the best of shrubs, year round, both for foliage and for structure, is *Cornus alternifolia* 'Argentea'. Its dark branches rise in horizontal tiers and, in winter, you are aware of the way that raindrops hang, catching the light, on the undersides of every horizontal branch. The leaves, in summer, are small and airy with much of white on their margins. *C. controversa* 'Variegata' has a similar though more spreading habit and its leaves are larger. They flush earlier and are often devastated by an April frost. Sometimes *C. alternifolia* 'Argentea' will rise to 4.5m/15ft, layer after layer – one fresh layer a year if it is in the mood. It then becomes a small tree. Mine seems to have come to a halt at 2.4m/8ft, but I keep hoping that it will change its mind and forge on up.

*Cotoneaster horizontalis* has to be mentioned several times in the year. This is the only month when it is entirely without leaves, as the new crop is already expanding in February. Its strong fishbone structure is powerful and it is good against a wall of any aspect, piling itself upwards without assistance. It is equally effective projecting horizontally from the top of a retaining wall, which is where the birds deposit its seeds. All but two of our many specimens were bird-sown. So stiff a shrub makes admirable support for clematis and other climbers, and if they shade out and kill parts of their host, well, it is dispensable and easily replaced.

*Spiraea thunbergii* is an extraordinary little shrub – old as the hills yet generally unsung. It will flower very early, in the bridal wreath style, and is currently covered along all its fine twigs with expanding flower buds, looking like miniature Brussels sprouts. After its early spring flowering, it should receive some annual pruning, cutting some of the old branches quite hard back and shortening all the flowered growth. In autumn, the linear foliage is long retained, only changing to warm yellow in late November and early December, before shedding. The way I prune it, this is never more than 1.2m/4ft tall. Its hybrid offspring, *S. x arguta*, is more vigorous and more obviously wreath-like in its flowering. It can become an ugly, woody specimen of 1.8m/6ft or more, but responds with the greatest good temper to being cut right to the ground, immediately after flowering. Where space is restricted, this can be done biennially.

Dogwoods of the bright-barked kinds are grown not for their shapeliness but for their winter colour, and frequent hard pruning greatly improves this, since the young wood is never brighter than in its first year. You can practise the short-life-but-gay style of pruning, cutting the whole shrub down to the ground at the end of March, each year. All its subsequent growth will then be pristine and produce bright colouring all over. This will weaken its constitution, in the course of time, necessitating replacement planting. Or you can prune out some shoots, say one third of the oldest, each year, in which case the shrub's life span will be indefinite. The one thing not to do is nothing. You will then get a huge, overgrown shrub, dull in every respect at every time of year.

I write of the *Cornus alba* type of dogwood, typically with carmine stems. A colony was planted by the horse pond, on the Lloyds' arrival at Dixter. It revels in a boggy situation and its stems are reflected in the water. I also grow the white-variegated-leaved cultivar, 'Elegantissima', as much for its foliage in summer as for its winter stems, though I am grateful for its dual role. There are two small groups at the back of our main bedding-out area, in front of the house, and they are among white Japanese anemones. All the shoots are pruned back to a 30cm/1ft stump, in spring, and the plants' health does not seem to have been seriously affected in the first twenty years. After a slow start, they are 1.8m/6ft high by the end of the season. We manure generously, I should add. They are underplanted with small bulbs flowering in early spring, before the dogwoods have been pruned.

Another shrub grown for its colourful young stems rather than for its shape (which is like a shaving brush) is a red-stemmed form of willow, *Salix alba*. I'm not sure which clone; my unnamed cuttings came from the moat-side at Scotney Castle, but they seem to be less colourful in my garden – not even a really bright orange. But a beautiful willow in winter, both for the habit of the shrub, which needs no pruning if given enough lateral space, and for its rich, deep reddish winter stems and fat leaf buds, is *Salix fargesii*. Its summer leaves are large, as willows go, elliptical but fairly broad.

## Young foliage

The bright green leaves that some bulbous or tuberous plants show at this time of the year put them at risk from treacherous English weather, but they are very well worth a sheltered position in a sheltered garden. *Allium neapolitanum* started into new growth in October and is full of promise, now, though it aestivates from June till autumn. Other alliums that behave similarly and are now showing strongly are *A. giganteum* (which I only wish was easier to grow and increase) and *A. cristophii*, which seeds itself everywhere in the most delightful way. It is a good partner for Japanese anemones, completing its growth just as theirs is surging forwards. Even common chives, in a mild season, will have poked up sufficient young shoots by the end of the month to be used in delicious chives and cream cheese sandwiches, or to add flavour to a soup at the last moment.

*Arum creticum* is in full leaf, from an October start, and not only is its colouring a particularly strong green, but the sharply cut, angled leaves are outstandingly smart. *A. italicum* subsp. *italicum* 'Marmoratum' is the darling of every flower arranger and is known as 'Pictum'. Its leaf veining is picked out in palest green, creating a marbled effect. Birds sow it everywhere and sometimes their choice, as in the crutch of an old wall fig, is a stroke of genius. But I try to be firm about weeding out seedlings of a less than brilliant variegation.

The South African *Nerine bowdenii*, as also the related *Amaryllis belladonna*, choose to make their new foliage now. It is no good trying to thwart their precocity by planting their bulbs deep. They like to be half above the surface and there get the good baking which promotes their autumn flowering.

Perhaps my favourite in the early-leafing and none-too-hardy category is *Gladiolus tristis*, whose thin, rush-like leaves are already nearly 90cm/3ft tall. A hard winter can kill

PAGE 30 A long-established house leek above *Cotoneaster horizontalis* on a frosty morning
PAGE 31 ABOVE Ghost figures in the winter garden
BELOW The topiary lawn in winter

it off so it is as well to grow some under glass, but after a series of mild winters it increases abundantly in the garden, both by clumping up and by self-sowing.

## Shrubs in season

Witch hazels and wintersweets are still flowering this month. It has often been written that the earliest-flowering rhododendrons of the new year, *Rhododendron mucronulatum* and the even earlier *R. dauricum* (both rather like azaleas to the untrained eye) look admirable in the company of *Hamamelis mollis*, their flowers being a contrasting mauve or purple. So I dutifully planted *R. dauricum* 'Midwinter' next to one of my old witch hazels, and it is true. They do coincide, but the rhododendron is so tempting to pick and its flowers are anyway so frost-tender, that I don't give it much of a chance to make a decent bulk.

The lily-of-the-valley-scented *Mahonia japonica* started flowering in November and continues into March, but reaches a peak now with its clustered strands of small, pale yellow bell flowers. You can bring branches of it into the house for a day but it is not really much use when cut and pilgrimages should be made to it, in the garden. Its leaves are among the less interesting in mahonias, whose foliage is generally a strong point. A specimen – and it is usefully shade-tolerant – grows very large, if allowed to, and stemmy, but a frequent lop-back all over, in spring, works wonders and in no way compromises the next season's flowering.

The winter-flowering shrub honeysuckle, *Lonicera* x *purpusii*, really comes into its own, now, having opened a few desultory flowers since late autumn. It is possibly at its best in the garden in February, but if picked in January, it makes a great display indoors – large branches of it, this being a fast and willing grower to 2.4m/8ft and more across. To

*Arum italicum* subsp. *italicum* 'Marmoratum', bird-sown in the crutch of a wall fig tree

prevent it looking unruly as a shrub, I give it a good thinning, after it has flowered, in early spring, removing plenty of old, twiggy growths. The flowers, borne in couples along young wood, are white (they look as though in need of a visit to the laundry) and heavily perfumed.

Sarcococcas have rather the same sort of heavy fragrance, by no means refined but welcome, especially at this season. Their tiny white flowers are strung along young shoots, but these are rather smart evergreen shrubs, belonging to the boxwood family. They don't like to be blazed on by too much sun. I have quite a number of them and they all flower round about now. *Sarcococca hookeriana*, its pink-tinged variety *digyna* and the rather lower-growing var. *humilis* (45cm/1½ft) all have a suckering habit, good for ground-covering or infilling purposes. I have never seen fruit on them but *S. confusa* is free with its black berries, ripe from the previous year when the next year's flowers are out. *S. ruscifolia*, at 1.2m/4ft, is rather taller than the others and makes the handsomest shrub. Its berries are dark red. With all these, I prune occasionally and when the mood takes me, by thinning out old branches.

The evergreen *Clematis cirrhosa* var. *balearica* is flowering away merrily, with its palest green bells, freckled with tiny dots within, if you look for them. The larger, bolder-flowered cultivar 'Freckles' is heavily marked brownish red within and this is the more readily seen because the flowers open out quite wide. It has a long season. Unfortunately, the foliage is coarse. My plant really belongs to my neighbours, who grow it on our dividing fence.

Obviously related to this are the hellebores, and some of the Orientalis hybrids are very similarly freckled within the flower. The one that is always out by Christmas but at its best in January is currently known as *Helleborus orientalis* Early Purple Group. It is deciduous, so you can remove its old foliage, before flowering, with impunity, and it has a mass of not very deep purple blossom throughout the month. As I have it in an entirely sunless position, I have planted it around with early-flowering snowdrops, to highlight the purple. And so I come to the bulbs.

## Bulbs

Flowering without protection from the new year is the very short-stemmed little *Iris histrioides* 'Major'. This is pale blue and very charming but less easy in cultivation than it once was. I'm not sure why. It certainly gets battered by wind and shredded by slugs where I have it, among the rhizomes of *Euphorbia griffithii* 'Fireglow'. These small bulbs are really most easily appreciated when quite thickly planted in large clay pans. Some I bring into the great hall (which is suitably chilly) as they are opening; some stand on an old chest in the porch and others on the paving just outside the porch. After they have finished their growth cycle, down in the frameyard, we repot for the next season, but first roll the dormant bulbs in a fungicidal powder to protect them against inkspot, which is a killer.

'Katharine Hodgkin', although classified as a Reticulata hybrid, is similar to *I. histrioides* in habit but far more robust. The flowers appear to have a spotted snake in their ancestry, and are rather sinisterly marked in shades of grey, pale blue and yellow, all of them fairly subdued, but they make a great display. 'George' is rather taller, and more obviously has *I. reticulata* in its blood, but is still early. This is purple and scented.

*I. winogradowii* is very close in appearance to *I. histrioides* 'Major', but soft, pale yellow. I much prefer it to *I. danfordiae*, which is a brighter yellow and certainly cheerful but lacking in refinement. Not that one is ardently seeking refinement at this time of the year, when anything is welcome that will lift the spirits, but if it's there it is welcome.

*I. unguicularis* is not bulbous, but comes in apropos, as a, generally, winter-flowering species. The commonest colour is mauve, its large, fragile blooms (large for the time of year) of silken texture. Its buds are lovely to pick for the house the day before they would open anyway. They may be borne at any time from late October to the end of March, this depending on the variety and on the weather. In every mild spell, you should visit them on alternate days, to gather the next crop. The plants are extremely untidy and should be sited in a hot position, handy for picking but not prominently in sight. The advantage in leaving the old foliage is that

this encourages the flower buds to make longer stalks for picking. And you should pick, rather than pull, because the flower buds are usually made in pairs, which develop in succession. If you pull the first one, it will break off together with the second, and the latter will not have had the chance to develop.

In normal seasons, most snowdrops belong to February, but it is a big group and there are exceptions. Chief among them at Dixter is *Galanthus* 'Atkinsii'. This is a strong, rather tall-growing hybrid that doesn't set seed but clumps up amazingly fast. It makes a great show in a damp, north-west-facing border which is primarily given over to *Euphorbia palustris*, *Aralia cachemirica*, *Rodgersia pinnata* cultivars and *Geranium wallichianum* 'Buxton's Variety'. All their remains are entirely removed in early December, the area is given a top-dressing of spent mushroom compost and the scene is set. When the perennials need dividing, the snowdrops have to be lifted, in big lumps. They are very forgiving. They are divided a little and most are returned, the rest being spread around other parts of the garden.

BELOW LEFT  *Galanthus* 'Atkinsii' as in-fill in a border of summer perennials (see page 123)
BELOW  *Galanthus* 'Atkinsii' highlighting *Helleborus orientalis* Early Purple Group in a dark corner

Another early hybrid is the giant 'Colesbourne'. A marginal note in the bulb book I was using at the time tells me that I bought it (one bulb) from Washfield Nursery on 18 February 1982. It has increased prodigiously, though only since Fergus's arrival have we concentrated much on spreading it from its original siting, which was and is among the crowns of *Polystichum setiferum* Acutilobum Group ferns. As these retain their greenery through the winter, we cut them back at the beginning of the month and they don't mind. 'Colesbourne' has broad, glaucous leaves and the inner segments – the bell of the flower – are all green apart from a narrow white rim. This grows up to 35cm/14in tall (I have just measured one). Very handsome indeed. When you gather snowdrops for the house, pulling (rather than plucking) the stems, holding your hand low down, is good practice for getting a nice length of stalk. If too weak and fragile right at the base, it is easily shortened. This works well also with narcissi and bluebells.

One of the pleasant little jobs that Fergus and I make time for, this month, is to look around for relatively undisturbed bare spaces, where snowdrops could and should be grown. It would greatly enrich their gardens if everyone were to do this. Just now, we have spotted areas in colonies of *Hedychium coccineum*, which is always late into growth, and among strong-growing varieties of *Fuchsia magellanica*, which won't mind being cut to the ground before the snowdrops appear.

I can relate nothing about winter aconites, which I have never yet been able to establish at Dixter, though I have made the attempt many times in many situations. I am still trying.

First of the daffodils to open, quite early in the month, is the tiny yellow trumpet *Narcissus asturiensis*. I have it growing in extremely poor meadow ground, so poor that grass is mostly replaced by moss, this being beneath a young oak. Only 7.5cm/3in or so high, the daffodil is quite unperturbed by the circumstances, but slugs do go for it.

## Self-sowns

The appearance of certain annual weed seedlings, in January, is always a signal that the year has turned. Notable are the redoubtable goose grass or cleavers – we're always at that – and ivy-leaved speedwell, *Veronica hederacea*, which is not too serious a weed and belongs only to the first half of each year, but can utterly wreck the appearance of carefully prepared spring bedding, so we have to take it seriously.

Other seedlings to appear now are those of self-sown hellebores and of the various biennial honesties, *Lunaria annua*. I think I have four different kinds of those and I try to keep them apart but it isn't easy. The two variegated kinds proclaim themselves at an early stage and you can spot the seedlings of the pure white-flowered kind by the rather brighter than normal colouring of its green leaves. This bright colouring is a character in most albinos.

## Food

There is, barring accidents, a plentiful supply of vegetables and saladings from the garden; leeks, carrots, salsify, parsnips, celeriac and Jerusalem artichokes among the roots, and they are dug straight from the ground. That gives the best flavour. As celeriac is not very frost-hardy, we cover the plants with hessian during frosty spells and that way they usually last till Easter. 'Pink Fir Apple' potatoes and shallots are taken out of storage.

So is Witloof chicory for my salads. The roots are packed thickly into large ornamental pots used for flowers on the terrace in summer. As I need them, a pot at a time (there'll be two or three pots in all) is brought into the house and stands in the darkness of the cellar stairs. In the garden, I can still usually be cutting a green chicory, 'Sugar Loaf', which, makes large, heavy hearts from a direct sowing in early July. I can only use a little of each at one time, but the rest keeps, wrapped, for a long while in the fridge.

Other salad ingredients include rocket (my favourite and with so much more flavour than what you, expensively, can buy). This, if too lush, will succumb to low temperatures, but September sowings will come through the winter more often than not, and I am also grateful to patches and odd plants that were self-sown from a previous crop. There is chervil, always easiest to grow for winter consumption; pak choi, mizuna, mega-cress (very tasty but not always available, so I save my own seed), lamb's lettuce from self-sown plants and, sometimes, winter radish.

Of brassicas, there are sprouts (two kinds, early- and late-maturing), the savoy cabbage 'January King', which I find has the best flavour, and, of late, the first of the purple-sprouting broccoli has been maturing mid-month. Most welcome.

I do not like January any more than the next man, but at least the evenings are getting noticeably longer. By the end of the month, we have won almost an hour of daylight in the afternoons.

Early purple-sprouting broccoli

February

Increase in day length becomes a headlong rush by the end of this, the shortest month of the year and the last of winter. According to the weather pattern established in January, this is, in temperatures and mood, either a winter month, prolonging the agony, or the beginning of spring. I like February: I like the word and I like the feeling of so much, in my garden, being on the move.

If it is mild, you may be sure of hearing the wiseacres telling us that we shall pay for it later. Well, there's not much we can do about that, is there, whether true or false? What they quite forget is to revel in the moment, accepting it for what it is. Dire events never take pessimists by surprise but they refuse to be caught up in the joys of living. 'Lure' is a word we hear a lot. Plants are 'lured' into premature growth or flowering, we are told, as though there were some evil genius, out there, pulling strings and drily cackling as he (she wouldn't be capable of such a thing) watches the approach and consummation of disaster.

On average, February is not a wet month. My grandfather (b. 1834) asserted (and I see no reason for gainsaying him) that the tag 'February fill-dyke' is a corruption of 'February full-dyke', referring to the condition of the dykes after the four wettest months. A recent entry in my small pocket diary for 13 February tells me that the temperature rose to 14C/15°F, that we had our after-lunch coffee (lying on rugs) in the orchard (where a sheltered, south-facing bank overlooks the rubbish heap), as also on the following two days. Also that tortoiseshell butterflies were feeding on crocuses and snowdrops and that there was a peacock butterfly on *Coronilla valentina*. Definitely elevating to the spirits.

Another good sign is that the great crested newts are back in the ponds. Till now, they had been hibernating, stiff and apparently lifeless, under paving slabs and in suchlike places. From now on, they abound particularly in the sunk garden pool, where they are a great source of interest to visitors from April on. I used to keep fish in this pond, but finally got fed up with the Koi carp, which bred like fury and stirred up the sludge so that you could never see into the water and you couldn't even see *them*, until they came up with a great commotion to be fed. Once they had gone, peace was restored and the water is now stocked, without any effort on my part, with natural fauna – including the newts. The water remains pretty clear for most of the year and you can admire the purplish underwater rosettes of *Stratiotes aloides*, the water soldier, which couldn't survive when the pond was never still.

## February flowers

On average, most snowdrops are at their peak this month. I love to pick a fat bunch – say a fistful of a hundred stems – and to have them near me indoors where I can inhale their honey scent. Bees go to them for their nectar. Without any intention of collecting, I do in fact have a good many named cultivars. Their differences may not be great, but they are interesting, and anything that makes you look at a flower with close attention

must be good – if not carried too far, one must add, so that you can't see the wood for the trees; this is the reason for some galanthophiles becoming galanthobores.

Snowdrops thrive especially where there is a bit of shade and the turf (if they are in a meadow setting) is a little less dense than out in the open. A few snowdrops among the foliage of *Cyclamen hederifolium* look nice. Another moisture-lover for part shade is *Cardamine quinquefolia*, a rather superior kind of lady's smock. The flowers are rich lilac mauve and they open over a long period. This plant has come rather late into my gardening life and I have not yet learned how to make best use of it.

But I do think I have got somewhere in combining a pale blue lungwort, *Pulmonaria officinalis* – it might be 'Bowles' Blue', 'Blue Mist' or 'Cambridge Blue', they are all very similar – in a carpet, with discrete clumps among them of the woodrush *Luzula sylvatica* 'Aurea'. This makes low tufts of greeny-yellow foliage, at its brightest at this time of year.

It would be easy (though dreary) to collect a wide range of pulmonarias, both for their flowers and, later on, for their foliage, though this is a good deal disfigured, in many cases, by mildew. A showy, foot-tall, blue-flowered cultivar, which I like a lot, is

PAGES 38–39 Winter crocuses in the front entrance meadow

ABOVE Snowdrops and *Cyclamen hederifolium* provide winter interest amongst dormant fern crowns

'Lewis Palmer'. Mine has happily seeded itself, still looking true to type, next to a hartstongue fern. Another good contrasting companion would be one of the stronger-growing celandines – the cream-coloured *Ranunculus* 'Salmon's White' (which surely needs to be balanced by 'White's Salmon') is the one I have provided.

February is the month of winter crocuses – *Crocus tommasinianus*, *C. flavus*, *C. sieberi* and *C. chrysanthus* with its innumerable variants. All of them adapt well to life in meadow turf and most self-sow. They give me a special thrill, the way they open wide in response to spring sunshine and, in shadow, to a little spring warmth in the air. This requires a rather special scenario and you may be almost certain that if you invite crocus-loving friends for a February weekend, the weather will be such as to keep the crocuses resolutely shut, or only half open, in a reluctant and slightly surly response to sunshine without real warmth. If I were a weekender and in danger of enduring three dull weekends in a row, I might miss the crocuses altogether. For this reason, I can understand why some gardeners prefer snowdrops. But if you're on the spot all the time, you are there to take advantage of the magic moments, and magic they are.

*C. flavus* (once *C. aureus*) is small but an intense and vital shade of pure, rich orange. It is fertile and self-sows. Clearly, it is one parent of the Dutch yellow, which is one of the

most popular of all crocuses. This is larger, but a less intense colour. Early-flowering, too, but although it makes fat clumps it is sterile and does not self-sow; you need to dig and split it up, after flowering, and spread it around yourself. It is the crocus that house sparrows have greatest fun with, tearing the flowers apart.

*C. flavus* contrasts well with *C. tommasinianus*, which is mauve, though such a discreet non-colour on the outside of the flower that you scarcely see it until shone upon. It is the most prolific of all crocuses. The clone 'Whitewell Purple' is a more definite colour and well worth having.

*C. chrysanthus*, shaped like an electric light bulb when closed and bowl-shaped when open, has an incredibly wide range of colour forms, some of them improbable if described without the flower in front of you, but they always look right. 'Advance' for instance, is pale yellow on the inside and mauve outside. My favourite is one bred by Ernest Bowles, 'Snow Bunting'. Cream-white with dark striping; sometimes a rather ragged petal outline and a gorgeous honey scent. It is one of the earliest in bloom, but often, alas, a different white crocus is sold under this name – it may be pure white, late-flowering and odourless.

Early narcissus are tremendously welcome. One that does well with me but that you seldom see in gardens is *Narcissus tazetta*, the species itself, parent of a large proportion of the bunch-headed kinds with the strongest (not the pleasantest) scent. It has a wide Southern European distribution in the wild; my stock was given me from Wakehurst Place (the outpost of Kew). Because it is on the tender side, I grow it under a warm wall. It has a very long flowering season and was already under way last month. The leaves are dark green, contrasting with white flowers (the cup, cream) in a large cluster which open successively.

'Tête-à-Tête' is deservedly popular. We are told that all stock of it is infected with virus disease, but it has tremendous vigour none the less. A small yellow trumpet, rather lacking in class, if I may say so, about 23cm/9in tall and tremendously willing. It looks nice with the pale yellow of primroses.

*N. minor* is a dear little yellow trumpet, 15cm/6in tall, with twisted leaves. It clumps up well, even in rough meadow conditions. As it is about half the size of, though otherwise similar to, our native Lent lily, *N. pseudonarcissus*, I like to keep the two of them separate. We have a lot of the latter in front of the house, where it self-sows. My mother raised the original batches from seed. It may not be at its best till March, but is nearly always finished by even an early Easter.

In a really cold winter, the tallish yellow *N. cyclamineus* hybrid 'February Gold' would not start flowering till March, but in other years it lives up to its name. I have it in a rather pleasing planting at the bottom of the long border, where it rubs cheeks with the margins of my main planting of Lenten roses, generally known as *Helleborus orientalis*

Fragrant *Crocus chrysanthus* 'Snow Bunting' growing in the meadow

hybrids. These look clean and pristine, because we remove their tired old leaves well before the display gets going. (If you leave this job too late, you find yourself removing some of the flower bud stems by accident, which is agonizing, and no one to blame but yourself, like losing at chess.) These hellebores are in mixed shades, mostly light colours, which show up better than the dark.

Behind them, as a back-up, is a narrow-leaved 'laurel', *Aucuba japonica* 'Longifolia'. A female, it is smothered in large red berries, in some years, and as they have only just fully ripened they are singularly fresh. There is a male near by, which I bought as 'Crotonifolia', though that should be female, according to the books. The name suits it because it is heavily variegated and you'll either love it or turn aside in disgust (poor, sensitive you).

The sub-shrubby *Helleborus argutifolius* has great bouquets, almost like a mop-headed hydrangea, of pale green flowers above handsome trifoliate leaves with mock prickles along their margins. It never lasts for long with me. Neither does *H. foetidus*, our native stinking hellebore, which I really prefer, but I don't mind its being short-lived, as it self-sows and is already looking its handsomest in its second year. After flowering, it is apt to go to pieces, but there will be others. It makes rich, dark evergreen leaves with narrow segments, above which the pale green inflorescence is well framed. The bell flowers are rimmed in purple. This hellebore often places itself at the foot of deciduous shrubs. It is shade-tolerant but comes truly into its own in winter, when the shrub is naked.

*H. x nigricors* is a particularly handsome hybrid between the Christmas rose, *H. niger*, and *H. argutifolius*, which used to be called *H. corsicus* – which explains the ugly hybrid name. This seems to be pretty long-lived with me (and I do not pretend to be a clever cultivator of the genus) and has bold leaves and long-flowering trusses of large white blooms. In the last part of its flowering, it will contrast well with a neighbouring clump of the cyclamineus hybrid daffodil, 'Jetfire' – yellow with a short, pale orange trumpet.

A few more shrubs are in flower. In a mild year, the

*Narcissus* 'Tête-à-Tête' with the foliage of *Geranium malviflorum* and verbascum

semi-double, pale pink *Camellia* x *williamsii* 'Salutation' will be in full bloom. I have mixed feelings about hybrid camellias. In so many, the leaves and general growth have been coarsened in the interests of flower size and, in my garden at least, they become disagreeably stemmy. This happened to my 'Salutation'. Knowing that camellias respond extremely well to a hard cut-back, I really laid into mine (*after* it had flowered, being always a believer in eating my cake and still having it). Not a leaf remained. It responded wonderfully. I lost the next year's flowering, but that was the only penalty. However, like most double camellias and some singles, it holds on to its dead brown blooms, which quite spoils the setting for fresh ones. I go crossly over the bush, pulling them off, from time to time but resent the necessity, and anyway cannot reach the high ones.

*Iris reticulata* taking its turn with summer-flowering *Geranium* x *riversleaianum* 'Mavis Simpson'

*Azara microphylla* flowers either this month or next. The first you know of it is the powerful scent of chocolate that reaches you at a considerable distance, on the air. The yellow flowers, which are on the undersides of the neat, evergreen leaves, are minute. You have to search for them and then wonder if it was worth it. However, this can make a nice-looking tree-shrub, though a hard winter can set it back. One of mine has had its shape spoiled by other wall shrubs near to it, but the second, a self-sown seedling from the first, grows out of paving on the terrace above. If that gets unduly stemmy, it responds well to a cut-back. My *Wisteria sinensis* took it into its head to climb into the azara and the result is so pretty that I have not restrained it.

On the lower terrace grows *Daphne odora* 'Aureomarginata', and that will flower from now till well into April, generously scenting the air with a heavy fragrance. The flowers are borne in terminal clusters on the young shoots and are purplish pink on the outside, almost white within. The evergreen leaves are rather ugly, the more so as the situation is too hot and sunny (but nicely sheltered from cold winds), and this turns it a rather sickly green. It is an admirable shade shrub in the south of England, but further north needs all the sun that's going, if it is to flower freely, or flower at all. Like *D. mezereum*, this is excellent on limy soils.

## More evergreens

I did not do full justice, last month, to the range of evergreen shrubs which hold me in such good stead, right through and beyond the coldest weather. Evergreens have to shed their leaves sometime and most of them lose the majority of them in May, when they are being replaced by young growth. This is a great topic for moaning with professional gardeners, who feel that autumn should be the time for leaf loss and resent the necessity for further, spread-out clearances at the start of summer.

*Daphniphyllum macropodum* is a great shrub, with rather rhododendron-like leaves, but much more attractive than the majority of those. Smooth ellipses, they are glaucous on the underside and the leaf stalks and main veins are red (in the strain grown in this country) throughout the winter. They grow in whorls and show up well at a distance on a largish shrub, perhaps 3m/10ft high. It looks tender but is not.

Next to this, and lighting up a shady wall, I have *Rhamnus alaternus* 'Argenteovariegata'. This has neat oval leaves with a white margin. Of rather upright habit, it is, although hardy, apt not to be wind-firm in the open but looks excellent trained as a wall shrub. I was given this idea by seeing it so treated against the old city wall alongside New College, Oxford – a planting instigated by Robin Lane Fox. The flowers, in spring, are insignificant, but when in bud, they swarm all over the young growths and are a warm reddish brown, which is as pleasing as it is unexpected.

Still largely in shade, in front of the wall is a rhododendron of the Ponticum series and very hardy, *Rhododendron hyperythrum*, which I first admired in Collingwood Ingram's garden at Benenden, nine miles from here. The elliptical leaves are strikingly rolled back along the margins. It flowers in April – pink in bud, fading white. On the other side of the garden, *R*. 'Seta' makes a neat shrub with small evergreen leaves and clusters of pink flowers, white at the base, and at their best this month. The shrub is no more than 1.2m/4ft high and unlikely to grow much taller, as I like to pick it rather freely, when still in bud. There's always a night frost to ruin the display at some stage, so I might just as well make the most of some of it indoors. 'Tessa', of upright, gawky habit, another small-leaved rhododendron, flowers this month, too, but I'm not too fond of its mauve-pink colouring.

*Trochodendron aralioides* grows near the daphniphyllum on the lower terrace. It is a 24m/80ft tree in Japan, but I have assumed that I can keep it to a height and spread of 2.4m/8ft. So far I'm all right. Its rhomboid leaves are astonishingly thick – smooth, yellowish green and nice to handle. Its panicles of green flowers in May make quite an impression, mainly on account of the wheel-like whorls of stamens.

Fairly new to me, but hardy so far, is a bright green, needle-leaved Australian shrub, *Grevillea* 'Canberra Gem'. It starts flowering this month, with small, bright pink clusters, and a succession of these opens for the next four months.

Dixter is not rich in conifers, but I love the group. In the long border I have a dear but rather sprawling plant, which I grew from seed gathered in the Carpathians, of *Pinus mugo*.

I like the contrast, there, with totally different kinds of plants. Another pine doing valuable service is the fastigiate form of *Pinus strobus*, which I have below the lower terrace, where the situation seems to demand a vertical. It is in very poor meadow soil, but evidently loves it. The needles are glaucous and have a curious way of closing upwards against the stems, especially in winter.

On the topiary lawn, some of the topiary pieces died (bad drainage, most likely) and I have replaced them with three (two of them very new, from our own cuttings) *Cephalotaxus harringtonia* 'Fastigiata', which has yew-like leaves – a little coarser. My idea, since no one currently here is interested in training new yew topiary pieces, is to have formal-looking shrubs whose shape will more or less (with a little help) look after itself.

Quite different, and a most important feature in the sunk garden, is *Juniperus sabina* (the one that smells of blackcurrants, when bruised) 'Tamariscifolia'. It is prostrate, with fans of tiny, slightly glaucous green leaves, which are the same colour throughout the year. I planted it on top of the wall which retains this garden and, in a great apron, it has cascaded down on to the floor, where it has spread out in an arc. Quite impressive, although I say it.

Shrubby evergreen euphorbias look good when there's no frost. They then become woefully dejected, though soon recovering when the temperature rises. Currently, one of the smartest in my garden is the clone of *Euphorbia characias* called 'Portuguese Velvet'. I have perched it on the corner of a retaining wall. The growth is compact and the shoots well furnished with glaucous foliage. On sunny days in February, you see ladybirds, freshly out of hibernation, sunning themselves on the shoot tips.

## The frameyard

Our most concentrated back-up area and also our sales and packing department are in the frameyard at the bottom of the garden. Most of the glass we have for protecting plants is in the form of standard Dutch light frames. Each one comprises a single large

LEFT *Helleborus foetidus* at the foot of *Cotoneaster horizontalis*, both self-sown
ABOVE *Daphniphyllum macropodum*

pane of glass, which lets in the maximum amount of light. The frame walls are solid concrete, which retains warmth pretty well. It is amazing how much can be achieved just with cold frames and no other form of protection.

Most of our newly made cuttings are put into double frames under lights. There is a frame within a frame – double walls with a cavity between and inner lights which are horizontal, not sloping like the outer. Condensation gathers on the undersides of the horizontal lights and there is very little loss of moisture. So it is snug, in there, and the heat accumulated by day is long retained at night. If heavy frost threatens, we further cover these frames with strips of hemp hessian. If there is frost and snow, everything is left just as it is. The cuttings and plants in the single frames do not need daylight while the outside temperature is below freezing. As soon as the frost lets up, off come the wraps, single frames are ventilated and the contents of the double frames examined for any rotting that may have been started by botrytis, the grey mould fungus. We apply a regular protective spray against this, every fortnight or so, and vary the active ingredient so that a resistant strain of the fungus cannot develop.

Soon after the war, we built a greenhouse, which is still in place. It, too, has solid walls, for the sake of insulation. The glass sides are half and the roof entire Dutch lights. There are benches all round, covered with grit, and the floor is earth. The great idea is to be able to retain a humid atmosphere when sun heat is strong. In this way we do not need to shade the glass at all.

Since Fergus came in 1993, we have greatly increased our nursery stock, without increasing the area in which it is grown. And two new greenhouses have gone up. One is alongside the old one and is the same size. In the original one, we aim to keep the temperature just above freezing, at its lowest. In the extension, we house our really tender, sub-tropical plants – ones we shall use in the garden in the summer – and here we aim (using an electric blower heater) to maintain a minimum temperature of 10C/50°F. But when we ventilate for a short period each day in winter, it may drop a little lower than this. The third, separate, house is a pit, which is an old device for retaining heat by sinking the lower half of the house below ground level. Plants love it in there and it is a multi-purpose house, but nothing is grown for display *in situ*. All the stock is held either for the nursery or for summer use in the garden.

We use soil-based John Innes composts, which I like for various reasons, chief among them the fact that soil provides a reserve of nutrients. Also, its weight gives more stability to the pots, when the wind is blowing. It doesn't dry out too quickly, either, and plants grown in a soil-based compost are the easiest to establish once transferred to a garden. The plants' roots will already be accustomed to a similar medium.

We provide our own loam by making stacks from turf skimmed off neighbouring fields and we sterilize this loam in a kind of blow-lamp device (called a Terraforce), which heats it and destroys all weed seed except clover! The smell given off by sterilizing soil is rather like chocolate.

I used to spend most of my working life (when I wasn't writing) in this nursery area, doing a large part of the propagation and potting myself. Now, no longer, so I'm not *au fait* with just what stock we are holding of each plant, but I don't mind having relinquished all that to younger people. In a way, I miss not being at the potting bench, aware, in summer, of the family of swallows being reared in the roof, sometimes of a blackbird family being brought up in a nest perched on tools (less used ones!) hanging on the walls. But there are so many cats around these days anyhow, that the birds have to go elsewhere. Fergus has two that live down here (and another old fellow living with him in Hastings), while Perry, whose family lives in the cottage just below the frameyard, has his own cat. My dogs, who are abject cowards when stood up to, are terrified of them and keep a safe distance. They, in their turn, are treated with disdain.

## Winter tasks

There are various routine winter tasks that we try to complete in the garden, before spring's arrival. Kathleen and Michael are plundering the stock beds for material to split and pot. With hardy perennials, this can be done at any time, but by February, things like day lilies, aconitums, crocosmias and phloxes are already shooting strongly, so the sooner they are dealt with the better for them. But the stock beds need sorting out themselves – weeding, rejuvenating, switching groups around (often for effect – they might just as well look as attractive as possible, and they can often suggest plant combinations to visitors) and manuring. Fergus doesn't like to get on to our heavy ground in sopping wet weather (although he frequently works on in such weather himself), but if a job is half done and it turns wet, he will finish it working off boards, which spread one's weight. And the others work with him! Winter digging is caught up with by the beginning of this month and the large clods turned over bear witness to the kind of soil we are on. But there are far worse clay soils than ours.

Where young trees have been planted in a meadow area, the competitive conditions of turf are hard for them to cope with, so we keep a cultivated area around them for the first few years. We weed that now, and then lay on a top-dressing of garden compost (made from the meadow grasses when they are cut). This, of course, also feeds the neighbouring turf, where the grass and cow parsley becomes far coarser than elsewhere, but this can't be helped.

We also clean out all the yew hedge bottoms, as they will die out if they have to compete with a lot of weed growth around their feet. And if ivy has invaded, that is pulled out too. Ivy accounts for the demise of many a neglected hedge, box as well as yew, and even rough hedges can be seriously weakened.

After the hedges have been cleaned, they are given a feed. This was of fish, blood and bone, at one time, but it has a remarkably caustic effect if it comes into contact with yew leaves. There was one year when the gardener on this job thrust his hand into the hedges with a fistful of fish, blood and bone, so that it should reach the centre of the hedge, but in every position where his hand had gone in, a dead brown patch of yew was the result. We are currently using the slow-release fertilizer Osmacote, but we apply it to the yew roots outside the hedge, as they normally spread far beyond the hedge itself. My father, aware of the greed of yew roots, set vertical sheets of galvanized iron between the hedge and any border that ran alongside. They are still there, though the yew roots have often managed to find an escape route over the top of them.

There seems to be a popularly held view that lawn-mowing should be entirely in abeyance between October and spring. I do not agree: a winter cut will make it far easier to cope with the dense mat of turf grass in the spring. The difficulty is in seizing the right moment for a mow, but it often comes in early February. It must not have rained, recently, else mowing will leave a slimy mess; the grass must be dry and it must not be frozen. If you get a succession of overcast nights and days, perhaps with a northerly wind blowing and no dew forming, the right moment materializes. Here, this year, it was yesterday, 4 February. Perry got round all the main lawns and alleys through the meadows, but when it came to the tricky little grass slopes linking the barn and sunk gardens, he needed the small mower, and it wouldn't start.

This is an old, old story. We all know about sending the mowers into dock in winter and the circular saw in for sharpening in summer, but any piece of machinery that has been given a rest for a while, far from feeling young and invigorated, gets into a state of torpor from which it refuses to be aroused – except by the expert. By the time the mower's problem has been resolved, the weather will have changed.

## Summer fruits

As a protection from birds, we have a cage for our raspberries, currants – red and black – and gooseberries. Sometimes it becomes a bird cage, until we have discovered the way they are getting in. I don't grow strawberries, as I can well live without them for long periods and when I want some, it becomes a treat, and I go to the local pick-your-own farm with a kneeling mat and that is enjoyable, with whole families around me at the same ploy. The cage is a substantial affair, made to a comfortable height for standing with chestnut poles and covered with fine-mesh wire netting. There are certain snags with raspberries: they have a wandering habit. Their suckers appear in the middle of gooseberry and currant bushes. It is more serious when the summer-fruiting kinds, which crop on the old canes, invade the autumn-fruiters, which crop on canes made in the current season. The latter are pruned by cutting them to the ground in winter. If they include summer-fruiting canes, these get cut down too and are not merely in the wrong place but never crop.

So, nowadays I am planting the autumn-fruiters elsewhere, outside the cage, as birds show little or no interest in them from August on. (There must be a reason, but I have not investigated it.) This leaves spare space in the cage, which I use for sweet corn, if I want any (I'm not too keen), and carrots. Both these crops are a great delicacy with badgers, so the cage is against them as well as birds.

This month, we clean off annual weeds. The great danger in long-lived crops is invasion by bindweed or some other perennial weed like black bryony or couch grass. We have to apply herbicides to them in the growing season. The summer-fruiting raspberries are pruned now, however, and so are the gooseberries and currants. A mulch of garden compost is applied thickly to the whole area, in the hope that this will prevent drying out in time of summer drought, as irrigation would, for various reasons, be extremely difficult to apply, as well as there being more urgent claimants. Usually this works.

Rhubarb is another crop that attracts perennial weeds. I don't think we have ever moved our rhubarb patch. That, too, is well mulched with compost. It is a most undemanding crop. Without any forcing, I can make my first picking at the end of March, and that is early enough for me.

## Pruning

All the wall-trained pears and the espalier Comice pears in the high garden are pruned by spurring back last year's young shoots. Branches are re-tied to their supports, when necessary. We don't spray these pears and their old branches are covered in lichens, which doesn't hurt them in the least. We do get scabby fruit if the weather is wet when the fruit is swelling – which isn't always, by any means. And the flavour of these pears is ambrosial when compared with the large, watery fruits, with perfect skin finish, that you would buy.

There are still fifty or so roses of various kinds, scattered around the garden, and they need some sort of pruning treatment. Mostly this is meted to them when convenient to us. If they are large shrub or vigorous climbing roses, like *Rosa* 'Kiftsgate', I believe in giving them a regular annual pruning by removing all flowered wood. This ensures that they never become too bulky. So often you see what people choose to call shrub roses that have been left entirely unpruned from the word go. They accumulate a tremendous amount of dead and useless wood inside them and become of ever larger circumference. This is a great waste of space, and I resent it even in my large garden. Besides, the rose is healthier if its wood is all reasonably young. So there is some catching up with rose pruning now, but it may start in November and finish in May.

Naturally, it is simpler to prune a deciduous shrub, like a rose, when it has no foliage on it and you can clearly see the whole plant's structure and what treatment will suit it best. That applies to all the deciduous flowering shrubs. You are supposed to prune a philadelphus immediately after flowering, which is a counsel of perfection, removing flowered branches so as to leave all that space clear for the new branches to develop in. But if you do, you will not only be working in conditions too congested and leafy to be able to see exactly what you are doing, but it is extremely easy to knock off brittle young shoots by accident. This is upsetting. By leaf-fall, all growth has hardened up and it is easy to work without doing damage. And you have the latitude to do the pruning at any time up to the flushing of a new crop of leaves.

## Logs to burn

In the house, I have two wood fires on open hearths. In winter, I sit in front of one of them for a large part of the day, writing on my lap-top (and I need to doze off in between active writing bouts). But at the end of the working day, I feel I'm justified in spoiling myself by migrating to my favourite room, the solar (where I have my record-playing apparatus), to read, listen and relax with a couple of whiskies and a tray supper, if I'm on my own. Or for conversation with friends, if I'm not. So, if the weather is not impossibly cold, I light the fire there around 6 p.m.

The logs needed for these fires are 53cm/21in long and an enormous amount of wood is consumed. Lenn cuts it for us in woodland that needs coppicing every twenty-five years or so, and he does that at weekends, making a beautifully clean job of it. The wood is cut the winter before I need to burn it. You can burn ash or birch green, but not anything else; it needs a summer in which to dry out. With our old tractor and trailer, we carry it up to a conveniently situated wood pile in the autumn, when the ground is, we hope, still dry and hard. (This is a countryside of mixed woodland and small fields, and the woods are generally situated on the steepest terrain, where cultivations would be awkward. So, fetching out the wood can sometimes be a tricky operation.)

We have a saw-bench and the wood is sawn in batches, ahead of when it is needed, and there is generally time to stack it in a wood shed before use. Straight from outside to the fires in winter, it can be superficially very wet indeed. Perry is in charge of wood sawing (though Fergus sometimes likes to take a turn) but it needs two of you – one to saw and the other to feed the poles to the saw-bench.

The fireplaces are re-stocked with the day's wood for burning, every morning. I try to hold off all fires by the end of May (but am sometimes reluctant, even then) and I migrate to another part of the house where I forget about fires (there's no joy in sitting in front of an empty grate) and the furniture is turned to face a large door, which opens into the garden and can often be left open till bedtime. So you feel in touch with outside while sitting comfortably within and relatively free from the attention of mosquitoes and other nocturnal buzzers.

I put a lot of money and effort into keeping my fifteenth-century heritage up to scratch, so I do not feel guilty about indulging myself with fires and they are a great joy. I nearly always light them myself, never using paper. If there are no live embers, my aim is to light an old, charred brand from the previous day, with a single match. Then, to blow that with bellows till there's a wide glow. I may, at this stage, help matters along with some bits of dried bark that have peeled off the wood to be burned, and dried off in the fireplace. I collect these. Then I put small bats of wood and some bigger ones on

Perry and Aaron at the saw-bench

top. I go out of the room at this stage and give the fire time to smoulder until it is ready to burst into flames. If I've no brands to start me, I may resort to a little kindling, which Fergus brings me from visits to Turkey, where it is sold in bundles. This is resin-rich coniferous stuff.

Lenn saves brushwood from the tops of the hornbeam he has felled (and hornbeam comprises at least two thirds of all the underwood). We collect that in the spring for use in the garden, supporting plants that need it and the double row of old-fashioned sweet peas that I like to have for picking, during six summer weeks.

## Seed-ordering

Either this month or, for preference, last, Fergus and I get down to the major task of deciding which seeds to order from which merchants, for the coming year. Thompson & Morgan and Chiltern Seeds are the richest quarries for a wide range of varieties, but to get all we want, we may need to turn to six or seven seed houses. First we go through the previous year's catalogues, which are marked with what we ordered then, and decide if we want to order the same item again. Then, through the new list, deciding what we want to order that's new. At the same time, we give thought and make notes on what we would like to use and combine in our various bedding-out areas. That's the exciting bit. The rest is rather humdrum, and I'm glad I don't have to do it by myself any longer, as once I did.

March

There is something sharp and aggressive in the very word. March is prepared to hurl every sort of weather at us. It is the first month of spring but winter still lurks in the wings, ready to return with an ugly leer. Snow is more frequent than in December. Yet it is a jokey sort of snow. As it sits perched on top of blue grape hyacinths and yellow daffodils, we can scarcely take it seriously and, indeed, it is gone within minutes, until the next squall arrives. Winds are vicious. It is unwise to grow many fragile early-flowerers, like *Tulipa fosteriana* 'Mme Lefeber' (more appropriately known as 'Red Emperor') with its huge expanse of red sail. All can be smashed on the first day. Large, early-flowering magnolias have a brutal time of it, too. I remember 'Cherry' Ingram (Captain Collingwood Ingram), who lived a few miles distant, phoning me one sunny March morning and summoning me to go and see his *M.* 'Charles Raffill', a splendid rose-red tree-magnolia. I explained that I couldn't that day, would the next day do? 'Yes,' said he, 'but you know how it is.' I did. A day in March is a long time in a large-flowered magnolia's season.

On average, this is the first of the dry months, too.

Whan that Aprille with his shoures sote
The droughte of Marche hathe perced to the rote,

Chaucer wrote at the start of *The Canterbury Tales*. Farmers welcome this drought of March, as their saying 'A peck of dust in March is worth a king's ransom' (with variants) bears witness. They need dry conditions so as to be able to get on with sowing and cultivating. We welcome dry conditions in March at Dixter, too. We have left it till now to finish clearing the borders of last year's herbaceous debris, to split and replant where advisable, to fork in mushroom compost or fine, well-rotted bark, and to spread on a dressing of Growmore (nitrogen, phosphate and potash) at some 95g to the square metre (4oz to the square yard). Of course, it's nice to have a shower to wash that off any foliage on which it may have lodged! It also makes it easier if the ground is damp and absorbent, for going along the flagstone paving cracks with a fine-spouted can, dribbling weedkiller. It is a boon to be able to get rid of weeds without having to lift the slabs, as once we used to. They never bedded back level.

I like to work with Fergus on the long border, whenever I can get out, and it takes a week or, at most, ten days to complete, not skimping anything. But, of course, there are always unpremeditated interruptions. Sometimes it's not all done before we open to the public, but at least they can see that there's work in progress. The huge old, green, wooden wheelbarrow is always a photographic attraction, especially with the Dutch, who consider it a huge joke. Let them laugh. (Snarl.)

Sometime this month, Fergus runs a volunteers' weekend. A group of students comes over from the Royal Horticultural Society's gardens at Wisley and there are other helpers to get all sorts of things straight. Fergus is in his element, moving from one group to another, apparently without hurry but covering the ground swiftly. In the evening, we eat in the great hall, a large fire blazing. I do some cooking but Fergus copes with the vegetarians. Finally, the students roll out their bedding, but I'm in bed before then. It's really good to get acquainted with new people like this and we keep track of a number of them for years afterwards.

## Meadows

The meadow areas are the most colourful and interesting, this month. In its first half, the Dutch crocus hybrids (*C. vernus*) are at their peak – purple, mauve, stripy, white – and not in the least demure. They have self-sown freely over the years and there are wonderfully thick areas of them that make your heart bounce, given a sunny spring day (and they do occur).

By the front path, they coincide with the Lent lilies, *Narcissus pseudonarcissus*, which are equally generous self-seeders. In the orchard, the crocuses form a swathe, roughly parallel with the long border and wrapping round the feet of the circular steps. They overlap the daffodils, but make good team-mates, as the daffodils are still short enough not to interfere with the crocuses' display. Finally, they fill the bath-shaped basin of the drained upper moat. Originally, my mother had them on the sloping sides, where she also planted her snakeshead fritillary seedlings. She thought the bottom would be too wet for them, but they thought otherwise, and soon seeded all over that.

At one end of this dry moat is a patch of summer snowflakes, *Leucojum aestivum*, and this usually reaches its peak after the crocuses have faded, when the wild celandines, *Ranunculus ficaria*, are flowering all over. In one or two recent years, however, we have been plagued by pheasants in the garden, after the shooting season is over. They come to regard it as a sanctuary but are nuts on the flowers both of *Fritillaria meleagris* and of celandines, with the result that the only display was from the snowflakes.

One of my mother's additions was *Anemone apennina*, in weakish shades of blue, pink

PAGES 56–57 The lower moat is at its brightest in spring, with wood anemones and primroses
ABOVE Lent lilies, *Narcissus pseudonarcissus,* naturalized amongst the leaves of a dormant
gunnera by the horse pond

and off-white. It is happy enough and interesting for its circle of far more numerous petals than our own wood anemones, *A. nemorosa*. These, although never planted deliberately, are abundant in many places, especially all around the lower moat, which is at the bottom of the orchard. A rather gloomy piece of water in summer, because of overhanging oaks, it is lively enough now and adopted by a pair (more than one pair, in winter) of mallard ducks. These blush-white anemones (the blush becomes more intense as the flowers age) grow in carpets, but are mixed in with clumps of wild primroses, the softest shade of yellow. There are also patches of goldilocks, *Ranunculus auricomus*, a small, bowl-shaped buttercup and the earliest of its genus to flower. The anemones open wide by day and with slight encouragement from the weather. The scene is as good as anything we have deliberately contrived.

Right across the garden in the horse pond area, the gunneras, *Gunnera manicata*, whose huge umbrella leaves will later, much later, shade everything out beneath them, are only just rubbing their bleary eyes. Their growth buds are fat snouts and covered with pale brown scales. It amuses me to give one of them a pair of eyes, with a couple of cypress cones from nearby, and then I lay my spectacles below them and just across the snout. When the first leaf begins to unfurl, it looks like an ear trumpet.

The gunneras are quite easily persuaded that spring has arrived and may show a little green even as early as February. That will almost certainly get frosted, but there is a whole quiverful of embryo leaves in reserve, and they win through in the end, new growth continuing as late as July. Meantime now, in March, the colony looks so dead, with its withered last year's foliage lying around, that I have been asked whether we have been dredging the pond. But − a case of youth and old age − small things like anemones, Lent lilies, fritillaries and, a little later, wild orchids, find a most agreeable niche in the gaps between the gunnera rhizomes and make a jolly display. They are able to complete their growth cycle before all becomes darkness.

The pond is looking clean, open and attractive, and with luck one will hear frogs or toads croaking, though very few breed any longer, whereas in the past there were many. The first aquatic in flower will be the large kingcup, *Caltha palustris* var. *palustris*. It is as comfortable on damp land as in water and here bridges the two elements. Just about as early is the bog bean, *Menyanthes trifoliata*, though you will still see it in flower in the north of Scotland in June. From shallow water, it pokes up short racemes of blush-white flowers, in which the petals are attractively fringed. Along the pond margin, towards the forstal (the approach drive), in which dogs are constantly being exercised (usually on a lead, I'm thankful to say) by their owners, the dogwoods are not pruned until the end of the month, and then only the oldest stems. These are interplanted with fat clumps (fat, because they love the boggy conditions) of the 'Gravetye Giant' cultivar

Self-sowers: Dutch hybrids of *Crocus vernus* with native Lent liles, *Narcissius pseudonarcissus*, in the front entrance meadow garden of *Leucojum aestivum*. I was told, by Mary Stewart, the Scottish romantic novelist, that they can be grown actually under water, and that she has done this. I have been unsuccessful so far. I cannot seem to stop the bulbs floating away before they obtain root purchase.

Next to the dogwoods and hard up against the forstal fence are two shrub willows, in full bloom now with narrow, yellow catkins, *Salix udensis* (syn. *sachalinensis*) 'Sekka'. It is a male clone. The young stems are often deformed, being flattened and twisted into scrolls, the entire surface now thick with pussies. Many of us (especially the flower arrangers) consider this an attractive feature, but conventional horticulturists are horrified. As they predominate on most judging committees, this plant is never likely to receive any award! Its propensity for twisted branching is strongest on the vigorous young wood following pollarding. Unpruned specimens become almost normal. I compromise, pollarding after a number of years. I find that if too regularly pollarded, this willow is apt to be attacked by the silver-leaf fungus and to die. It is beautiful in summer, too; the leaves arch over to and below the horizontal. As their upper surface is glossy, they catch the light and this is especially noticeable as you drive down the forstal towards sunset and the willow leaves are all gleaming as they catch the low light.

Perhaps this is the moment to mention that most of the wild pussy willows, popularly known as palm and expected to be flowering on Palm Sunday, are great, smoky puffs of yellow this month, though their flowering time varies a lot according to genetic factors, exposure and where you are. These are male plants of the goat willow, alias sallow, *S. caprea*, and it is always a joy to see these heralds of spring. They are besieged by bees, collecting their pollen.

Parallel with the side of the forstal there is a north-facing hollow, whose cliff-like escarpment indicates where excavations ceased centuries ago, when iron ore

was quarried here. This is where I have made my principal attempts to grow rhododendrons, but, with a few blessed exceptions, they don't like me much. Bulbs do, though.

My main colonies of the European dog's-tooth violet, *Erythronium dens-canis*, are here and they are at their peak for ten days mid-month. First, and very suddenly, you see a dark, chocolate-coloured cluster of unfurling leaves, with narrow flower buds nestling at the

centre. Within a very few days, the leaves have expanded, showing a marbled pattern of chocolate and green, while the buds have stretched upwards on 10cm/4in stalks, only waiting for a warm morning to open their nodding blooms into a kind of lampshade with rosy-mauve petals at the horizontal or, if feeling expansive, reflexed. They look quite different from anything else and I try to make a point of visiting them every reasonably pleasant day. Their clumps alternate with those of *Narcissus minor*, which is just the right diminutive size as a companion, and of primroses, which I had to introduce here, but they are well away, now. In a month's time, but I may as well mention it here, quite a different, albeit similarly coloured, erythronium, the American *E. revolutum*, will be flowering on the bank. I have only lately introduced that, but it has taken off and is spreading fast. It seems to have a running rootstock, whereas if I want to increase *E. dens-canis* we have to split the clumps after flowering and spread them around ourselves. It self-sows only a little. There are huge colonies of *E. revolutum* in the Savill Gardens at Windsor Great Park, and I find that encouraging. One is experimenting all the time, with different species that might adapt well to one's own conditions, but there is nothing pressing about all this. It's something that can be done when opportunity arises.

LEFT European dog's-tooth violets, *Erythronium dens-canis*, in a meadow setting
ABOVE A developing colony of hoop-petticoat daffodils, *Narcissus bulbocodium* var. *citrinus*

Another colony that I have started – in a most unpromising piece of ground where, otherwise, nothing much more than mosses will grow beneath an oak – is of the pale yellow form of hoop-petticoat daffodil, *Narcissus bulbocodium* var. *citrinus*. It doesn't spread fast but does self-sow and is clearly in its element. Such a charmer.

Fergus has given a start to snowdrops in this area – *Galanthus* 'Atkinsii' – and we also seem to be establishing with some success the rather small-flowered doronicum, or leopard's bane, with yellow, spring-flowering daisies on 75cm/2½ft stems, that you see so much of in woodland in the north country and Scotland.

There is one other meadow area which should be looked at now, next to the boiler room at the east end of the house. There are ancient lilacs, now in bright green bud, and then a deep hollow, once a pond but drained by my father into the lower moat. However, we also drain into it surface water from the high garden area, and there is a leaky hydrant by the raspberry cage, which is never dry for long, however much I plead for corrective action. That drains into the hollow and we have now taken advantage of the inevitable and planted it with kingcups (*Caltha*). There are also clumps, here, of a handsome red-flowered comfrey which I first collected from a ditch-side in Romania (Transylvania), some twenty years ago.

Around this hollow is a lively spring display of goldilocks, *Ranunculus auricomus* – our largest colony, by far; lady's smock, *Cardamine pratensis*, in contrasting mauve; and wood anemones. On the bank, just below Big Dick, the big yew, is a favourite tree willow, *Salix daphnoides* 'Aglaia'. This is a male, but, for many weeks before flowering, it is covered with silver-white pussies, the young stems being deep crimson red. It presents me with a cultural problem. If you never prune it, young growth, with its bright winter colouring, is much reduced, but if you do cut it back rather sternly, it dies. I am now on to my third or fourth specimen. I shall probably not prune it and see what happens. It looks nice all through the year.

One way and another, we have quite a number of different willows and these are a favourite host plant for the toothwort, *Lathraea clandestina*, which is easily established on them, although it may wander to pastures new. So I have it on the willows by the horse pond and also on *Salix alba* 'Sericea', which I grow for its pale grey foliage, in the long border. Toothworts are total parasites, without any green in the plant at all. This one, which comes from southern Europe, has clusters of bright purple flowers – like an aniline dye but also easily mistaken for crocuses at a distance – from February to April and it can make a great display, as it does along the Backs by the River Cam at Cambridge. Mine are fun, but I could wish that the show had a bit more punch in it. The plant is most easily established by transferring a lump from an established colony to near the roots of your chosen host.

Alders are the poor relations of birches, in the popularity stakes, but I have a weak spot for them. They like the same moist conditions as willows. We have a native *Alnus glutinosa* in the horse pond area, which my brother Oliver planted during the war, but the house cow (a Jersey), which we kept in those days, ate its leader so that it has two trunks. There is a hollow between these two which is filled with rain water for most of the year. I like that (don't ask me why). But of late, a self-sown seedling has appeared right on the bank of the horse pond and that has streaked ahead. It flowers in February — a purplish colour, while the dormant leaf buds are blue.

My showiest alder in flower, however, is the Italian alder, *Alnus cordata*, which is planted by the lower moat. The male catkins on that are clustered like the fingers of your hand if you held them straight and parallel. At this stage, they point in any direction — often horizontally or upwards — but on flowering, this month, they hang like any other catkin and they are fat and prosperous-looking, not a bit skinny like a hazel's. A good bright yellow, too. The wind soon blows them off.

## Shrubs and trees

This isn't a flowering shrub garden, mainly because such shrubs are apt to be bulky and dull throughout the summer. I don't want that sort of garden. Another factor, operative until recently, was the prevalence of bullfinches. Families of bullfinches were around all winter and spring and they stripped the buds, of both flowers and leaves, from a great many of the flowering and fruiting types of tree and shrub. I think because of the return of the sparrow hawk — since the prohibition of the use of the pesticide Aldrin (which made so many birds sterile) on farm land — bullfinches, which are rather a favourite food with them, as are wood pigeons, are now under control.

I can now again grow plum trees without losing the entire crop at the blossom bud stage. They flower in March and are very pure white. I always hope that 'Early Rivers Prolific', which needs a pollinator, will coincide with 'Victoria', which doesn't, but which can act as pollinator to others. But 'Rivers' Early Prolific', as it should be called, is just going over as 'Victoria' is coming out. If I had a colony of wild blackthorn nearby, I suppose that would do the trick — it has an amazingly long season. As it is very white itself, people mutter 'a blackthorn winter' when the weather turns cold, which it is bound to do at some time when blackthorn is flowering. None of which helps my 'Early Rivers'. I'm lucky if I get a decent crop from that one year in three, but it is my favourite culinary plum.

There are some shrubs which I feel I must have. A bit of forsythia, for instance, so that I can bring budded branches of it into the house shortly before it flowers outside. *Kerria japonica*, again yellow-flowered, I must also have. I am growing the single 'Golden Guinea' cultivar. As with some of the early-flowering spiraeas — *Spiraea* x *vanhouttei*, for instance, desperately dull in the garden for most of the year — you can divide your stock and pot some of it up, in the autumn, so that it can be either brought indoors, when flowering (unpopular with whoever has to clear up its fallen petals), or, my preference, stood outside my porch to welcome me (and anyone else) when I go in and out.

One or other corylopsis seems essential to me, but I must have a scented kind, which

the dwarfest and largest-flowered species, *Corylopsis pauciflora*, is not. So I have the lemony-scented *C. glabrescens* (which I noted in Cherry Ingram's garden), and that is fine, with dangles of pale yellow blossom, nice to pick.

I cannot altogether avoid camellias. I twice planted my own-propagated 'Lady Vansittart' at the end of a north-facing shed and twice it was stolen. So, taking the hint not before time, I planted the third one at the end of another shed where the public don't pass and that has flourished. What I like about this *Camellia japonica* cultivar is the neatness of its leaves and the agreeable twist on them. The double flowers are generally pale pink, often pink with a few red petals, and occasionally all red. Not really a selling point, and they still cling to the shrub after turning brown. The neatly double red 'Margherita Coleoni' – which, again, I struck from a cutting, years ago, and it was years before I could get it identified – is rather good about a timely petal-shed. The vulgar streak in me gravitates to 'Mercury' (from Jackman's old Woking nursery), which is large, bright red and slightly open in the centre of a loosely doubled bloom. I have that next to *Magnolia* x *loebneri* 'Leonard Messel' and they flower together without quarrelling.

Of course, one must have a few magnolias and I am delighted with this one, which has quickly made a small, twiggy tree. You can admire its promise all through the winter and it flowers over quite a long period, now – a soft, clear and definite shade of pink, the flowers small but compensatingly numerous. With its *M. stellata* parent, it shares the advantage of opening its buds over a long period so that if one lot gets frosted, which is probable, they will soon be replaced.

*M. stellata* has been here, in the right angle of two retaining walls close to the daffodil orchard, since before I was born but has never made a large shrub, as it is not on good soil. No matter, it is large enough and I always welcome its reliable display of spidery, pale pink blossom. Some of its branches are very old and lichen-covered, but others, arising from those which I had cut back, are younger and more vigorous. That's a good feature in magnolias – they respond well to a hard pruning, but you must feed, too.

On the high wall dividing the upper and lower terraces, we have another original, *M.* x *soulangeana* 'Lennei', and that has a long season, starting this month. It is a large, loose-growing hybrid and, with its lax habit, takes up a lot of space if planted out in the open, so its position against a wall, where you can tie the main branches in, is ideal, although it scarcely needs wall protection from the hardiness angle. Some of the branches of mine trail on the paving below it. They are not much in the way, so I allow that and it gives the opportunity of looking down into the flower, by way of a change from always looking upwards.

The blooms are quite large, electric light bulb shaped, deep mauve-pink on the outside, off-white within. The colouring is not refined but this magnolia makes a great display and never fails, even if occasionally interrupted by frost.

The chalices of *Magnolia* x *soulangeana* 'Lennei' with *M. stellata* behind

## Scillas and hyacinths

Under this magnolia is a colony – one of several – of *Scilla bithynica*, another Cherry Ingram acquisition. It is a very pale blue species – rather too pale, at times – and a prolific self-seeder, so that a colony is soon built up. There is deepest shade under the magnolia in summer, but it is still leafless in March, so the scilla receives all the light it needs. I also grow it, among common male ferns, *Dryopteris filix-mas*, outside our larder. The ferns are deciduous and currently dormant, their old fronds cleared away. I am now trying to establish the scilla in rather shaded areas of rough grass, where the turf is not too thick. This seems to be working. Odd that *S. bithynica* is so little seen or offered.

Another scilla we have is 'Rosea', the pink-flowered cultivar of *S. bifolia* – not so nice as the bright blue *S. bifolia* but still welcome. I've not thought of a good companion for that. No good putting out a suggestions box, as the public are not yet with us.

The best-known scilla, *S. siberica*, comes on gradually and may not be at its peak till the end of the month or later. This really is unadulterated and rich blue, the flowers bell-like and pendent. It grows splendidly under border conditions but does not last for many years in turf, with me. With some of my friends, it does.

Under the dogwoods at the back of our main bedding-out area, in the solar garden, is a pleasing little colony of dwarf bulbs: a late-flowering snowdrop that Beth Chatto gave me which she has named 'Finale'; a clump of yellow *Narcissus minor* (which increases rapidly in cultivated ground); and a *Scilla/Chionodoxa* hybrid, x *Chionoscilla allenii*, a robust grower. This is the way we like to make use of spare space in spring. The bulbs will have finished flowering by the time I prune the dogwoods.

We also have the chionoscilla contrasting with the young, greeny-yellow foliage of *Valeriana phu* 'Aurea', the chionoscilla clumps being among the somewhat rhizomatous valerian shoots. Later, the valerian grows up to 90cm/3ft or more and has moderately undistinguished corymbs of white flowers.

By the end of March, most of the florists' hyacinths are in flower. Whether categorized as early, mid-season or late, they all seem to flower more or less together in

x *Chionoscilla allenii* with the young foliage of *Valeriana phu* 'Aurea'

the garden. There is something about their waxy artificiality that I find most endearing and the scent is swooning, borne on the air. If you can leave your colonies undisturbed (which may be none too easy in a busy garden) they make up into thickly flowering groups. The flower spikes will vary a lot in size, but whether fairly large or small, it doesn't matter; the mixture of all sizes is just what's needed. They can be very long-lived. I think it was in 1927 that my brother Oliver had appendicitis which prevented him from accompanying my parents to one of the spots where a total eclipse of the sun was expected (it was cloudy, of course). He was brought a pot of white *Hyacinthus* 'l'Innocence' in hospital. The bulbs were later planted at Dixter at the foot of an espalier pear and they are still there.

My favourite established colony is in the long border, of 'Ostara', which is deep blue. The pale yellow 'City of Haarlem' is a good mixer, though I don't seem to keep it for very long. I have had it around a clump of *Lathyrus vernus*, which is a reddish-purple, non-climbing pea, flowering now and next month, and also beneath the branches of *Spiraea japonica* 'Goldflame', which is brilliantly copper-coloured on its young shoots. Most gardeners prune this in spring, but if you do, it doesn't make a good foliage display till considerably later. I prune it in July, immediately after flowering, which gives it time to make new growth on which to flush an abundance of early shoots next March.

## Walls

Any figs that need tying in to the walls should have been dealt with by now. They are grown mainly for their leaves as wall decoration, and their pale grey stems also look good in winter. To fruit well, as little pruning as possible should be practised, as they fruit from the tips of their previous year's young shoots, and a great many of these will have to be removed if the tree is to be trained into the wall. So we try to get away with doing this operation only every third year. If we leave it for too long, not only does the weight of the fig branches cause them to break away from their ties, but the projecting growth is a nuisance to the flower borders in front.

Peaches should have been pruned and trained before they flower, which is usually in early March. They need quite a lot of treatment, cutting out old, fruited wood and tying in young shoots, whose optimum length will be about one foot. The apricot, on the other hand, keeps most of its old wood from year to year, flowering (even before the peaches) and fruiting mainly from spurs off that wood. Over-strong young shoots that come forward have to be removed, but if they are positioned so that they can be tied in without bending them unduly, that is ideal. They can extend the tree's range against the wall and also replace tired old branches. The flowers are white, with deep crimson-red calyxes.

The old wall pears, which date back to my father's time, are spur-pruned and tied, where necessary. A number of them have the undignified role of giving support to ornamental climbers. The Japanese quince, *Chaenomeles speciosa*, makes an unruly shrub

which is most difficult to control in an open site. It flowers mainly on second-year wood, with long wisps of the young shoots projecting outwards. On the whole, a wall position is the most satisfactory. I have a nice deep pink one that was a favourite of my mother's and I am growing the blue *Clematis alpina* 'Frances Rivis' up it. The two coincide towards the end of the month.

Many of our retaining walls are colonized by large old pads of aubrieta, and this is aubrieta time: shades of mauve and purple, with a few that are reddish. I do nothing about growing choice, named varieties and I certainly don't cut the plants back after flowering, to keep them neat. Why should I want them to be neat? They keep themselves neat enough. But the Mexican daisy which colonizes all our walls, *Erigeron karvinskianus*, does need a tidy. It flowers non-stop (opening white and ageing pink) from May to November but now needs to be cut back as hard into the wall cracks as you can reach. This also gives breathing space to my dear rusty-back fern, on the lower terrace. It is still looking as fresh as ever.

Periwinkles will grow in walls or as ground cover. We have a number of clones – the typical blue, white, purple, double blue and double purple. All these are *Vinca minor*. The largest, showiest colony was planted by my mother along a very low piece of retaining wall with a yew hedge above it. It is a south aspect, which encourages freest flowering. Another service we do for this colony is to strim all its old growth back, every other year. Nearly all the blossom is produced from ground level and in this way you are enabled to see the flowers without competition. They were all white, when first planted, but some have reverted to the blue of the wilding, and the mixture is nice. March is their great display month, although you can find a few blooms at almost any season. On the whole, the greater periwinkle, *Vinca major*, makes too untidy a colony but I do have some of 'Variegata', whose foliage is splashed with areas of cream. That's good under a shrub, as its variegation is just as bright in the shade and it lights up dark places. You can cut your plants hard back annually, to promote young shoots and to keep them in order.

At this season – or perhaps in February, but before they are showing flower buds –

we also take the strimmer over the large colony of *Epimedium pinnatum* subsp. *colchicum*, which makes such excellent ground cover beneath the branches of the old *Malus floribunda* crab. The epimedium foliage is good evergreen material for most of the year but is tired by now and anyway the strimming allows you fully to enjoy the spring display of bright yellow blossom, quickly accompanied by coppery young foliage.

Mention must be made of violets – the sweet-scented *Viola odorata*, now in its prime. The big Lutyens seat, down by the topiary lawn, catches the late morning sun so that, if we're drinking champagne before lunch ('The best time to drink champagne', said Sir David Scott, 'is at 11 o'clock on a Sunday morning when everyone else is in church') and there's sunshine but an edge to the wind, this is the place to sit and sip and bask, with the dogs stretched out on the lawn. Just in front of me, in a gap between lawn and paving, is a ribbon of white violets. I love that. They come in a range of colours – white, pink, buff yellow, mauve and typical violet – and are endlessly obliging about where

LEFT Large old clumps of aubrieta hanging off the walls on the back drive. *Bergenia stracheyi* is in the foreground.

BELOW The pale grey tracery of a wall-trained fig next to a fruiting peach in flower

they'll grow, happy in sun but also excellent in quite deep shade, where their stalks grow longer, should one want to pick a bunch to have near one's nose indoors. And the flowers, together with primroses, can decorate a green salad, after it has been dressed.

There is a huge dawn chorus of birds, by the end of March, but my favourites, the blackbirds, are the loudest, shouting the odds at one another. Why can't we sound as beautiful, when we're being aggressive?

## Hedges

We shall have got around to cutting all the rough hedges quite early in the month. If any yew or ilex hedge needs to be halved, this is also the best time to be doing it. The evergreen ilex – *Quercus ilex* – hedges have widely spaced units but were allowed to grow high, to 3.6m/12ft or more, and extremely thick. On their garden side, a great deal of border was gobbled up. Their olive-green colouring makes a pleasing change from yew and they do provide very necessary shelter from the prevailing south-westerlies. But we decided, as one needs to with any hedge, in course of time, to reduce their bulk by 'halving' them. You cut all the branches along one side, back to the central trunks. Half measures are useless; if you merely reduce the branches, leaving long stumps, some will break into new growth, others won't. But if you go right back, you may be sure (almost) that strong new shoots will break freely from the trunk.

We did that, first, on the sheltered border side and a lorry from the London Zoo fetched the prunings, which are ideal browsing material for giraffes. After a couple of years, we gave the same treatment to the hedge's other side. This not only spreads the shock, but ensures that you don't lose all the hedge's shelter value at once. The hedges form a horseshoe arc, and we are now tackling the stretch on the windward side.

When yew hedges are trimmed, you can never take them quite as far back as in the previous year. So, over the years, their bulk is sure to increase. If you never do anything to redress this situation, you end up with unbalanced monster hedges such as you see at Crathes Castle or Powis Castle, for instance – fun, maybe, but very far from what was originally intended. In our case, I resent losing too much border space, in some situations, while in others, neighbouring paths are so much overlapped that they can no longer be used.

The sweet violet, *Viola odorata* 'Alba', tucks itself into odd crannies

This is when we halve our yews. It looks ugly and stark, at first,  but the wounds are soon healed. For the rare cases where they are not, we keep a few spare plants by us with which to stop gaps. Any self-sown yew seedlings that are spotted in the garden are potted up and grown on against an emergency.

## Bamboos

We try, at least every other year but every year would be better, to thin out our bamboo clumps. They make wonderful features, not so much as a hedge but as key specimens, solo or integrated with other plantings. Old canes – culms, they should be called – live on but gradually lose vigour and they get in the way of developing new canes. They also give the bottom of a colony a choked-up appearance, in which masses of old foliage accumulates. If all this is sorted out, you will be able to see through and past the remaining canes once more and it all looks far more appetizing.

It is quite hot and protracted work. I like to take a kneeling mat with me and a saw and to work around the outside of a colony for a start, sawing every cane I decide to remove as low as I possibly can and flush with the ground. This makes the job so much easier to do, next time it comes round. As with all pruning, I always remove the obvious duds, first, after which it becomes clear which of the doubtfuls (doubtful when you started, but no longer so) should go. The outside of the colony is easiest to reach, in the first instance, but removal of dud material there will later allow you to reach into the heart of the clump with comparative ease.

## Seed-sowing

We still rather shy off much seed-sowing, in March, largely because we know how time-consuming it will be (and Fergus likes to do the major part of it himself) and how even more demanding the seedlings will be for undelayed attention once germinated. There is still, always, so much catching up to do out in the garden. I nag a bit to have lettuce and parsley and celeriac sown, in pots, and sweet peas and a few other things.

As for outside, the ground is usually far too dour, still, to receive seeds kindly. We did have ideal conditions, one dry year, and I got Perry to sow some broad bean seeds. About one third of them didn't germinate but the rest did so well with their extra growing time that they easily compensated and gave as good a yield as the beans we held back to sow at our normal time, in late April, all of which germinated.

By the end of the month, we have put the clocks forward and everything seems different. The hawthorns are bursting into leaf. The borders are filling out – young cardoon foliage is looking especially handsome. It's go, go, go, and we have reached that stage when we cease to stop and stare. That is a great mistake. We should always make time to look and to take things in. Otherwise what's the point?

April

Keats captures the flavour of the month in his opening to *The Eve of St Mark*, as folk are being called to evening prayer:

The city streets were clean and fair
From wholesome drench of April rains;
And, on the western window panes,
The chilly sunset faintly told
Of unmatured green, vallies cold,
Of the green thorny bloomless hedge,
Of primroses by shelter'd rills,
And daisies on the aguish hills.

Definitely not summer yet.

But the swallows are back. House martins count as swallows for the purposes of seeing the first (which I never seem to, anyway). 12 April is cuckoo day, in Sussex (don't ask me why), but cuckoos, the loud monotony of whose persistent call we used to swear at, are now so rare that it is sometimes May before I hear my first. Still, the dawn chorus is terrific and the fact of its being so loud at Dixter is a pleasant reminder of the fact that our sort of garden provides a great many suitable habitats for nesting birds.

## Daffodils

It is (or should be, unless the season is ridiculously early) the month of the daffodil. I always reckon that 12 April is a date one should be able to rely on for a good display, in our daffodil orchard – some are earlier, some later. First to flower is *Narcissus* 'Princeps' – marketed to us as 'Princeps Maximus', to make it sound more important. It is like a glorified, tetraploid Lent lily. My mother picked most of them in tight bud, 'cooked' them in the bathroom hot cupboard, and would then send them to family friends.

Next comes the mainstream 'Emperor' – a yellow trumpet and always reliable for a fortnight's display but no longer. Its last day, before fading, coincides with the cherry blossom opening on an early white-heart variety, which has made a very large tree by the lower moat. I remember that being planted in the early 1930s. We never get a crop, of course; the birds have that, but I can buy such beautiful, succulent cherries locally that that's no deprivation.

All these daffodils and narcissi were planted in large groups. Coinciding with 'Emperor' is 'Minnie Hume', a white narcissus mixed in with another, smaller white one, 'Lillie Langtry' (or it might have been 'Mrs Langtry') named after King Edward VII's favourite, who was popularly known as the Jersey lily.

A little later comes 'Barrii', sold to us as 'Barrii Conspicuus', this being named after the Barr family's famous bulb house. It is a yellow narcissus, the small cup being

PAGES 74–75 The daffodil orchard with 'Emperor' in the foreground rimmed with orange. A lovely scent wafts from a big swathe of this. We are then done with the maincrop until the poet's narcissi follow much later, in May.

My mother considered that all should be dead-headed, after flowering, not by merely pulling the flowers off the still green stalks – that would have been an immoral shortcut – but by picking or pulling stem and all. We children were bribed with a penny a hundred, and everything was counted – by us. That was an accepted part of the rules. Meantime, the garden was opened for free to all parishioners on a Sunday when the daffodils were at their peak, and we were engaged to pick bunches of them to give to each group. We still open in the same way, but I'm afraid the daffodil picking has lapsed. So has the dead-heading. The daffodils soon become engulfed in the rising tide of grasses and other meadow components.

I do not grow many daffodils in the borders, because their foliage becomes really unsightly, there. I can think of some gardens which appear to be finished for the year when their over-generous display of these and Spanish bluebells is past and there is nothing left to see but 'flopping masses of decay', as Farrer aptly put it. Still, there are a few. One of the most spectacular, early on, is a white narcissus called 'Aflame', which has a large and brilliant scarlet cup. The flower nods slightly on its stalk, but I have a group in the high garden that can be seen as you walk up steps towards it. The cup bleaches very quickly, but retains its colour if picked young for indoors. Then, I have the Triandrus hybrid 'Thalia', a bunch-headed pure white narcissus, whose leaves are reasonably discreet. It is a fantastically generous flowerer and for a long period. That, under a bamboo, looks nice with the blue flowers of *Brunnera macrophylla*.

Occasionally, I use a narcissus for bedding. One combination that has worked well is a carpet of the single, pure white *Arabis* 'Snow Cap' (a seed strain), interspersed with the yellow, orange-centred Cyclamineus daffodil, 'Jetfire'. Both have finished flowering mid-month, so we can follow with an early-flowering annual such as *Osteospermum hyoseroides* 'Gaiety', with bright orange daisies, maybe combined with the light blue *Asperula orientalis*. And they, again, will be followed by a third display. This, if you like seizing such opportunities, is the advantage of really early spring bedding.

Another good subject for it, while I'm on this theme, is *Bergenia stracheyi*, say with purple aubrieta. This bergenia has small, neat foliage and an abundance of deep pink flower clusters. It will have finished by mid-April and can be moved to a reserve (you must have that), as can the aubrieta, cutting it back as you move it. The site is now clear for the next brainwave!

## Meadows

The meadows have much to offer besides narcissi; indeed, the latter are deliberately excluded from some areas. The first of our local wild orchids, *Orchis mascula*, is in its prime. It is a strong grower, sometimes a foot tall, with quite long spikes of distinctly reddish-purple flowers. Rather a nasty smell, but you're not obliged to push your nose into them. The leaves can be heavily spotted purple. These are Shakespeare's early purples. We have them scattered around but strongest in the upper moat, where snakesheads are still flowering and there is a handsome contribution from dandelions. The pale blue Spanish bluebells have a stronghold, here, but they also come in pink and white, in the orchard.

The wood anemones, *Anemone nemerosa*, are mainly over but I have an excellent late-flowering clone, called 'Lismore Blue', from the Duke of Devonshire's south Irish property at Lismore. Wild anemones are quite often blue, in that part of the world. 'Robinsoniana' is a well-known example, which I also have, but 'Lismore Blue' is better shaped and neater. It is near the horse pond.

Blue is a precious colour, in a meadow, as so many of the wild flowers are yellow daisies or buttercups. Near the front path, *Camassia cusickii*, with tall racemes of light blue stars, will be in bloom by the end of April, swiftly followed by my most successful foreign import, the American *C. quamash*, my strain of which has deep blue stars on foot-tall stems. This clumps up well but also self-sows, the seeds not ripening till August.

Early purples, *Orchis mascula*, with Spanish bluebells in the upper moat

## Pots

Michael Crosby-Jones is an extremely good maker of flower pots, near to us, so we are easily tempted to buy the nicely shaped kinds that he would make specially for us, if he needed to. Then, of course, we need to buy bulbs to fill them. But then, we buy so many bulbs that we need more pots in which to plant them . . . The April display is especially lively, our main shop window being either side of the entrance porch, but we also assemble pots for display in other parts of the garden.

Hyacinths look and smell wonderful when gathered together in large pots and I buy at least twenty-five of each variety at a time. They do more than one year, but are eventually planted out. Of the late kinds, one of the most successful is the old double red 'Hollyhock' – a compact cultivar which needs no staking. (Others may need it but probably don't get it.) 'King Codro' is an intriguing late-flowerer; deep blue but with green tips to its petals. It lurches about, rather, but is endearing, like some friends who have a weakness for the bottle, but always remain charming under the influence.

Narcissi can often be flowered in the same pot for two or three successive years. They always catch you on the hop, in summer, by making new roots long before you had expected them to. By the time you have awoken to the situation, the best course is just to scrape away the old top layer of soil and replace it with a rich soil-based potting compost such as John Innes No. 3. *Narcissus* 'Quail' is an excellent, multi-headed, long-flowering jonquil, deep butter yellow. 'Winston Churchill' is a multi-headed Tazetta – the scent is quite different from a jonquil's and not so friendly. This has an orange cup but prominent white doubling in the centre.

You can choose any tulips you like for pot work. I am fond of the early, deep yellow, single *Tulipa* 'Bellona', which is also sweetly scented, but all too often have been sold the wrong tulip under this name. A protected position will enable you to grow double tulips, especially the heavy-headed late doubles, without them being snapped off beneath the weight of rain. 'Princess Irene' is a winner of subtle colouring. It is shortish, with glaucous foliage, the petals a mixture of soft orange with a purple flush on the outside – even of the inner three segments. 'Couleur Cardinal', similarly short, has dark stems and deep red flowers flushed purple without. The colourings and inner markings of tulips are inexhaustibly varied and subtle.

Other plants we display outside the porch, now, always include the climbing *Tropaeolum tricolorum*. Its sheaves of blossom consist of pixie-cap flowers in three colours: red outside, yellow inside and a burnt rim around the mouth. *Euryops pectinatus* is a tender shrub (though it can be grown outside along our south coasts) with feathery grey foliage and rich yellow daisies. Then, I have a scraggy, tender rhododendron, with deliciously boudoir-perfumed white flowers. Fergus brings out, as early as he dares, the yellow-variegated form of *Agave americana*, to give solidity to the scene. That will stick around till October. We also like to put *Geranium maderense* on display, if it is flowering, but it can be ruined by a late frost.

## Tulips

I will here give my concentrated attention to this favourite flower (favourite with Fergie just as much as with me) in its garden roles, although it continues through much of May, so I shall have to return to it. The advantage of the later-flowering kinds is that they have a better chance of not being battered by rough weather. The mid-April-flowering *Tulipa* 'Rosy Wings', for instance, which is an old-fashioned cottage tulip (before that category was eliminated), has elongated blooms of great style. They are desperately vulnerable to wind and seldom give me more than a week, but their prosperous clump has been in the long border for many years.

As regards their treatment, our tulips fall into two categories: those that are treated as bedding plants and are lifted and dried off after flowering; and those which we can treat as permanencies, because they are growing where they will not be in the way at any stage. Our heavy soil seems to suit tulips uncommonly well, and some of these colonies are now thirty years old.

One of my favourites is the Darwin hybrid 'Red Matador', which is growing within the embrace of *Pinus mugo*. It is strong red but with that subtle pink flush on the outside which characterizes many tulips. When the bloom opens, it reveals a magnificently marked and coloured centre. Another permanent site is within a group of giant fennel, *Ferula communis*. The spring foliage of this perennial is an undulating duvet of finest, bright green filigree, so with it I grow a tall red tulip, 'Halcro'. Again it has that pink flush.

I think tulips combine spectacularly with euphorbias. With *Euphorbia* x *martinii*, which is fairly low but shrubby, with pale green, red-centred 'flowers', I have the Viridiflora tulip 'Spring Green' and a third, in this party, is the green-flowered *Tellima grandiflora*, with scalloped basal leaves. Who said my tastes were loud and brash? With the bright yellow-green *Euphorbia polychroma* and more of *E.* x *martinii* behind it, I have two lily-flowered tulips, the scarlet 'Dyanito' and the orange 'Ballerina'. This is not so modest, but near by, with the sheaves of *Gladiolus tristis*, which is palest green, there is the mauve-flowered variegated honesty, *Lunaria annua* 'Variegata', and as blue a tulip as lilac knows how to be, 'Bleu Aimable' (often misprinted Blue Amiable). When tulip foliage is dying, it isn't a nuisance, like daffodils, but remains compact and is easily absorbed by its neighbours.

ABOVE  Pots outside the porch
RIGHT  Lily-flowered *Tulipa* 'Ballerina' with *Euphorbia* x *martinii*

Tulips have many roles as bedding plants. For instance, the lily-flowered 'China Pink' above a carpet of pink pomponette daisies (alas, it becomes increasingly difficult to find seed of the latter as a separate colour). I like to bed out 'Florestan' carnations, treated as biennials, and their hummocks of glaucous foliage are an ideal background, in spring, for tulips, especially a rich red, black-centred one like *Tulipa eichleri*. Any biennial, or perennial treated as a biennial, will make a good partner. We like tulips with our lupins, whose own young foliage makes a delightful background to any-coloured tulips. Bedded-out sweet williams can make a terrific early summer display, but you'll want to pep them up in spring – with tulips, of course. In cases such as the last two, the tulips will not need to be lifted until the lupins or sweet williams have themselves completed their display, so the bulbs will have dried off and will be ready to harvest, anyway. But if they are with spring bedding, like bellis or forget-me-nots, they'll still be green. No matter. Don't imagine they need to be replanted, to finish off. Just lay them out on racks in a cool, airy shed and they will automatically withdraw their reserves from their leaves back into the bulbs. When the foliage is quite sere, we harvest the bulbs (rubbing off any dirt) and, if we have the time then, but if not, later, we sort those bulbs which look large enough to flower the next year out from those which don't. All are hung up, safe from mice, in open-mesh bags, dangling

from a horizontal pole (and appropriately labelled). The tiddlers will (sometimes not till early winter) be lined out in a reserve area and will there build up strength to be used again for display, in the year after their rest. In this way, our stocks of tulips never need to decline, but that doesn't prevent us from buying a lot more, each autumn. Where will it end?

## Blossom

This word blossom has a particular connotation – the spring blossom of cherries, plums, peaches, pears, almonds and apples, whether grown for fruit or for ornament. We do not have a lot of it, because ornamental blossom trees tend to be rather large passengers, once they have flowered. Also, there was the bullfinch problem. But some we do have, and also a certain number of flowering shrubs.

I am fond of pear blossom, for its sickly sweet scent; also for the distinct manner in which the flowers (which are always dead white) are borne in clusters. There is a large espalier pear on the solar chimney breast. 'That must be terribly old,' a lady visitor said to me. 'Well,' said I, 'how old are you, for instance?' 'I was seventy last week.' 'That's just about the pear's age,' I told her. 'Not so very ancient, is it?' She agreed. That must be ten years ago. The pear is in good order, although it has lost a few of its horizontal branches. I hope the lady has done no worse than lose a few of her teeth. It is a culinary pear and excellent value as such in November, though its name label has long since vanished.

The old wild pear that was here, in front of the house, before we came to Dixter and either side of which yew hedging was planted, is quite a sight in bloom, although it was better still before we had to decapitate it, following the 1987 storm, which left it rocking. At least two species of parasitic fungi fruit at its base, each autumn, so I suppose its days are numbered. Yet another old pear, a nineteenth-century survivor, is in the peacock garden, and that is a beautiful shape, especially noticeable when flowering. From being vertical at its base, the trunk divides, about 1.2m/4ft up, into two horizontals, and these become vertical again, after another 90cm/3ft or so. My sister and I loved to hoist ourselves on to the horizontals, when we were children, and sit there.

LEFT *Tulipa* 'Red Shine' in front of *Prunus glandulosa* 'Alba Plena'
ABOVE *Gladiolus tristis* with tulips 'Bleu Aimable' and 'China Pink', forget-me-nots and honesty, *Lunaria annua variegata*, in the barn garden

The crop of small pears is prolific and always scab-free, but no one is tempted, more than once, to eat them.

I no longer have any 'Bramley Seedling' apples, since the two big storms of 1987 and 1990. Their rich pink blossom was handsome. But we still have our old *Malus floribunda*, planted when we came to Dixter. It has fantastically twisted trunks, long concealed by ivy. This has been replaced by a carpet of *Epimedium pinnatum* subsp. *colchicum*, of which I have already written. The crab blossom is at its best mid-month, while still not quite out, and is then a lively shade of pink, but it soon bleaches. There used to be six 'John Downie' crabs, in front of the house, this being the best for jelly-making, though the fruit is subject to scab. Growing on particularly nasty clay, they never really throve and only one now remains – pink as the blossom opens, then fading white.

The morello cherry is trained against a north wall in the barn garden. That is pure white, and we have just now planted, alongside it, the double form of *Prunus cerasus*, called 'Rhexii'. It should make a beautiful companion in its flowering season, but does not fruit. I have two of the bush cherry *P. glandulosa* 'Alba Plena' in the barn garden, wreathed with double white pom-poms along all the previous year's young shoots. I prune it hard, after flowering, to encourage plenty of new growth, so it is never more than 1.2m/4ft tall. Some 'Red Shine' multiple-stemmed tulips looked spectacular in front of the prunus. We have to spray that with fungicide, before flowering, as it is subject to a blossom-wilt disease, which otherwise quite ruins the display right in the middle of the season. There is a bonus in the autumn, when the cherry's foliage turns pink.

## Other flowering shrubs

In the cats' garden, next to the boiler house, an ancient colony of lilacs comes into bloom. They never receive attention and are covered in lichens, but are exceedingly good-tempered and make a charming display. There's no scent to compare with the common lilac's, *Syringa vulgaris*, though other species may be fragrant in one way or another. For instance, *S.* x *persica* 'Alba', a slender-stemmed shrub, only 1.5–1.8m/ 5–6ft high, with glacier-white blossom; that is, white but with the faintest hint of blue. I prune out a lot of its flowered wood, immediately after flowering, and we also need to spray it against a fungal disease which attacks leaves and young stems. The public love it, and with good reason. Another popular dwarf lilac is *S.* x *meyeri* (*S. palibiniana*), whose habit is extremely stiff. The mauve blossom has a rather cheap scent. This can grow too large for the space it deserves, but I cut mine very hard back and it responded excellently, being no more than 1.2m/4ft high for the time being.

I ought to get the fine-leaved *Rosmarinus officinalis* 'Benenden Blue' (a collection of Cherry Ingram's from Corsica) in harness with *Coronilla valentina*. I find the rosemary as hardy as any *R. officinalis* and it is tremendously free with deep blue (not the usual grey-

*Malus floribunda*, above a carpet of *Epimedium pinnatum* subsp. *colchicum*

blue) blossom. The coronilla, which I mentioned in February in connection with being visited by an early butterfly, has its main season in April, although it may flower at any time from autumn on. It is densely covered with heavily scented, bright yellow pea flowers. Growing no more than 45cm/1½ft high, it could go in front of the rosemary. Both have a rather lax habit, so they could intertwine. Why hadn't I thought of that till this moment?

A great feature, early in the month, are the four clipped specimens of *Osmanthus delavayi* on four corners of the barn garden. Many visitors are short-sighted in their appreciation of a garden. They'll notice and enquire about one of the osmanthus, entirely failing to appreciate that the quorum is made up with three others. There are, I have worked out, about one quarter million of the little tubular white flowers out at this time. Their scent is carried far on the air. They remain white for a mere week; then start noticeably changing to brown, but the scent does not abate for a long while. They are clipped over as soon as the display is past.

Rather a nice apron in front of one of the osmanthus is made by the celandine, *Ranunculus ficaria*, which I found in a nearby shaw and named 'Brazen Hussy'. Its bright yellow flowers show up gleamingly against purple foliage. It is planted on the site of *Crocosmia* 'Lucifer', whose green spears take over as the celandine takes its bow and exits. Celandines in borders can be a menace and every year I have to eliminate plants which have found their way into some unwanted spot. I know of some gardens where they have taken over completely. They are sensitive to herbicides, but if there are other plants around, the task of elimination is not simple. Another of these osmanthus looks good in a strong combination behind *Phormium cookianum* 'Tricolor' and the dwarf, heavily cut-leaved form of cardoon, *Cynara cardunculus*, which I had from the Chelsea Physic Garden. In front of them, some of the mauve-flowered, variegated-leaved honesty.

I do not pride myself as a rhododendron-grower, but a group of the magenta-flowered evergreen azalea which we used to know as *Rhododendron obtusum amoenum*, now

Bushes of *Osmanthus delavayi* define the corners of the barn garden

*R.* 'Amoenum', makes a knock-out display near the forstal. With grass for a background, it looks just right. I also have a *R.* x *loderi* 'King George', which never fails to flower profusely, although different parts of the bush flower at different times, spreading the season. The scented flowers, which are as much as 12cm/5in across, open pale pink and fade to white.

My best magnolia, now, aside from *Magnolia* 'Lennei', already described, is *M. liliiflora* 'Nigra'. That has a long season, lasting well into May. The flowers are elongated, their petals wine purple (blackcurrant wine) on the outside, pale inside. It is prolific on a dense, not over-large bush. We regularly, every other year, layer its lowest branches. On lifting them rooted, after two years, another lot of layers is put down. The other showy magnolia is 'Galaxy', which makes a stiff, upright specimen, occupying little lateral space, an advantage where I have it. This is a hybrid between the last and *M. sprengeri* 'Diva'. It has sizeable pink flowers and makes a good show from an early age.

## In the borders
By the end of the month, the borders will almost have filled in with fresh vegetation and little soil will be showing. This is largely thanks to the running theme of forget-me-nots. They make an interrupted haze of blue through much of the garden and this will last till the end of May. They weld various good combinations, for instance with the bronze, evergreen foliage of *Libertia peregrinans* and the pale yellow young foliage of *Spiraea japonica* 'Gold Mound'. The forget-me-not haze needs to be, and is, balanced by strong foliage such as that of the cardoons, oriental poppies and delphiniums. Even the day lilies' straps have their own strength, while hostas are coming along. Not that I grow many, these days, as I cannot be bothered to fight the snails and slugs which ruin their appearance.

Other features which I think noteworthy would include the milk-and-roses form of *Lathyrus vernus* called 'Alboroseus' with the rich, reddish-purple heads of *Bergenia purpurascens*. The usual purple *L. vernus* is nice with an old *Narcissus cyclamineus* hybrid called 'Queen of Spain', which is a light lemon yellow and not too vigorous. A group of deepest purple-brown *Fritillaria pyrenaica* rises behind the grape hyacinth *Muscari armeniacum* 'Blue Spike', which has a rather fluffed-out inflorescence. One forgets entirely about such plants for most of the year, until suddenly, there they are.

Of euphorbias that shouldn't be taken for granted, *Euphorbia amygdalloides* var. *robbiae* grows in all sorts of places. It is somewhat unaccountable, as a disease often wipes a colony out, but it is adept at flourishing where you had not intended it. We have an ancient colony, perhaps forty years old, at the very dry foot of a row of ash trees in the frameyard area. Another in the risers of some Lutyens steps. Others, again, self-sown, on the kitchen drive wall, where they hobnob with aubrietas and primroses. This is a notably sunny spot, and the euphorbias are said to like shade. But sun or shade is all the same to them, and when in a basking spot, their lime-green inflorescences change to ruby red in July, which is totally unexpected. The last happy place in which I would mention this spurge is beneath a stretch of yew hedging, in front of the house, where they consort brilliantly with self-sown wallflowers and bright purple honesty. This euphorbia's foliage makes dark, evergreen rosettes from which the flowering stems rise to 45cm/1½ft or so. The only attention they need (but it is often neglected) is the removal of all that has flowered and the foliage below, at summer's end. This cleans the colony in readiness for a new crop of leafy rosettes.

I grow both *E. griffithii* 'Fireglow' and my own 'Dixter'. Of the two, rather contrarily, 'Fireglow' has made the stronger colony. Both must be grown in full sun for their best colouring. 'Fireglow' is the brighter red but its green leaves are rather dull. 'Dixter' is a deeper red and the whole plant, leaf veins and stems included, is suffused with purplish red.

*E. palustris* comes out at the same time and is my and Fergus's favourite, in its season, so long as the colony is strong and happy, which it is, on my wet, heavy soil. Its substantial inflorescences are lime green and about 75cm/2½ft tall at the time of flowering, though taller later. And they sparkle – literally. I suppose there must be a tiny crystal of nectar in the centre of each flower, and it catches the sunlight, especially towards the end of the day. Nothing could look fresher.

Rather on a par with euphorbia colouring and often mistaken for a spurge is the monocarpic umbellifer *Smyrnium perfoliatum*, a 60–90cm/2–3ft plant which can be worked

into all sorts of places. I like it, for instance, with the parrot tulip 'Orange Favourite'. But the smyrnium (like *Eryngium giganteum*) is rather a law to itself. You start it from fresh seed, scattered where you want it, preferably in part shade; then wait for three years or so, before you get the first flowering. The plants appear each spring, unless you officiously weed them out, but the first year, only a pair of seed leaves, followed by dormancy; the second year, a pinnate leaf or two. Finally the flowering, in which the large, stem-clasping bracts (or are they stipules?) are the most prominent feature, and they,

as well as the corymbs of tiny flowers, are brilliant, mouth-watering lime green. After that, the plant dies, but once it is established and self-seeding, you won't lose it and may even moan about how prolific it is.

A spring grouping that I enjoy has the Jacob's ladder *Polemonium* 'Lambrook Mauve', which is a low, clumpy plant, in front of pale yellow *Thermopsis villosa* (45cm/1½ft), which has loose spikes of pea flowers; magenta *Geranium macrorrhizum*, and a very strong Spanish bluebell, *Hyacinthoides hispanica* 'Chevithorn' (it is virtually sterile but makes fat clumps of large, pale blue bells).

The last flower I shall mention is probably the most exciting of the month, *Arum creticum*. I mentioned its sharply angled, glossy green leaves in winter. Now, late in the month, it carries its bright yellow arum flowers, in which the spathe makes a spiral near to its tip. In the wild, I am told, it is most often a much less interesting cream colour, but the yellow form is rightly the one always seen in cultivation. Flowering may not last longer than a week, so the excitement really deserves a party in its honour. Then the plant rapidly goes to rest and is seen no more till the autumn.

I feel obliged to mention one new pest that turns up around this time, though sometimes earlier: the lily beetle. It is bright red, rather handsome and hard-textured, so not too easily squashed. It feeds on the foliage of all your lilies and fritillarias. On sunny days, it sits on top of the foliage, often in mating pairs – and you must catch it, not getting so excited that you bungle, because as soon as the beetle sees what you are at, it drops to the ground and is totally invisible. It continues, with batches of slimy larvae, generation after generation, to ruin your lilies until August, and you really need to have someone chasing it up every day. I suppose if all your lilies were in colonies there might be some spray to apply, but if lilies do well for you, they'll be self-sowing among other plants and be all over the place and hard to locate.

LEFT *Tulipa* 'Spring Green' with lime-green *Smyrnium perfoliatum*
ABOVE *Smyrnium perfoliatum* growing amongst forget-me-nots

## Vegetables, salads and seeds

Towards the end of the month, we sow all our broad bean seed and most of the peas — both in considerable quantity, as they freeze so well. There'll also be outdoor sowings of such as parsley, lettuce and beetroot.

Purple-sprouting broccoli and kale should be cropping well, but I always hope for a good surplus, to which I add sprouting Brussels sprout shoots, all of these for freezing. I well know that there'll be a hungry gap in respect of garden produce, at the turn of May and June. Spinach develops quickly at this time of the year, so we may sow that now, but I am loath to if I expect to be away in June, as is often the case. Any $F_1$ brassicas that need sowing this month or next will be done under controlled conditions, in pots, under glass. There's never much seed in a packet and what there is is expensive. We sow leeks in pots, too, transferring them to their purpose-made trenches in June.

April is a remarkably good month for fresh salads. All the saladings that overwintered successfully will be growing like fury, trying to run up to flower and I, in my turn, try to keep up with thwarting their intention and eating the young shoots. There'll be no lettuces. Witloof chicory may hang on from secondary shoots and there'll be secondary growth on the sugarloaf chicory that I was cutting all winter.

We need to consider whether to make a new globe artichoke bed and generally the answer is yes. I like to have a bed for each of the two varieties I grow. 'Gros Vert de Laon' is the hardier and more reliable; 'Grand Camus de Bretagne' is my favourite, but there are usually winter gaps in their bed. Actually, I find that after two years, my best policy is to start a new bed, gaps or no gaps. So we do this with rooted offsets (only very slightly rooted and only one shoot per offset), heeling in a few spares to replace those that miss. All being well, the old beds will crop from late May to early July, and the new bed from July on. Artichokes are madly extravagant of space, but I aim to be able to eat them most days from May to November. And I haven't a friend who doesn't enjoy them with me.

Sowings of flower seeds are all done under cold glass and they will be going on, frantically. Even more testing is the seedlings' subsequent treatment. They are so easily spoiled through not being handled in time, being allowed to get drawn and overcrowded. I don't do any of this myself, nowadays, depending on Fergus and Michael to do the right thing at the right time. The first hurdle is to spot germination as soon as it has occurred. The seedlings need full light from that moment. Actually, it is quite

*Arum creticum*

exciting going over your seed pots each morning, to spot what has happened since yesterday. I am always trying to impress on my seed-sowers that they should not sow too thickly, which is the temptation if plenty of seed is available. There's no point in having masses of seedlings crowding each other out before you are ready to take them to the next stage. Pricking out or potting seedlings up individually takes up an immense amount of space, which needs to be organized in readiness for them. Space is also needed for individually potting all those rooted cuttings which were overwintered under glass. This space is found in the cold frames, by moving overwintered stock of saleable plants out into the open. Most of it is hardy enough for that.

Meantime, the house and gardens are open to the public again and there should be an Easter surge, much depending on the weather. I only wish Easter could be fixed and on a sensibly late date, mid-month. The May bank holidays are always a lot busier. After all, one has to expect a good deal of pretty poisonous weather, in April. The whole countryside is a garden but there's a case to be made for viewing it from the confines of a well-heated car.

Everyone is madly busy in their gardens. Even those who wanted to have nothing to do with theirs from September for the next six months become aware, by the Easter holiday weekend, that something drastic really must be done. So our nursery trade makes a welcome recovery and unflappable Brenda Common is back on sales, in the afternoons.

My study becomes one of the public rooms, being part of the original house, so I need to change my way of life, which I do gradually. It is difficult to give up fires suddenly but if the yeoman's hall, in the added building, has the sun on it all afternoon, it warms up nicely, so I can write there, with the help, if the sun is not obliging, of two gas heaters. And, of course, I want to be out there, quite a lot of the time, planting or preparing for planting or whatever. So I don't want a book round my neck between spring and autumn, and I try to confine writing to my regular pieces for the *Weekend Guardian* and for *Country Life*.

Sometimes I need to creep through the crowds, back to my study to print something that needs to be posted or faxed. I try to do this with minimum disturbance to the guides and to the parties that are being shown round. At least everyone is aware that the house is a lived-in home. Not a museum.

April tonight must pass away,
Tomorrow's sunrise brings us May,
What else it brings us — who can say?
Not you nor I.

This much is certain — April's tears
Foster the glory Summer wears,
And Love grows strong thro' doubts and fears
And cannot die.

Lines by my grandfather, Basil Field, 1834–1908

May

The very word May, short and direct, seems full of light and ready to become airborne. Man compares himself with the world around him, with the birds shouting their songs, the trees bursting into leaf; old or young, in imagination or in fact, he feels himself a part of this great creative impulse.

*Im wunderschönen Monat Mai, als alle Knospen sprangen,*
*da ist in meinem Herzen die Liebe aufgegangen.*
(In the wonderful month of May, when all the buds burst open,
There love sprang up in my heart.)

Thus Heine, at the start of his *Dichterliebe*, unforgettably rendered for voice and piano by Schumann.

The poet's love affair, which started in May, ended in bitterness and recrimination when he was jilted. We are not told which month that happened, but it must have been November, for sure, when the leaves were falling. Those who sing the praises of May most highly are the same who revile autumn as depressing. But I think if you have a gut sympathy with the natural cycle of the year, the charms of autumn are as vital as the forward impulse of spring.

Temperatures are all over the place, in May, but one of the moments that I'm strongly aware of is when, near noon, I'm beneath newly leafed trees, the sun is standing really high and the shadows are short. The sharpness of spring will be present for a long time, but the closeness to summer suddenly makes itself apparent.

The belt of ash trees on our west flank is still unyielding, in the first half of the month; no rustle of spring from them; only the empty sough of winter. Yet even they have to relent and put on their summer apparel, by the end of the month. Their character is utterly transformed. I wish we had a horse chestnut – I haven't even planted one yet; it's not so easy to fit one in, if your mind is capable of visualizing the finished product. This is not a tree garden, but there is no greater magnificence, as you stand, looking up at it from the outside, than a white horse chestnut in bloom. No other flowering tree can touch it, either for sheer bulk or for panache. (The pink-flowered kinds are only a weak shadow of this.) But we have oaks on our boundaries – stag-headed and by no means fine specimens, but no matter. Their young foliage is fresh as fresh, in May. By the forstal, they make a fine, though suitably distant backdrop to the horse pond, with its fringe of dogwood, underplanted with snowflakes – *Leucojum aestivum* 'Gravetye Giant', which continues in bloom well into the month.

Bluebells are still at their best in the shaws and woods around us, but they flower most freely after the underwood has been coppiced. One area, in Weights Wood, where a solid stand of sweet chestnut is cut for fencing every twelve years or so, is particularly rich in bluebells. Like other woodland flowers, they are most prolific after light has been

PAGES 92–93 Fading daffodils are soon engulfed by orchard wild flowers

admitted. But these are a good ten minutes' walk away and it's surprising how easily one can miss making the effort to go and look, when there are so many distractions on one's doorstep. It's the same story with the wild cherry in Four Acre Shaw (eight acres, actually, but the shaw is named after its adjoining Four Acre Field). It is a single tree but with attendant sucker saplings around it. As these are all of the same clone, no fruit is set; cross-pollination is required for that. So we never find new cherries popping up here or there, as we do the wild service tree, *Sorbus torminalis*. I have a strong young specimen of that in our old orchard – one that I found as a seedling in a nearby shaw margin. It flowers, late in the month, with corymbs of white, hawthorn-like blossom, but this is hard to spot as the tree has no background. I never thought of that when I planted it. One should really give more thought to the placing of such permanencies as trees and long-lived shrubs. It isn't practicable to move them, once established.

Hawthorns make excellent, long-lived small trees and our own native species develop a lot of character in their shapes. So I'm proud of the double, pinky-red *Crataegus* 'Paul's Scarlet' that I created some forty years ago, taking my scion wood from the specimen in a friend's garden and budding it on to a self-sown seedling in our rose garden. When the scion was strongly established, I moved the entire plant over the boundary yew hedge, into the adjacent orchard. In its good years, it makes a great display, but if the previous summer was wet early on, its foliage gets scab badly and drops off prematurely. That will mean a dearth of blossom the following May.

## Meadows

The tail end of the narcissus season is most strongly represented, in the orchard, by *Narcissus poeticus* var. *recurvus*, the poet's or pheasant's eye narcissus – white, with a tiny red rim around its small cup. It has the best fragrance of all. But that is liable to good and bad years and, as with the double red hawthorn, a wet May makes its foliage go down to fungal disease prematurely and before the bulb has built up reserves. Result: virtually no bloom the next May. This pheasant's eye has a double form – loosely double and very charming – which does not flower till two weeks later. You see a lot of it in the north of Scotland, Orkney and Shetland, where it has often been planted along the roadside. Unfortunately, at any rate in the south, many of its flower buds are liable to blindness. But I love to pick such newly opened blooms as there are and to arrange them with purple honesty and lime-green *Smyrnium perfoliatum*.

There is a great surge of growth in the meadow areas, one of whose most exciting features is the huge quantity of green-winged orchids, *Orchis morio*, which have naturalized since my mother and I introduced them from the wild in the 1930s. Their natural habitat was permanent pasture, but when all of that disappeared during the war, because there were ploughing grants, the orchis went too. So what would now be considered an act of vandalism and illegal turned out to be an act of rescue and conservation. Life is full of contradictions. We used to sally forth with a huge, bushel-sized trug basket between us and a fern trowel. Orchis tubers are not generally deep at all, but we took no risks and dug each up surrounded by a good wodge of soil. It was the same with other orchids but one thing I have learned is that you can expect to be able to naturalize the species that anyway grow wild in your locality, but not those that come from quite different habitats, like, in our case, the bee, fragrant and pyramidal orchids from calcium-rich soils.

The so-called green-winged orchid has no green on it to warrant the name. It varies a lot in height, but is on average dwarfer than *O. mascula* and a cooler, less pink shade of purple. Another local orchid with which we are successful, and which flowers in May, is the twayblade, *Listera ovata*. It has two broad, opposite, basal leaves and a spike of perfectly green flowers. It is difficult to spot them in a largely green sward, but once you've got your eye in, you'll realize that they are everywhere (where there are any!).

An enchanting little deciduous fern of undisturbed, permanent pasture puts in its appearance in spring: the adder's tongue, *Ophioglossum vulgatum*. Only a few inches tall, it has one glossy green leaf, like an arum's spathe, and this encloses the reproductive 'tongue', equivalent to an aroid's spadix.

Clovers are seldom included in seed mixtures recommended to those starting a meadow, because their nitrogen-fixing properties encourage just the kind of coarse, lush vegetation which you least want. But in an old, established meadow, clovers are very welcome and the red ones, really magenta, are out now, in force. They contrast with our three main species of buttercup. *Ranunculus bulbosus* is the first out; then the tall, widely branching meadow buttercup, *R. acris*, which has a neat double form, worthy of border space; third, the creeping buttercup, *R. repens*, which can be a ferocious weed, in damp borders, spreading by overground stolons. That has a neat double form, which I have so far failed to establish in our new meadow area, the topiary lawn. Perhaps it finds too much competition from the wild kind already there.

One of the showiest additions to the meadows, this month, is the dazzling magenta *Gladiolus communis* subsp. *byzantinus*. We have to add it where we want it, as it does not set its own seed in our strain, but, once established, it persists. There is much of that in the borders, too, and it dies away discreetly without occupying space that will leave a gap. I wish I grew the meadow saxifrage, *Saxifraga granulata*, of which there are colonies at Kew and Hatfield House, but I have never obtained stock.

Moon daisies (or ox-eyed daisies), *Leucanthemum vulgare*, are an integral feature of a varied meadow turf, but I find that their populations come and go. In the upper moat, for instance, they used to be thick all over, but there are now scarcely any.

This is a mystery; I believe that they get killed out if there is a drought year, but there may be another reason. However, they spread into the garden proper and are a link between the wildness of the orchard and Lutyens's formal landscaping, where they invade the paving cracks in and around the circular steps. Red valerian, *Centranthus ruber*, is here, too, and in the terrace retaining walls overlooking the upper moat. I allow this invasion, joyfully, but as soon as the plants are fading, they receive a hard cut-back and order is restored. Likewise on the back drive, where the display in April was from aubrieta, *Euphorbia amygdaloides* var. *robbiae* and primroses. Now, there is a great wave of moon daisies.

With the moon daisies and valerian on the circular steps, I should mention a third prominent feature, a hummock of the shrubby *Convolvulus cneorum*, which has grey leaves all the year but is now covered with white convolvulus flowers. It is sited on a ledge, which suits it because this is a fairly tender species and needs the best possible drainage if it is to survive our winters. I have tried it in other places with little success, but here it has survived for a number of years.

## The pond areas

At times in its life, the lower moat in summer has been a continuous green sheet of duckweed, *Lemna* species. Now, we have none of that and I believe this to be on account

LEFT Green-winged orchids, *Orchis morio*, have seeded themselves abundantly in the meadow garden
ABOVE Infillers that need no extra space, *Gladiolus communis* subsp. *byzantinus* and Dutch *Iris* 'Blue Triumphator'

of the 'wild' mallard (probably bred to be shot). Two or three of them spend much time here, and others on the horse pond. In spring, they try to breed, invariably without success, but they never give up. Each pond also has its pair of moorhens. Although so much smaller than ducks, they are aggressive and never allow themselves to be ousted. Scary by nature, they do get used to us to a large extent, and it is nice to watch their precise, yet jerky, movements when one has the time. That is generally when we take after-lunch coffee by the horse pond.

Our largest *Gunnera manicata* are in the partial shade of trees, by the lower moat. Their leaves are vast and visitors soon make a track through the long grass to have themselves photographed beneath a leaf. But most of the colour is out in the sun, by the horse pond. Here there are gunneras too, with the added interest of being conspicuously in flower. The multi-branched inflorescence could be compared with the scales of a fir-cone but stands erect more obviously like a penis – a great attraction.

There are plenty of flowers, now, in and around the pond. On the banks, masses (too much, really) of the water dropwort, *Oenanthe crocata*, which is like a larger, more poised version of cow parsley, *Anthriscus sylvestris*, and lacks the latter's sickly flower scent. So it is good for cutting and arranging with its natural partner, also present in quantity and partly submerged, the wild *Iris pseudacorus*, with clear yellow flowers on 90cm/3ft stems.

Three other irises grow around here. In shallow water, one called 'Gerald Darby', with pale purple flowers on dark purplish stems. Then, also emergent, *I. versicolor*, which is principally reddish purple and white. I used to think that this was purely a border plant, until I saw it naturalized in a large boggy area in the Outer Hebrides, one summer. Mine is regularly devoured, after flowering, by the brown larvae of an iris sawfly. It has to survive these attacks as best it may. I daren't spray, here, as the pond is stiff with fish and much other life. The last species is *I. sibirica*, which is bluish purple. I have that in the high garden where I enjoy its colour contrast with scarlet oriental poppies, but it is a dull dog, after flowering, and its lengthening leaves sprawl over the neighbours. In the margin of the pond, what it does after flowering passes unnoticed.

Happiest in water a foot deep, or slightly more, is the golden club, *Orontium aquaticum*, which is a handsome aroid with sinuous flowering stems. Lacking the spathe of most aroids, it just has the spadix, which is yellow at the tip and white behind it. A striking plant.

Underwater oxygenators can be terrible take-over plants and I am always having one or other of them foisted on me by owners of fish, who no longer want to look after them, bringing them to and tipping them into my pond from a can, together with the underwater plants that the fish lived with. I'm not making this up; we have actually seen it happening. I am battling with one of these take-over plants now, a species of hornwort. But the well-behaved oxygenator which I really love is the so-called water violet, *Hottonia palustris*. It makes clouds of lacy foliage, arranged in loose rosettes, and appears throughout the winter dressed in bright green. In spring it may flower or it may not. The decision is probably dictated by how congested the colonies are. If not congested, they flower, throwing up primula-like candelabrums of palest mauve blossom to about a foot above the water. The display is very pretty.

There are willows on the bank between the pond and the forstal, which we pollard every third year. But at the bottom of them is a colony of the water saxifrage, *Darmera peltata*. Its rhizomes are right on the surface and it flowers, with domes of pink blossom on fleshy pink, hairy stems, before its umbrella leaves (like a mini-gunnera's) appear.

## Scents

On a bank set back from the horse pond is a deliciously scented shrub, which started flowering in April. This is *Elaeagnus umbellatus*. It is not quite evergreen, losing the last of its old foliage in late winter. Now covered in young, greyish-green leaves together with thousands of tiny greenish flowers, it gives off this spicy aroma, which is carried on the wind into the high garden, some distance away, so that everyone wonders where it comes from. Near by, I also have the silver-leaved *E.* 'Quicksilver' (till lately known as 'Caspica'). Its flowers are pale yellow, similarly scented, and they open a couple of weeks after the other's have finished. You should plant one or other of these near a sitting-out place. As a foliage plant, 'Quicksilver' is the better for earning its keep, but it is not so prolific a flowerer.

Among other notable scent-wafters, in May, is the incense rose, *Rosa primula*, which has glandular foliage emitting this remarkable fragrance, especially after rain. The shrub is nothing much to look at. It congenitally suffers from a die-back disease, as do others of these early, yellow-flowered roses – 'Canary Bird' and *R. hugonis*, for example – but it always recovers in the course of the summer. It flowers in May, but that's no selling point. Another aromatic-leaved rose is the sweet briar, *R. rubiginosa*, at full stewed-apple strength on its young shoots. (More on that when it fruits in autumn.)

*Azara serrata* is a vigorous evergreen shrub, which generally, for safety, needs to be grown against a sunny wall. That is smothered in bright yellow clusters of bloom, late in the month, and it smells strongly of fruit salad. I told a potential customer this. 'I don't like fruit salad,' said she, coldly. In colour, it contrasts strongly with the rich blue evergreen *Ceanothus* 'Cynthia Postan', sharing the same wall. If you come and see my example, you will be able to work out how to do it better yourself.

The May-flowering daphnes are night scented and it's too chilly to be sitting out of an evening, so I should site them near a door which you have to go in and out of, even at night (to the deep freeze, maybe, or perhaps you go to the gym after work). The scent of *Daphne tangutica* is heavy, heady stuff, and this is one of the great survivors. Furthermore, it can be relied upon for a second crop, in the summer. The flowers are purplish on the

PAGE 100  Looking across the young foliage of *Gunnera manicata* to the horse pond
PAGE 101 ABOVE  Golden club, *Orontium aquaticum,* in the horse pond
BELOW  Water violets, *Hottonia palustris*

outside, white within. I actually prefer *D. pontica*, which has rather smart lance leaves in loose rosettes. Its flowers are green and show up well – if you're looking for and at them. But their lemon scent is out of this world. (Now where shall I turn for superlatives?)

And the first of the climbing honeysuckles is out; they are night-scented. I have a particular weakness for *Lonicera caprifolium*. I haven't a good specimen at this moment but I have a strong plant to put out. I wish one wasn't always looking for places for climbers. This is a pale honeysuckle and the leaves (or leaf-like bracts) below the flower cluster are joined and totally encircle the stem.

It is the season of *Clematis montana* and its many variants. Always be certain of equipping yourself with one that has the strong vanilla scent. This is often at its strongest when the flowers are almost over. My white montana, which was never a named clone but serves me excellently, is powerfully scented. The pale pink 'Elizabeth' is another winner. There are plenty more, and you can go on a sniffing quest.

*Wisteria sinensis* flowers in the second half of May – some racemes earlier, if they lie against a warm wall. Although its racemes are of only moderate length, this is the best of wisterias, all-round. Get yourself, from a reliable and accountable source, a vegetatively raised (not a seed-raised) clone. The clone that is still most often grown has been around since the early nineteenth century and it usually has a second, light but welcome, crop of flowers in August. Mine is an old plant that was growing against the house, over a balcony and round a corner as far as the terrace doorway. When there had to be house repairs, I decided to get rid of it. However, it had in the meantime layered itself in quite a different direction and I found it growing over my 'Lennei' magnolia. From there it has progressed into *Azara microphylla* and on to the 'Brunswick' fig. It is physically and emotionally irresistible.

I have lately planted another wisteria, of which I am equally fond, and I only hope it will be happy against the south-west-facing oasthouse wall. We have made a good place for it but once its roots go beyond that, it's into some pretty awful stuff. This is *W. venusta*. It has short racemes of well-spaced, large white flowers and the summery fragrance is the same and as good as in *W. sinensis*.

## Clematis

Of *Clematis montana* I have written. The largest-flowered and most dramatic clematis are in bloom before the end of the month. They are all subject to wilt disease and I rather despaired of them until Fergus came to Dixter in 1993, but he now makes a regular practice of giving their roots a drench with systemic fungicide (varying the ingredient, so that the fungi don't build up resistant strains) and this also eliminates trouble from powdery mildew, which afflicts many of the Texensis and Jackmanii hybrids later in the growing season. This has made a tremendous difference. I have to say that the early-flowering whoppers are not nearly as useful garden plants as those that flower on their young shoots and for far longer, later on, but it is nice to see them, all the same.

One of my oldest plants is 'Marcel Moser' growing up a post supporting the hovel roof, in the exotic garden (the old rose garden). It is similar to and of the same vintage (within a year) as 'Nelly Moser', but has longer sepals. Of course, it bleaches in the sun. Of the many more modern hybrids of similar appearance, 'Bees' Jubilee' has been a success and one specimen, planted inadvertently, is bountiful and regular as clockwork. When we were making good places in which to plant rhododendrons, near to the forstal and on the steep north-facing bank, we used old potting soil and this contained the roots of pot-grown clematis turned out from the nursery as dead. Not all of them were and this 'Bees' Jubilee' was a survivor. It is now in harness with a large-leaved rhododendron. I see that a wild honeysuckle has joined the throng, but I shall have to control that. We have plenty of them around already, some in the most unlikely places.

In the long border I have 'Lasurstern', a big blue, white-centred clematis that I've had for fifty years or more, either moved and divided or layered from its original position. This one was meant to grow over a *Viburnum* x *burkwoodii*, but I got tired of that, so the clematis now has to make do with pea-sticks for support. Many of my clematis get stranded in this way. 'The President' (which is purple) at the back of the border was on *Spiraea* x *arguta*, but I fell out with that, so the clematis has to make do with a pole. That's all right.

A twining climber that is at its best for flowers in May, although it can be even more spectacular for pendent racemes of scarlet berries in September, is *Schisandra rubriflora*, both male and female plants, side by side. In flower, the male is a little more prolific, but there's not much in it. The flower buds are like cherry stones and they open into red lampshades. This is hardy and does not even require a sunny wall.

## Spring bedding

The bedding plants that we use for spring display vary, to an extent, from year to year; enjoying a change is a part of the point of all bedding plants. There are only a few official beds, and they don't even look like that, as the bedding is largely integrated with other plants. Others of the bedders are scattered around and through the borders to liven them up when so much is still green.

Sometimes I have polyanthus primroses. I like the $F_1$ Crescendo Red strain, and worked up stock from small beginnings – you don't get much seed in a packet of $F_1$s. That's how the seedsmen make their living. You cannot replant polyanthus in the same

*Clematis* 'Marcel Moser'

ground indefinitely, which rather limits your choice, after a time. Polyanthus are currently taking a rest but I have a lot of seed-raised auriculas, which are fun. They can be highly specialized florists' flowers but mine are not – just a pleasant mix of, mostly, rather sombre colours. I have rogued out the wishy-washy, indeterminate ones. The scent of auriculas is strong and it is different from that of polyanthus and primroses. Stock takes up a lot of reserve space, in summer, and I daresay there'll be another change of policy, some day. There's nothing much you can grow with auriculas – not that I have thought of, anyway.

I must have some wallflowers, in spring, but again there are changes to be rung. The traditional type of wallflower, which we called *Cheiranthus cheiri* (or Cheerianthus cheeryi, in parks parlance) but is now *Erysimum*, is sown in the seed bed with the brassicas, this month, ahead of their flowering a year later. A lot can go wrong with this crop. It is not entirely hardy. It hates waterlogged conditions and in some pieces of ground, when growing on in a reserve area, it gets club root. We are now finding that the dwarf strains make large enough and more compact plants than the tall, and have gone over to them. When we bed out, I insist on close planting, with no gaps between units. The accompanying tulips have their own groups near by, but not dotted between the wallflowers. In a large bedding scheme, it is nice to combine two or even three single-colour wallflower strains, as it might be 'Ivory White' (palest yellow fading to white); 'Primrose Yellow' (a little deeper than the 'White'); and 'Fire King', or some other intense orange. These I plant in separate colour blocks in front of the house. Tulips with which to combine them might be the burnt-orange lily-flowered 'Queen of Sheba', or a good late yellow like 'Mrs John Scheepers'. Another idea: a purple wallflower, which is sombre, with a brilliant yellow Cloth of Gold type. You then need twice as many

plants of the dark variety as of the bright one. Of course they are grown separately, through summer, and put together on planting out. Purple and bright yellow could be combined with groups of pale yellow or white tulips. You might like something different. But it is worth massing the wallflowers so that these scrawny plants support one another in the event of high winds.

Dutch iris rise above the self-sowing annual *Limnanthes douglasii*

Another type of wallflower that I like to grow is the Siberian, which is dazzling, uncompromising orange and with its own sweet scent. It is rather later than the others and at its best in late May. I like to see patches of it in the long border and it is nice with the pure white *Allium neapolitanum*. It also beds out well with the similar but dwarf mauve *Erysimum linifolium*, and that is excellent with the late orange tulip 'Dillenburg'. We do not sow the Siberian wallflower or *E. linifolium* until early July, otherwise they flower prematurely in the same year and the plants are weakened.

Some autumn-sown annuals are already at their best in May. The five-spot, *Nemophila maculata*, which has purple spots at the tips of its off-white petals, is not too good at roughing it outside through the winter, so we raise that under glass, pot the seedlings individually and plant them out in March. It is the same story with *Omphalodes linifolia*, which is like a refined, grey-leaved gypsophila. Then cornflowers: we sow the blue *Centaurea* 'Jubilee' strain in early October and bring them on, some in large pots, to stand outside the porch, others in 10cm/4in squares, to plant in the borders in March and they'll flower on till July. *Cerinthe major* 'Purpurascens' is treated like this. In the garden, I planted a few among some of the yellow erythronium hybrid 'Pagoda', which flowered in March and is dying off now. The cerinthes never gave up all summer.

My chief self-sowing annual, exceedingly lively now, is *Limnanthes douglasii*, the poached egg flower. Above that and a permanency in one corner area is a blue Dutch iris. There's another ancient colony of these bulbous irises that my mother planted in the year dot, under the cedar-shingled barn (which has no gutter). It is yellow and white and never fails. I have already mentioned the self-sowing and Fergus-distributed forget-me-nots, which persist through the borders for most of the month.

One of the best perennials for spring bedding, though rather unusual in this role, is the double-flowered pink campion, *Silene dioica* 'Flore Pleno', which I best liked under the 90cm/3ft *Allium hollandicum* (*A. aflatunense*) 'Purple Sensation', also bedded out in the autumn. The campion has to be found a damp reserve spot in which to spend the summer, after flowering, the alliums being harvested and dried off.

The annual viscaria, as we used to call it, is really a silene, the blue form of which looks rather like flax. There is a bright pink strain, called 'Rose Angel', and a mixture of pink and blue; also one that is near to red. This we sow in autumn and grow on in individual pots for planting out in March, to flower from May through June. But that, too, is good in 12cm/5in pots to stand outside the porch.

## The borders

I have touched on many incidentals in the mixed borders, especially the bulbs and bedders, but more needs to be said about their permanent contents. These are largely green, through May, and foliage is of great importance: for instance that of veratrums, *Veratrum album* being the species that I grow best (or that grows best for me). These liliaceous perennials develop very slowly from seed, and there's not a lot of scope for

division of old clumps. This can be done, but it sets them back something chronic. Still, once they're there, they're there and, apart from slugs, I have nothing to worry about. They even self-sow, a little, which is flattering. *V. album*, as also the others, has large, rounded and pleated leaves. It will flower in July.

The cardoons go from strength to strength, with their big, grey, deeply toothed leaves. The bright green foliage of oriental poppy, *Papaver orientale* 'Goliath', likewise lance-shaped and toothed, looks well in front of the cardoons. But you do need to anticipate the latter's huge spread and not plant anything too close to them. If you have done so, some of the outer cardoon leaves may need to be removed. The poppy's huge red blooms, on upright, almost (but not dependably) self-supporting, 1.2m/4ft stems, are opening late in the month. Near by, they flower in front of *Viburnum opulus* 'Compactum', which has white lacecaps. In one of our stock beds, I have challengingly planted 'Goliath' next to the tall, semi-double buttercup, *Ranunculus acris* 'Stevenii', which is brightest yellow. That is an eyeful, but my aim is to make a trio, here, with a white cloud of *Crambe cordifolia* behind the other two. Unfortunately the crambe hates my heavy, wet soil.

One of the best leaves, before we have to surround it with a palisade of pea-sticks, is that of *Clematis recta* 'Purpurea'. I think the scarlet type-plant of *Papaver orientale* looks super in front of that, in the high garden, but some would disagree (have done, in fact). But it pleases me and that, surely, is enough!

Splendid in its May dress is my clone of the ornamental rhubarb, *Rheum palmatum*. Its jagged-margined leaves are red purple, on emerging, and remain purple on their undersides, which are still well displayed for several weeks. The flowers, by contrast, are white. All around this, I have late red tulips. The rheum is at the back of a deep border in the barn garden – because I want other plants to have grown up in front by the summer, when most of its leaves have died off. So I have a large patch, in front of it, of *Astilbe chinensis* var. *taquetii* 'Superba'. This has beautiful young foliage, pinnate, crimped and curled and rather hairy. All in among the astilbes we have established a self-sowing colony of the allium-like *Nectaroscordum siculum*, 90cm/3ft tall with umbels of bells in green and chestnut colouring. If isolated, this bulb can be rather a nuisance after flowering, but in with the astilbes it can do what it likes, disappearing in its own good time.

Libertias are out in May, with narrow, linear, evergreen leaves and white flowers that look triangular. *Libertia formosa* was my principal species in the wall garden/barn garden area, and it sows itself freely, sometimes in the steps dividing the two gardens. When near to *Euphorbia griffithii*, it makes a good contrast. Plants do not age gracefully and I find it best to replace them after about three years, allowing seedlings to take over. But it is a stodgy plant, its flowers close up against their main stems, compared with a form (it must be a hybrid, I think – it is certainly sterile) of *L. ixioides* given me from her Dublin

Colonizers of Lutyens's circular steps

garden by Helen Dillon. On this, the flowers spray gracefully outwards. In one spot, it makes a nice companion behind the blue (nurseryman's blue) perennial cornflower, *Centaurea montana*, now in its first flush. After this, I cut the centaurea back, we spray the resulting young shoots against mildew, and it flowers a second time in August.

I will mention that this is self-sown too and I should like the reader to be aware of the numbers of plants which I am talking about that do self-sow and whose seedlings we encourage, when they are in a suitable spot. Mostly, of course, they are not, but I should think a quarter of all the plants in the barn and sunk gardens are self-sowns.

In parts of the high garden, *Geranium rubescens* is a great unifying theme from late May till early July. It is biennial and has deeply cut foliage with red petioles. The flowers are like a glorified herb robert, *G. robertianum*, magenta-coloured. The trouble is that if we leave too many of its seedlings, there is too great a gap when we need to pull it out in early July. We have successfully overcome this by threading plants (raised from seed in pots) of the ladybird poppy (red with black blotches) through the border where the cranesbill has been removed. Sun roses are flowering now, and at the front of one border there is *Helianthemum* 'Red Orient' (which we should be calling 'Supreme') next to a white 'perennial' single stock and the geranium behind them. But this sort of combination is apt to change from year to year.

I am very fond of the stock (*Matthiola*) and it has the true stock scent. Under the right conditions, on light soil, it is a self-sower and there are chalk cliffs on the Isle of Wight and elsewhere where it is naturalized. But on a heavy soil like ours, it is uphill work. The leafy overwintering crown is apt to rot from botrytis. If it escapes that (and Fergus sometimes applies a protective spray), it flowers and seeds but seldom does a second year. I remember a huge old plant at Tintinhull, in their white garden, which must have been three or four years old. Never mind; our soil sometimes turns up trumps.

There are several early-flowering geraniums flowering now. I have a particular fondness for *G. albanum*, which has nicely rounded flowers, quite close to the ground (unless there is a challenging neighbour for it to climb into), and of a chalk-pink colouring. When it has had its turn, it dies back, so you can grow it among perennials that come into their own later in the season. In my case, these include *Hedychium densiflorum* (all hedychiums are late developers) and the giant reed grass, *Arundo donax*, in a position where I grow it right next to a path (for the sake of the distant view).

Then there is *G. x oxonianum* 'A.T. Johnson', which it is easy to have too much of because it is one of those ideal lazy gardener's ground-cover plants which covers the ground (and all the neighbours) and flowers for months and months in a raucous shade of pinky mauve, getting increasingly untidy all the time but totally unnoticed by its owner, who should have cut the whole thing back after its first flush. Well, I have dispensed with most of that but there is one rather useful (that dangerous adjective) group behind our *Fuchsia* 'Riccartonii' hedge, recently cut to the ground, so the geranium shows up. If you get yourself in the right place, where several paths meet (two of them mud paths surrounding a stock bed), there is a good view of various plant shapes and colours: the geranium at your feet, shouting loudly; behind, a single clump of the variegated grass *Calamagrostis* x *acutiflora* 'Overdam' (this is a case where I believe that a singleton grass may be more telling than a group); a vivid 1.2m/4ft fennel, *Ferula* 'Cedric Morris', with shining green leaves and lime-green umbelliferous flower heads; in the distance, an excellent weigela, *Weigela* 'Praecox Variegata', thick with tubular blossom, now, of a more intense pink colouring than *W. florida* 'Variegata' and with a sharper leaf variegation. But I have the latter bang in the middle of the long border, where I believe it to be the oldest ingredient. The flowers are deliciously scented and I like their soft pink colouring with the pale yellow on their newly expanded leaves. Neither weigela turns dull, after flowering, as the green-leaved kinds do, so they earn their keep through to late autumn.

I feel that I am running into space trouble and must forego mention of many plants now looking good, but I cannot omit the old-fashioned double crimson-red peony, *Paeonia officinalis* 'Rubra Plena', which hangs over a carpet of London pride, *Saxifraga umbrosa*, a haze of tiny flesh-pink flowers. Behind these two, the white Portugal broom is in full bloom. I've kept that for very many years − for a broom − by conscientiously pruning it immediately after flowering.

I have been reminded of a few other essentials. The yellow peony with beautiful rounded foliage, *Paeonia mlokosewitschii*, is something of a joke. I originally grew it from seed and planted a whole row of it in a spare plot, while I made up my mind where to grow it in the garden proper. I never did come to that decision, because I am so acutely aware of its short flowering season of barely a week and it's not a plant that you can hide away for the summer. So there, in its row, it remains and makes a tremendous show, when the sun opens out its flowers, for all of five days in early May.

Then I nearly forgot lilies-of-the-valley, which I adore and should like to pick every stem of, for bunches to bring into the house or give away. That intermingles with the London pride and I must say its fortunes are chequered. It is one of those cussed plants that not only doesn't want to stay put, nor to grow where you'd like it to grow, but is inclined to take umbrage for no apparent reason. Still, I have it here and there.

*Iris tectorum* is in the high garden, and I'm working on that but am apt to let neighbours swamp it when my mind is elsewhere. Its broad leaves are very fresh at its

Fennel, *Ferula* 'Cedric Morris', *Geranium* x *oxonianum* 'A.T. Johnson' and *Calamagrostis* x *acutiflora* 'Overdam' in the high garden

time of flowering and the flowers, with their huge, floppy standards, on quite short stems, are a lovely blue, which I far prefer to the albino. This is the Japanese roof iris but I have never seen it, nor a photograph of it, on a roof. That would be good. I expect it suits the Japanese climate, which is tremendously humid in the summer. The iris would need to find its moisture somehow, somewhere.

## Work

There is particularly frantic activity in the nursery, frameyard and sales area. The two Bank Holiday weekends are our busiest for sales, in the year. We get a great many parties, from abroad, especially America, around the time of the Chelsea Flower Show. Some of them, at their request, I show round, usually rather small and select parties which don't flinch at my price!

There is a tremendous amount of pricking out to get through and later sowings need to be made, for instance of tender annuals like zinnias, quick-developing annuals like marigolds and cosmos, annuals which we shall not want to use in the borders till July, and tender vegetables like cucumbers and gourds. Cannas and dahlias, brought out from their winter quarters in the cellar, are rubbing the sleep from their eyes and need some attention. Dahlias from which we want to take cuttings (rather late, but useful for September–October flowering and for rejuvenating stock), are put into a close (but unheated except by the sun) frame, where they soon shoot away. We should like to get the cannas shooting faster, but haven't the right accommodation, so we have to wait for nature to lend a hand.

In the borders, with everything growing like mad, most of our preparatory work has been done and it is a question of staking or in other ways supporting plants as they need it and not too long before, as the sight of masses of stakes or pea-sticks is not one that elevates my spirits. So delphiniums, for instance, may not be staked until already 1.2m/4ft high. We hope that the lupins won't need staking at all, but if a wind gets at them halfway through their flowering, there has to be a quick rescue operation before all their laid spikes have become crooks and turned upwards.

I'll leave comment on the herbaceous lupins till June but the tree lupins, *Lupinus arboreus*, are at their best before that. I saw these wild on the shores of the Olympic peninsula in Washington state, and was impressed by the amount of wind they will take. In our gardens, they get blown to bits before they are three years old, but young stock grows fast and they are great self-sowers. Their evergreen foliage is always cheerful in winter. Now, in May, they cover themselves with pale yellow spikes and their sweet scent has none of the peppery quality of the perennial kinds. They make billowing specimens and created, I thought, a fine background to one of my globe artichoke beds, just as it was about to crop.

Evening light on the long border

The one drawback to the growing of any lupin, these days, is the large and prolific grey aphid which so quickly ruins them, unless you are on the watch. We spray with something nasty, but one spraying is not enough. The aphids' waxy coating is highly resistant. This aphid came to Britain from America. But our own various species are active and rapidly multiplying and there are cases where we cannot wait for ladybirds or hoverfly larvae to do the clearance job. Honeysuckles, viburnums, morello cherries, hellebores, shrubby euphorbias, cardoons and artichokes; also, next month, broad beans; these are some of the host plants on which we may need to perform a rescue act.

There are certain perennial weeds that we shall never be rid of but at least we can prevent them from getting worse. For instance, a creeping vetch, *Vicia sepia*, which gets into paving cracks and also into the roots of other plants. Wearing rubber gloves and carrying a cup of ready-diluted Roundup, Fergus, or whoever, takes a small paint brush or piece of sponge and, making sure that it is dry enough not to drip, applies this systemic herbicide on the weed's fresh leaves.

Tulips are always producing rogues as well as virus-infected, broken flowers, so we mark these plants in order to be able to sort them out, later on, from the colour and variety that was intended. Life is never simple where you are dealing with living things. But you cannot be bored, not in your own garden. In a friend's, you can accept their problems with the greatest equanimity.

June

The trouble with June is the speed with which it flashes by. Everything is coming to maturity, but is still young and fresh. There is little dead-heading to worry about, unless you are a rose-grower. The meadows reach a peak, in respect of their wild flower content. The horse pond scintillates. The borders are full of zest; there is much green in them still, but also a great deal of colour from early summer perennials.

A well-known feature of gardens where a lot of bedding out was practised was the June gap. This is the period between the removal of spring bedding and the settling in of its summer replacements. At Dixter we try to eliminate this with June-flowering bedding, using either biennials having an early summer season, or early summer perennials treated as biennials. That works fine while it lasts, but I have to admit that we then run into the danger of a July gap!

## Early summer annuals, biennials and mobile perennials

Herbaceous lupins make a grand display in early June. Their leaves are satisfying in the run-up to flowering and then the flower spikes themselves are an interesting combination of vertical and horizontal: upright spikes composed of horizontal whorls of flowers. Their warm, peppery scent is welcoming, too, and the sight of pollinating bees.

However, after they have flowered, there is little you can do for lupins other than dead-head them. Occasionally they will be inspired to carry a worthwhile second crop, in July, but more often there'll be nothing on offer except mildewed foliage. So we sweep the lot away and replace with summer bedding. Meantime, another batch of lupins for next year is being raised from seed and the seedlings will be lined out for the summer to grow on in a reserve area. We like to choose two single-colour seed strains, grow them separately and then mix them when bedding out in the autumn. Thus, we might have pink and yellow one year, yellow and blue another, or blue and red in a third. It should, of course, be understood that the modern lupin often already combines two colours in each flower – the top half, for instance, may be blue and the bottom half white. This adds to the excitement. Total mixtures of colours, which are the easiest to obtain from the seed merchants, are all right in their way, but it is good to be able to exercise some colour control.

Our lupin treatment has another advantage: that we can bed them into different areas of the garden in different years. In fact, as I write, we plan to have a grand mixed lupin display of what purports to be a fairly dwarf strain, in our main (wind-exposed) bedding-out area in front of the house, in May–June next year. It will be interplanted with tulips for the spring and will be followed by rather later-than-normal summer bedding, in late June. That may entail a July gap, but this bedding will continue well into the autumn if it includes dahlias, say, and bedding verbenas or rudbeckias.

Foxgloves have the same flowering season as lupins – I mean the biennial strains of our native *Digitalis purpurea*. Sometimes we save our own seed from a good white one that is growing in isolation. We like the 'Glittering Prizes' strain, with heavily spotted glove

fingers, or the all-apricot-coloured strain. I see no point in dwarf foxgloves – their height is no disadvantage even in the smallest garden; nor in strains in which the flowers are arranged all round the spike, rather than on one side, as is natural. The one-sided kinds always look towards me, in my experience, and they are graceful. Foxgloves leave a gap after the end of June and we have to be ready to deal with that.

I made an interesting experiment with Canterbury bells, which are naturally biennial. We sow them in April and either grow the seedlings on in pots (some in large pots are good for display) or line them out for the summer like the lupins and foxgloves. In 1998, we planted out some not very large, pot-grown plants in autumn, interplanting them with *Lychnis* x *haageana*, grown on in pots from spring-sown seed. This has brilliant scarlet flowers and is a short-lived perennial, probably best treated as a biennial. It is half the height of the Canterbury bell, but perfectly able to make its mark. The bells were a mixture of single-flowered kinds, which I like best. The white, mauve and purple ones obviously contrasted well with scarlet. I was a little nervous about the pink-flowered Canterburys, but in fact they turned out to be perfectly acceptable – you must take my word for it. The main display was in June, but as the bed is where I pass daily on my way to culling a salad, I dead-headed the bells as they turned brown, and

PAGES 112–113 June in the long border with *Allium giganteum* prominent
ABOVE Pink and yellow strains of lupin with *Weigela* 'Praecox Variegata'

this induced them to produce a very acceptable second crop. By that time, the lychnis had finished but we had made a direct sowing among them of the annual *Papaver commutatum*, the one with crimson flowers and a black spot at the base, and that took over. The planting of zinnias with which we had intended to replace the Canterbury bells, if they had completed their flowering at the normal time, in early July, never had a look-in. No matter; the experiment had been interesting. If I can convey something of the fun and absorbing interest that one can get from varying experiments of this kind, I shall have done OK.

So, I have touched on annual poppies, in this case the ladybird type. Another we grow is the double-flowered strain *P. rhoea*s 'Angel's Choir', which has a great colour range only excluding the scarlet of field poppies, to which it would naturally revert. And we like the Turkish *P. tauricum*. All these, and other members of the poppy family with exceedingly fragile roots, we sow in plugs, thinning the seedlings to one in each and planting them out without need of root disturbance. Those sown in March will flower in June and are excellent gap-fillers – for instance where forget-me-nots have been pulled out.

We have made quite a June feature, in recent years, with the pure white umbellifer *Ammi majus* (much used as a cut flower in the Netherlands and Germany) and a deep 'blue' larkspur, quite close to the wild type. I think *Consolida* 'Blue Cloud' is as near as you will get to it from a commercial source, but we save our own seed. Both were sown in the autumn and brought on in pots under cold glass. Grown this way, the ammi will reach a height of 1.8m/6ft, so the 90cm/3ft larkspur goes in front of that. Another good partner for ammi is the columns of willowy, fresh green leaves of *Helianthus salicifolius*, which we rate more important as a foliage rather than a flowering plant.

An annual/biennial that I dote on is the truly sky-blue *Cynoglossum amabile* (there are several obvious trade names). An early March sowing – or a September sowing if you can overwinter your stock under cold glass without its damping off – should have it in flower before the end of this month. Growing about 45cm/1½ft tall, it mixes well, in a harmony that should soothe the most easily shattered nerves, with the young glaucous foliage of blue lyme grass, *Leymus arenarius*. We plant the cynoglossums out in April, or even May.

The clean cheerful orange of the annual daisy *Osteospermum hyoseroides* is a regular feature at Dixter, as Fergus and I are both so keen on it. This is quick-maturing and you don't want to keep it waiting if, following a spring sowing and individual potting, it is ready to go out. It mixes well with blue, for instance the annual woodruff-related *Asperula orientalis* which is one of the few blue-flowered umbellifers) or with the bulbous *Brodiaea laxa* (now moved to *Triteleia*).

LEFT ABOVE *Ammi majus* with blue larkspur
LEFT BELOW *Cynoglossum amabile* with *Leymus arenarius*

St John's Day being 24 June, *Anthemis sancti-johannis* is so named for flowering at that time. We find this to be best treated like a biennial. It is the cleanest, most uncompromisingly orange daisy imaginable (needing twig support, even though only 60cm/2ft tall) and I love it in the long border with the magenta *Geranium psilostemon* (which never, in photographs, comes out its true colour, most of the blue element being lost). We may tone these down with apricot foxgloves and 'blue' larkspurs.

Of rather similar habit are the florists' pyrethrums, and they have a great freshness, in June. We like the crimson, yellow-centred kinds and the seed strain is listed as 'Robinson's Red'. We sow in the spring of the previous year and line the plants out to grow on, but as they hate disturbance in autumn, we do not move them into their flowering quarters till the early spring. They are already showing new growth in February.

*Salvia sclarea* is a bold, upstanding biennial, 90–120cm/3–4ft sage with an inflorescence of mauve flowers and rosy-mauve bracts. On light soils it is self-perpetuating but on our clay we need to raise it under controlled conditions. Which we gladly do, as plants with a presence such as this are invaluable and it has a long season. I like *Lychnis coronaria* in front of it. This comes into its own at the end of the month, with stiffly branching grey stems (and leaves) supporting a 75cm/2½ft structure with brilliant magenta, moon-shaped flowers. It is a self-sower and although technically perennial, it is at its best in its second year from seed and should never be kept beyond a third. It creates a range of daring combinations for itself, and it is up to us to accept, encourage or reject them. One such (next month) is with the scarlet *Crocosmia* 'Lucifer'. Less abrasive but equally effective, this month, is its positioning in front of the bright green foliage of *Grevillea* 'Canberra Gem', which has itself only just gone out of flower but continues to be an evergreen asset year-round.

Those of us with long-established gardens are sure to have *Eryngium giganteum*, known as Miss Willmott's Ghost. But we depend on its self-sowing, as its tap root makes it an unsatisfactory subject for raising in pots and planting out. And so, each year, it will be somewhere different from where it was last. Starved plants may not flower for several years but under good conditions it should be biennial. I thought it looked pretty good in front of my old colony of *Melianthus major*, now just getting under way after being cut to the ground at winter's end.

ABOVE   *Osteospermum hyoseroides* with *Triteleia laxa* syn. *Brodiaea laxa*
RIGHT   Self-sown *Eryngium giganteum* in front of *Melianthus major*

## Perennials in season

It is, or should be, impossible to discuss perennials without at the same time including some shrubs and other categories of plants, since they all help each other. And, of course, bulbs are perennials.

What are penstemons? Soft shrubs, really, and at winter's end, I either cut the old plants hard back, to sprout more vigorously from low down, or I leave them to flower a little earlier on the growth they brought through the winter. A third alternative is to start them again each year from cuttings, taken late in the summer of the previous year. This gives the most level results. I like the combination of *Penstemon* 'Drinkstone', which is a soft shade of red, with the rich purple spikes of *Salvia x superba* and the flat heads of a pale yellow achillea. 'Moonshine' has nice grey foliage but the yellow is a bit too bright. I prefer the sport from *A.* 'Taygetea' that turned up in my own garden and which I called 'Lucky Break'; this grows to 90cm/3ft and is a soft though distinct yellow.

The salvia has great staying power and, being a sterile hybrid, can be relied upon to flower a second time in September. Similar at a lower level, in June, though with no great tendency to flower a second time, is *Salvia nemorosa* 'Ostfriesland' ('East Friesland'). That would be a suitable companion for *Anthemis sancti-johannis*. The anthemis that is now coming into its own is the pale yellow *A. tinctoria* 'Wargrave', though there is some confusion between this and 'E.C. Buxton'. Quite by accident and in a stock bed, it flowered with *Yucca gloriosa* 'Nobilis', with an impressive candelabrum of waxy, cream bells. This yucca is less stiff than ordinary *Y. gloriosa* and it has an interesting bluish cast. Also, it is less inclined to flower out of season, which is an advantage, as you can plan accordingly. *Y. gloriosa* has the irritating habit of trying to flower so late that its

inflorescence is arrested by cold weather in mid-growth. Such a waste of effort.

To return to the anthemis, it, and others of the same species, may grow inconveniently tall, to 1.2m/4ft, on older plants, needing a lot of support; and they are subject to powdery mildew. Then, suddenly, the whole colony exhausts itself and you may find that there's nothing left for next year. The solution I adopt is to take soft cuttings from its mossy young basal growth in February. These, potted individually, will be ready to use as bedding plants by May, and they will flower non-stop from late June till late autumn, given just one dead-heading. No mildew and just one cane and a tie for each plant is sufficient. The height of these youngsters will not greatly exceed 60cm/2ft.

This is the month for old-fashioned pinks – *Dianthus plumarius* and its many hybrids. Nothing could be pleasanter nor better convey the feeling of summer than to walk into the orbit of a cushion of pinks that is wafting its unique fragrance. Alas, they hate my heavy soil and, apart from a few stalwarts wedged into dry-walling cracks, they need frequent renewal, which I usually overlook. Moreover, many of the hybrids which will flower freely as young plants cease to do so on reaching middle age, although the plant remains healthy.

I always grow a batch of 'Rainbow Loveliness', treated as a biennial, and that has a deliciously sweet scent on the air, but it is not the typical pink scent. Its seed ripens in late July and we sow it forthwith for flowering the next year. I also grow the carnation-like (though classified as a pink) 'Haytor's White', which is neatly double, is scented (good for a buttonhole to wear to Glyndebourne opera) and flowers over quite a long season. Which means that it also needs fairly frequent renewal. Long-flowering perennials usually make you pay this price.

I don't really go in for the early-flowering kniphofias (pokers) but a super form of *Kniphofia caulescens* given me by Helen Dillon does flower in June, although September is

*Allium cristophii* with *Geranium* 'Ann Folkard' and *Salvia nemorosa* 'Ostfriesland'

the normal flowering time for the most widely distributed clone. Helen's has the usual coral-coloured flowers but its chief excellence resides in its amazingly bold and substantial leaf rosettes, which are the expected glaucous colouring. They do not split, after flowering, into the normal cluster of new crowns that provide the usual opportunity for multiplying this species. It scarcely proliferates at all and it would need a more expert propagator than myself to discover how to overcome this obstacle. However, my plant, now four or five years old, makes an arresting corner feature and it has *Trochodendron aralioides* behind it, now in flower. The flowering panicles of this are fresh, bright green and their main feature is a circle of stamens which look like the spokes of a wheel (*trochos* is Greek for a wheel).

On another nearby corner, the feature is a clump of *Stipa gigantea*, now flowering; a grass which ideally lends itself to an important position of this kind. It makes a 1.8m/6ft fountain of oat-like flowering panicles, which are rose-tinted while young and last until high winds blow them to bits in the autumn. This is a see-through plant. There is a low wall, nearby – we are on the lower terrace – just right for sitting on when you're part of the way round a tour of the garden, and you can look through the stipa to the tall 'blue' panicles of *Campanula lactiflora*, coming into its own at the end of the month. Beyond that a view of two tall clumps of giant reed grass, *Arundo donax*, with glaucous leaves. In the distance, the three white cowls of the oast house. These were wooden but are now fibreglass. They still need a good wash every few years. One more thing worth saying about the stipa. I first planted it too close to the corner. As people turned this, they bumped into the obliquely spreading stipa stems and bent them – which meant that they had to be removed. So I moved the stipa back and all is well.

Many campanulas are at their peak in June. *Campanula persicifolia*, whether white or blue, is a great self-sower; our heavy soil suits it to perfection. As it is shade-tolerant, it often sows itself under a hedge or shrub and then peers out from that at a height of 60cm/2ft or so. In this way plants provide the ideas for us. The blue version would combine well with *Pimpinella major* 'Rosea', a 90cm/3ft, June-flowering umbellifer – native, but quite insignificantly white in the wild, whereas a fairly intense pink strain is a very good colour indeed (Fergus doesn't rate this highly, however; I shall have to bully him).

I suppose *Allium cristophii* is just about the best species for general garden purposes. It has large globes of stiff, lilac-mauve segments, and these persist, so that even when the colour fades the globe retains its presence for a long time. It is the sort of perennial that can be fitted into many places. Given a start, it will go on with the good work by self-sowing. I am pleased with it among Japanese anemones. It peps them up before their season but does them no harm.

*A. moly*, only 23cm/9in tall, is bright yellow. Its display is brief but it is a good filler between the bottom of yew topiary and the adjacent lawn. Among it, we have a self-sown spotted orchid, *Dactylorhiza fuchsii*. With its mauve spikes this works so well that I shall make an intentional planting with more of it. The natural hybrid *D. x grandis* is

larger and more important-looking, therefore deserving border space, which I have lately given it.

I am not a great fan of astrantias. I dislike their self-sowing habits, the seedlings are always of inferior quality and, like *Alchemilla mollis*, they have a tough rootstock and quickly become quite an effort to extract. Still, I must have some. 'Sunningdale Variegated' for its young foliage, which was at its best last month. The selection of *Astrantia major* made by Margery Fish, which she named 'Shaggy'. It has a large, irregular ruff of pale green bracts. But be warned; it is often sold untrue to name as seedlings are passed off as the real thing. Lastly, *A. major* 'Ruby Wedding', which doesn't have a rather miserable little inflorescence like many of the red kinds and is not too dark to show up well. In fact, there is a self-proclaiming gleam on the bracts. We liked this next to the *Geranium psilostemon* hybrid 'Ivan'. It is as strong a colour as the species but has a larger flower.

June is a great month for cistus. One of the most persistent and long-lived is also my favourite, *Cistus × cyprius*. Its large white blooms, a fresh crop each morning, have a maroon blotch at the base of each petal. But the leaves are also interesting: a dark, solemn green with a touch of blue in them which, in cold weather, may be heightened to the colour of lead. The bush grows to 1.8m/6ft and has a lax habit, so that it leans on its elbows. It can grow as it pleases and can do no wrong in my sight. It is apt to harbour weeds in its depths, which demand a grovel to extract. Over it, I am rather unwisely growing a vigorous hardy cucurbit, *Thladiantha dubia*. It would cheerfully envelop and exterminate everything in its path, so we practise a restraining act twice during the growing season. It is a male clone and covers itself with small, yellow, cucumber-type flowers in later summer.

Few gentians are for my style of gardening, but I have *Gentiana lutea*, a strong three-footer with whorls of yellow flowers above strongly ribbed foliage, not unlike a veratrum's. I have been unable to think of any appropriate companion for that, so it just explodes, soon running to seed.

Under a deciduous escallonia, near by, I have a colony of the evergreen *Saxifraga stolonifera*, which is an overground runner with loose rosettes of scalloped, hairy leaves

ABOVE The dragon arum, *Dracunculus vulgaris*
RIGHT *Rosa* 'Cornelia' behind *Rodgersia pinnata* 'Maurice Mason', with *Hosta* 'Buckshaw Blue' (now replaced), *Carex elata* 'Aurea' and *Euphorbia palustris*

beautifully marked in different shades of green. To everyone's surprise, that bursts into flower in June, with open sprays of lopsided white blossom, about 30cm/1ft high.

This is at one end of the north-west-facing bed with heavy soil where I had a January display of snowdrops. They have now been displaced by its perennial contents. There's a vigorous form of *Rodgersia pinnata* freely producing 90cm/3ft panicles of blossom in a good shade of pink. Slugs and snails pay no attention to this but I replaced the glaucous hostas that I used to have in front of it, because their foliage became a reproach far too early in the season. Instead I have *Geranium wallichianum* 'Buxton's Variety', which will not start flowering till next month but whose sharply jagged and well marked foliage is already an asset. Behind these, *Euphorbia palustris*, now fading, and *Aralia cachemirica*, with boldly pinnate leaves and still coming on. Right at the back is a rather puzzled-looking Hybrid Musk rose, 'Cornelia'. 'Why am I here?', it seems to be asking and I really cannot remember why, but it seems happy enough.

Some plants seem born to be soloists. In a fairly shady barn garden border, we have a good colony (which Fergus overhauls and replants every other year) of the dragon arum, *Dracunculus vulgaris*. In spring, its speckled shoots look like a team of adders disappearing underground. In fact they are emerging and expand into fascinating leaves, constructed on the same principle as *Helleborus foetidus* and *Adiantum pedatum*, with leaflets radiating from an arc. The large purple arum flowers open late in the month and on the first day smell of carrion, which attracts pollinating bluebottles. After that the smell subsides, each bloom lasting for three days. The total display is brief but a great event. It sometimes coincides with our local flower show but I have to be careful which blooms I select to enter. I did once get a First in the 'Any Other Flower Not Mentioned in the Schedule' class.

In the wall garden, the highlight for me now and till the autumn is *Paris polyphylla*. It grows in a shady border and you might not notice it at first, since it is green in the midst of a lot more green – the filigree lady fern, *Athyrium filix-femina* 'Plumosum Axminster', is one striking neighbour. The paris rises 60cm/2ft on a naked stem and there produces a whorl of lance leaves. Next come the floral parts, also in whorls, finally crowned by a central knob, which is the developing ovary. This amazing structure is all in muted shades of yellow (the stamens), purple and green. The ovary gradually enlarges and splits open in October to reveal brilliant orange seeds.

The giant fennels, of the genus *Ferula* (not to be confused with *Foeniculum*, the strongly aniseed-smelling herb), flower this month if they intend to flower at all. Fergus and I collect any of the spines that we can get hold of as there's not a dud among them. We discovered some beauties when in east Turkey in May, some years back, but there's never any seed collector there at the right moment to bring stock to this country. There must be many species just waiting. Every ferula has wonderful filigree foliage and all are different. The one most grown here is *F. communis*, and this now suddenly runs up to 2.4m/8ft within a few weeks, carrying corymbs of lime-green blossom. You cannot miss it.

There is quite an event, late in June, in the peacock garden, where the topiary peacocks are linked by double hedges of the bushy michaelmas daisy, *Aster lateriflorus*

'Horizontalis'. Between these double rows I have ribbons of a purple English iris, *Iris latifolia*, the last of all the bulbous irises to flower. Its foliage can die off here unnoticed, being concealed within the asters' growth. If you look across to the house from this area, you'll see a white 'Kiftsgate' rose flowering in the branches of a damson plum. And you'll be struck by its scent, if you approach a little

nearer. We make an effort to prune this each winter, removing the previous year's flowered growths. If you don't do this, the whole thing becomes an uncontrolled monster and will soon bring its support crashing to the ground. I don't want that; I rather like damsons, in their September season.

There's a lot of honeysuckle about in June, not least the wild plants which seed themselves around the garden. You suddenly become aware of their presence in the evening or early morning, when you walk into their scent's orbit. I see that one has reached to the top of the bay tree, without my being previously aware of its presence; and there is another growing over a *Cotoneaster horizontalis* in the sunk garden. The late Dutch honeysuckle, *Lonicera periclymenum* 'Serotina', was a selection from the wild, found on one of the islands off the coast of Holland, and it has particularly rich dark red buds. I grow that on a pole close to the house and it is fully out by the end of June.

Another wilding with garden selections is the common elder, *Sambucus nigra*. 'I am very fond of the Elder-tree,' wrote Miss Jekyll. 'It is a sociable sort of thing; it seems to like to grow near human habitations.' She associated it with farm buildings and planted a group at one end of her potting shed in her frameyard. As a bush it is fairly nondescript, but in flower it is transformed, every branch being lined, on its upper side, with flat corymbs of cream-white, scented blossom. These swags give structure to the whole bush. In the garden, we grow two kinds for their blossom. The earlier is 'Guincho Purple', with purple leaves and fairly small flower heads in which the anthers are pink, so the inflorescence is slightly flushed. If I make elderflower cordial with this, that is pink, too. The cut-leaved *S.n.* f. *laciniata* is the other and that has particularly large flower heads. A seedling from this, which looks an exact replica of its parent, has turned up on the fringe of the sunk garden and I have let it remain. These flowering elders are pruned in winter by removing their flowered wood. This encourages them to produce strong new growth. Some gardeners grow 'Guincho Purple' entirely as a foliage shrub, but I think it makes a rather heavy and gloomy lump. The elder which I do grow entirely for foliage,

LEFT Storm clouds brewing over the peacock garden
ABOVE *Paris polyphylla* with the lady fern, *Athyrium filix-femina* 'Plumosum Axminster'

giving it a hard cut-back all over, in winter, is *S.n.* 'Marginata'. It has a broad marginal variegation, pale yellow at first but maturing white. This variegation is not diminished in a shady position, to which it will give light. Elders put up with a deal of shade.

I make my elderflower cordial by putting half a dozen large, recently opened flower heads in a saucepan, together with five lemons, halved and their juice squeezed, 340g/¾lb of sugar (I have cut down on this from 450g/1lb) and a gallon of boiling water. This is left to steep for three days before being strained into bottles. It is not for long keeping.

## The ponds

There are wild honeysuckles around the horse pond, one of them overhanging the water, another twining up an oak sapling which we pollard, but, for the sake of the woodbine, not too hard. That is close to the forstal and looks welcoming as I drive home. The ponds are tremendously lively, now. There's no need for the tinkle of running water to be aware of a pond and the wild life that congregates in and around it. Rising fish make quite as much noise as I need and there is a constant coming and going of birds. Often, a blackbird nests in the dogwoods. It skims low over the water as it goes to and fro for food, and every time its shadow passes, there's a scurrying swirl from disturbed and scared fish. Of course we do get herons – one heron at a time, because they are strictly territorial. So I suppose a shadow could be a threat. I'm glad to have the fish thinned out a bit.

The waterlilies are all in bloom, now. They have quite strict hours and professional photographers, who are crazy on long shadows, usually miss them at their best. They are not fully open much before 11 a.m., by which time photographers have removed

themselves, moaning about the hard, flat light. By 3 p.m. on a hot day the waterlilies may already have started to close, though it will be an hour later in less fierce weather. I have some half dozen varieties. As I don't want them to mix and as I also always want to be able to see plenty of the water's surface, I get a water garden specialist to come each year and relieve me of stock

*Nymphaea* 'Rose Arey' in the sunk garden pool

around the perimeter of each colony. It is a mistake to grow over-vigorous varieties (usually concentrated among the white- and yellow-flowered kinds), as they take over far too much water and, in becoming congested themselves, their leaves grow out of and above the water so that you can no longer see their flowers. Most of mine are crimson or a reasonably strong shade of pink but I have lately added an exciting yellow called *Nymphaea* 'Texas Dawn'. Its flowers present themselves several inches above the water's surface – during the first day or two, that is. On the third day they sink back to the surface and on the fourth they're done. I find that if you pick waterlilies to float in a bowl, they'll close towards the end of the day (some people manage to keep them open with paraffin wax), but the next day they'll open wide again, so for a lunch party (though not for dinner) they'll be co-operative.

One of the brightest features at the horse pond's margin is Bowles's golden sedge, *Carex elata* 'Aurea', and it retains a good colour till August. This is also an excellent border plant, where the soil is damp, and contrasts effectively with hosta and rodgersia leaves. But don't plant it in shade, or much of its brilliance will be lost.

On the horse pond's bank, the combination of gunneras with a contrasting bamboo in their midst now shows up as intended. Gunneras, like irises and other rhizomatous plants, tend to march ever outwards, but to leave the centre of their colony vacated. It was at this stage that I planted the bamboo, *Thamnocalamus tesselatus* (formerly *Arundinaria tesselata*). It is clump-forming, with no running tendencies in our climate, and the abundant foliage is a slightly greyish green.

In the sunk garden pond, the oxygenating water soldier, *Stratiotes aloides*, has risen to the surface, for the summer. Its leaf rosettes are purple when under water, but turn green where they have come up into the open. The waterlily 'Rose Arey' has a nice starry pink flower, with rather pointed petals and it gives you the rare chance, if you kneel by the water's edge, of testing whether it really is scented, this being supposedly a selling asset. Well, it is scented, but nothing to get excited about. You'll do better to be watching newts, and lots of visiting children and their parents do. Water is always a draw. I hope that, in these nannying times, we shall never be obliged to put up a barrier to stop children (or anyone else) from falling in. I have, several times in my long life, and am none the worse for the experience. The water is 38cm/15in deep. I have to admit that it is wet.

## Meadows

Wild flowers in the meadow areas reach a climax, this month. They are dominated by yellow daisies, of which there are several species but the commonest is *Leontodon autumnalis*, the autumnal hawkbit, which flowers from June to October. To see its display at its best, you have to catch it right. The flowers are not fully open till mid-morning and they follow the sun, so you need to have the sun behind you. By early afternoon the flowers are closing. This has seeded itself into the topiary garden lawns in a big way, since I started to let them grow long, a few years ago. The topiary pieces, themselves shaggy with young growth, seem to be swimming in the deep sward and there is much white clover, conveying its honeyed fragrance. Here, and elsewhere in the poorest soil, the dominant grass is common bent and that flowers at the end of June and in early July, a lovely soft pink, though much paler on dewy mornings. Rather similar, at a higher level, is the impression made by a couple of smoke bushes, *Cotinus coggygria*, which become hazy immediately after flowering, pink at first but easily dew-laden.

Wild orchids, whose seeds are so light, are moving in without assistance, but the early part of this month sees wonderful displays of spotted orchids, *Dactylorhiza fuchsii*, in its principal self-appointed strongholds. These are in the orchard, in the prairie, which was once an orchard, and in the shady hollow next to the forstal (where, also, there is a late, heavily fragrant azalea, *Rhododendron arborescens*, flowering). The orchid's spikes are dense and in varying shades of mauve, some so intense that they would be worth selecting, if I could be bothered.

My mother, who used to raise them from seed, added meadow cranesbills, *Geranium pratense*, to a number of areas and that is as good a blue as you'll find in any cranesbill. Then there is the indigo-purple *Iris latifolia*, of whose role in the peacock garden I wrote earlier. Whenever we replant this, there is masses of surplus stock and we find that it is perfectly able to maintain itself under competitive meadow conditions, flowering well in some years, poorly in others, but totally undemanding.

## Fruit and vegetables

This is not a good month for garden produce as I make no effort to bring on early crops. On our soil, it is so much easier to have them coming in late. There'll be spinach; also, if we've been on the ball, early calabrese, from a protected sowing.

And the first ambrosial flush of globe artichokes. Such a spate of them; how can I bear to remove myself from their orbit? When I'm away, I leave instructions that every one must be picked and eaten and, on the whole, I find a willing following. When I'm there, it's artichokes every day, for me, and no satiety.

There'll be green gooseberries all month and it is best to freeze these while they are still on the small side. In the second half of the month, the large and squishy 'Malling Delight' raspberries will be ripening. As soon as we see first colour in them, we spray against the raspberry beetle, whose maggots would otherwise spoil a dish of the ripe fruit. We are also on the lookout for sawfly caterpillars on gooseberries and redcurrants.

## Work

Routine mowing and edging, staking, weeding and irrigating, if necessary, goes on. But one of the most important jobs to get done is the planting up of the exotic garden for its late summer and autumn display.

There are a few rose bushes (about ten) left here – a *Rosa* 'Mrs Oakley Fisher', with single apricot flowers, given me as a cutting from Sissinghurst by Vita Sackville-West. Several bushes of a polyantha rose, 'Madge', with trusses of blush-pink double flowers that smell of *R. arvensis*. I quite often don't prune this until after its first flowering. No one lists it any more, so I feel responsible and we sell a few raised from cuttings and on their own roots. One 'Ballerina', classified surprisingly as a Hybrid Musk; it has big panicles of single pink flowers.

Quite a lot of plants in this garden, grown mainly for their foliage, are hardy and remain out year-round. There's a patch of *Phormium cookianum* 'Tricolor', which flowers pretty regularly, in early summer, and it has a fascinating structure. The hardy Japanese banana, *Musa basjoo*, has its thick fern-frond overcoat removed, early in the month, although it may poke a bit of new greenery out from the top in any mild spell from February on. *Eucalyptus gunnii* seedlings, which we keep for several years if their juvenile foliage has a good blue colouring, are cut hard back, so as to keep their growth in the attractive juvenile state. But we also grow on replacement seedlings every two or three years. It makes a good 1.8m/6ft of young growth in one season.

The cut-leaved sumach, *Rhus glabra* 'Laciniata', is hardy and suckers all over the place, so we now lift these and pot them up for sales. The main core plant is cut to the ground. Paulownias and tree of heaven receive similar treatment, so as to procure the largest leaves possible on their young growth. The pink-variegated box elder, *Acer negundo* 'Flamingo', I keep pretty hard-pruned as that encourages it to go on producing new young foliage, which has the colour, through most of the summer. The *Yucca gloriosa* just need to have their old leaves pulled away. Steady the plant with your other hand as you do this, otherwise there's the risk of losing an entire branch. The phormiums need tidying in the same way. The other one here is 'Sundowner', which has pink striping along with green and purple. It's not as hardy as 'Tricolor' and may take time to recover after a hard winter.

Otherwise, Fergus and I are discussing at every step how to arrange our planting of dahlias and cannas and of exotica that have overwintered under heated glass – cacti, succulents, streptocarpus, foliage begonias and many other exciting foliage plants. We have an old bodge, filled from a hose with water, into which we can dip our cans as required, always planting with a big dose. All this is hard work and there's masses of debris piling up at every stage, but a lot of fun, too.

To be writing about June without devoting a section to roses shows what sort of a gardener I am. I often love the perfect bloom, or a climbing rose hung with great swags of blossom. But for much of the year, rose bushes are hideous and there's no way to be rid of them. They simply refuse to disappear into the ground and return the next spring, all pristine and ready to delight. Far from it; they are grumpy, surly objects, just longing to inflict vicious wounds, so I am happy to leave them to your care and to visit you when all is song and dance.

July

This is the warmest month. At last, the evenings and nights have ceased to be chilly and it is right for picnics at Glyndebourne opera, which is less than an hour's run from Dixter. It is also right for taking our evening drinks to the top of the long border. About seven of us can fit on to Lutyens's seat. It has two return bits at the ends and the one nearest the orchard gives you the best view of the long border itself, but in the gloaming it is just as good to be looking towards the sunset sky, against which the ash trees are silhouetted.

The seat, which gets little sunshine at any time, is also good to visit (if not already occupied) by day, when one may be quite glad of shade and the top end of the border reaches a climax by the second half of the month. Best in the morning, while sunshine slants across it from behind and before the light becomes too hard and crude and shadows almost cease to exist.

Indoors, everything is totally different from the winter. I am banished from my favourite room, the solar, as there is no fire to act as a focus. The same in my study, the parlour, below, which has become a public room. That can be rather gloomy, after 10 a.m., when the sun leaves it. The great hall is at its luminous best at 6 a.m., when sunshine floods into it from the north-east. The quiet of long summer mornings is so good. Many birds stop singing – I miss the blackbirds after the second week – but goldfinches carry on, and swallows, which are nesting in the kitchen yard, using the clothes line to sing from. The garden is wonderfully refreshed; hydrangeas and mulleins have regained their vitality. The smoke bushes are beginning to smoke and are laden with dew. The phone is silent; there's no one around to bother you, unless an early photographer. I know they need the early morning light but I do rather resent their presence, seeing that the whole of the rest of the day will, of necessity, be a crowd of incident.

## Running repairs

Fergus and I frequently make a practice of meeting in the garden, early. We are still doing a great deal of planting, in July, for it must be remembered that our aim is to keep the interest going for another three months. With the garden empty, we can do things near to paths without getting in anyone's way. And, most important, we can think – I mean, think creatively on how to carry on with the show. Fergus makes a list of what's available for planting from the frameyard and we work out what to replace the June-flowerers with – the lupins, sweet williams, *Erysimum linifolium*, *Ammi majus*, larkspurs and early cornflowers. There's always something going over that needs attention.

If the plants, like alstroemerias or delphiniums, can't be moved out, we tuck in annual climbers to grow over their skeletons, notably blue ipomoeas (which can no longer turn yellow with cold, as they do even in June) and the related *Mina lobata*, with little sheaves of tubular flowers in orange, yellow and white.

For replacements, we largely depend on cannas and dahlias (late-struck cuttings) or bedders raised from late-sown seed. We lean quite heavily on nasturtiums, sown individually or in pairs, in small pots, outside. Some of them are climbers; more are of the bushy types. There'll be some tuberous-rooted begonias, excellent for rather shady places. As we use so little heat, these are sown in June the previous year and the small tubers overwintered under the greenhouse bench. The next year they'll be raring to grow on and will be individually potted to be planted out now and flower till November. I like the cascade types but I grow them on the flat. Their flowers are small but brilliant.

We have got the hang of and enjoy growing *Coleus* (now *Solenostemon*) hybrids for bedding. These are generally known as tender pot plants with brilliantly coloured foliage in a range of patterns and colours. You seldom see them bedded, but I did, when I was young, and I was impressed. Our problem (self-imposed, I suppose) is to grow them without the assistance of heat. But, in fact, a May sowing brings the plants on very handily to be used as replacements for other bedding in early July. The seed is what's offered on the market; there are some restricted colour strains, others are mixtures. The seedlings are potted individually and kept happy under glass until we are ready to use them, by which time the glass is well enough ventilated and the outside weather friendly enough for the change to the outside world not to come as too great a shock.

We want to make quite an impact with a largish area and it can be part-shaded. Coleus rather like that. We set all the pots out on the path and I then arrange them, grouped by their general colouring and vigour (leaving out a few of the dullest), and with consideration of which will look best as neighbours. They take time to establish, but from mid-August for the next two months are making a great display. Really exciting – or disgusting, according to how you view coleus. Their range is amazing.

Late-sown zinnias and *Tithonia rotundifolia* 'Torch', which is like a zinnia but brilliant orange and up to 1.8m/6ft tall (avoid the mini-version, 'Goldfinger'), are good standbys. Also *Ricinus*, the castor oil bean, for its handsome foliage. There are several strains.

PAGES 130–131 The end of the long border, including *Verbascum olympicum*, *V. chaixii*, *Clematis* x *jackmanii* 'Superba' (trained on a post), *Hoheria lyallii* and *Senecio doria*
ABOVE Phlox and *Mina lobata*

## Trouble-shooting

We used to be passionately keen on the stately 1.8m/6ft tobacco plant *Nicotiana sylvestris*, as good for its leaves as for its flowers, but all nicotianas have become such an effort to grow successfully, since a killer downy mildew has swept the country (at least in its southern half), that we have given up. Powdery mildews can be controlled by regular spraying and Fergus is hot on that, but with so many plants now affected that never used to be, it is an effort. We no longer find monardas worth the battle. Clematis, especially of the Jackmanii and Texensis kinds, are seriously mildew-prone, but we can combine their spraying with the simultaneous control of the fungi causing clematis wilt disease.

Gardening is an artificial practice. The plants we grow are largely man-made and are seldom bred for freedom from disease. On top of that, we herd them all together under artificial conditions or we feed them up and expect them to perform glamorously. But it is a set piece of three-dimensional drama and to keep the show running we cannot or should not be surprised nor aggrieved if we run into a range of frustrating obstacles. The picture created is a work of art, in its ephemeral way, and I believe it is worth the effort.

Another problem is that of soil-borne diseases. Affecting those of us who like to grow annuals are the numerous cases where a plant – an annual aster, cleome or zinnia, say – having grown healthily up to a certain point, suddenly turns up its toes. This trouble becomes endemic to a certain piece of ground, so we adopt the modern method of coping with the situation by fumigating the soil. We use Basomid or Dazomet, digging in quite deeply the powder which, on becoming damp, releases a gas that kills all seeds and fungi in the soil. It is quite a performance and not simple when applied to a patch of ground surrounded by perennial plants or shrubs, but it can be done, if they are sealed off from the treated area with plastic sheeting and the same sheeting is used to cover the area so as to prevent the gas from escaping. These chemicals, understandably, are not available on the retail market. We tend to wait to apply them in summer, because they work so much more speedily in warm weather – perhaps two weeks of covered ground followed by another week while the ground is being freed of the gas. You then test the soil with sensitive and fast-germinating seed like mustard, rape or turnip, to see if it is by now safe to plant what you want to grow. The treatment releases nitrogen from the soil so you avoid extra feeding to the succeeding crop.

There are always spells from spring to autumn when the plants are short of water, and these are most likely to occur when evaporation is at its highest. My father installed a deep-bore well, which pumps water (nowadays by electricity) to the highest point in the garden, where there are two reservoirs; the water enters the first, where it can rest and deposit, then moves into the second, which is used for all purposes in the house. The garden draws from the first reservoir. The pipes clog up and there have to be pipe-clearing operations: air is blown through them at high pressure, two or three times a year. This makes it worse before it makes it better and there are crises when we are without water. Still, having our own, unchlorinated, is bliss, in my opinion (and I'm not alone in that). We could go on to the mains, but have not.

My father also laid irrigation lines underground throughout the garden. Most of those have had to be replaced. We can reach nearly everywhere when we need to but, neither the flow nor the pressure being great, it's quite a business getting round with the hoses at sufficiently regular intervals, so we start early and end late. Fergus makes things as easy as he can for me when I'm on the spot and he's not, and I have a notice, 'SPRINKLER', which is laid out in the bathroom so that I cannot miss it before going to bed. After a while, I get into the routine and remember to turn it off without prompting. If starting it off in the morning again is simple without involving too much hauling around of hoses, I do that, on letting the dogs out first thing.

It is true that we have a water-retentive soil, but even clay dries out, leaving huge cracks. We do what we can to increase water-retentiveness by incorporating a lot of bulky organic compost and manure into the ground and on to it as mulches, but there comes a time when extra supplies of water are clearly urgent – you only have to look at the hydrangeas to know; phloxes, likewise.

## Hydrangeas and phloxes

It is sensible to grow the plants that like you (and to disdain those that don't). Those raised peat beds that are created by rhododendron- and other calcifuge-plant-lovers forced to garden on alkaline soil are always pathetic. On a one-of-each basis, so as to be able to include as many varieties as possible, they are hopelessly spotty and never make a unified impression. But if you grow the plants that naturally enjoy your company, it is very different.

Hydrangeas like moisture; they do not like too alkaline a soil but if, like ours, it is neutral or thereabouts, you have the opportunity of obtaining a rich red colour from those, like *Hydrangea* 'Westfalen' (a hortensia – that is, bun-headed) or 'Geoffrey Chadbund' (a lacecap) which will give it to you. On really acid soils, they will inevitably be deep blue. That's all right in its way but is apt to look (even though it's not) artificial. It makes me feel slightly uncomfortable. On the other hand a hydrangea of light colouring, like 'Générale Vicomtesse de Vibraye', a hortensia with the advantage of considerable hardiness, looks better when a light sky blue than when light pink. I do not in the least mind pink hydrangeas, but the blues can be rather nice.

Well, if your soil is sort of in-between, you can quite easily (though with some labour) convert it to a sufficiently acid condition with weekly waterings with a solution of aluminium sulphate. Or you can spread the crystals over the ground above the plants' roots and thoroughly dissolve them from a hose or watering can. Do this from about late February till the flower buds are colouring. Within a couple of years, it will be working a treat. However, if you want a good strong pink or red and it is apt to be muddy mauve, a lime dressing will operate in the opposite direction. Or you may be perfectly happy to relax and let the colours come as they please. The fact is that hydrangeas are generously flowering and colourful shrubs with a substance that is often lacking among perennials. And they have a season when flowering shrubs (apart from white-flowered kinds) are not all that numerous. There are hypericums but most of those are in rather lifeless shades of yellow.

I have hydrangeas just about everywhere but there is a principal planting. I introduce other ingredients, because I don't think that the hummocks of hydrangeas all on their own provide sufficiently varied shapes. The giant reed grass, *Arundo donax*, which rushes up to 3.6m/12ft and more in a season, makes a wonderful break. So does the 1.8m/6ft *Campanula lactiflora*. And there is great variety in the surroundings. For instance, for two weeks mid-month, we have *Clematis uncinata* behind the hydrangea area and against the house: a great foaming mass of tiny white flowers among neat evergreen leaves. The eau-de-cologne scent wafts right round two corners of the house.

Some hydrangeas are particularly rewarding because of a long flowering season. 'Madame Emile Mouillère' is one of these; a white hortensia, already flowering early in the month. As the flowering heads become unsightly, sometime in September, you remove the branches carrying them and the display continues on the young shoots, often even into November, if frost holds off. Another with a long season is 'Ayesha', a hortensia which is medium pink with me and is distinguished from all others (to date) by its incurving florets. They are highly polished, like china. This needs a sheltered wall position in order to flower freely and I have it so that the eye takes it in together with *Buddleja* 'Dartmoor', which hangs over the wall from behind it. The buddleia, actually growing in the wall garden next door, is tall and vigorous and has heavy multiple panicles of light purple blossom which are perfectly designed to hang voluptuously over walls. 'Ayesha' flowers on and on, provided that it brings its old wood through the winter. In that case, it will flower both on the old wood and on the new. If it doesn't, it will be so busy making new wood that this will be too soft and sappy to flower at all and will become an easy victim to the next winter's frosts.

I am fond of many of the lacecaps, too, and I think they mix perfectly well with hortensias, if you want them to. Of the other, really winter-tough kinds of hydrangea, an outstanding example that comes into its own late in the month is *Hydrangea arborescens* 'Annabelle'. It flowers on its young wood and can therefore be pruned quite hard back each winter. But if you prune it too hard, the young shoots will bear enormous bun-heads on rather weak stems, which will flop. So we leave (or I leave – Fergus enjoys a hard pruning) some growth on last year's stronger young shoots to carry the smaller flower heads. In either case, we find it advisable to provide some support (discreet, of course). 'Annabelle' is pure white and can be excessively dominant if placed in a too prominent position. So I have learned to site it at the back of the long border. Even though it grows only 1.2m/4ft high, it makes a quite sufficient impression from there,

Hydrangeas are enlivened by the giant reed grass, *Arundo donax*, and foreground plants

and doesn't jump at you prematurely. It fades gracefully and when bleached to beige is one of the good features in the border's early winter aspect.

Phloxes have no structure to speak of but their domed heads give a pleasant bumpiness to the great eiderdowns of exciting colour for which I so value them. And they waft a summery scent, strongest while there is still dew around. I wouldn't be without that. The great thing about phloxes is that they should be robust and willing, healthy growers, devoid of the dreaded phlox eelworm. The best way to acquire them is by asking for a bit from a friend's garden in which you can see that they are flourishing. The name doesn't matter. Colour doesn't matter a lot either. I like bright pink or mauve phloxes as much as the soft colours, but avoid anything that's wishy-washy or indeterminate. The earliest-flowering kinds of *Phlox paniculata*, from which most of our border phloxes derive, will be out early in July or even earlier and they quite frequently give you a second flowering in September. One in particular, a light shade of purple with a paler centre (I wish I knew its right name; it was given to my mother and me by Dr and Mrs and Miss Burgess, many years ago, so we have always called it phlox Burgi), is an especially generous flowerer, scarcely pausing to take breath. White phloxes are very, very white and have dark leaves; they are apt to stare, so don't overdo them. This does not apply to *P. paniculata* 'Alba', which is soft white and, like the prototype phlox, the mauve *P. paniculata*, is tall, light of texture and graceful. These two, unlike the others, do need support but are worth it.

## The month's perennials

This is the climax month of the year for flowering plants as also for many insects. Butterflies, alas, are in pretty short supply, these days. But there are masses of meadow browns, with their floppy flight, and towards the end of July, the annual hatch of peacocks is suddenly with us. Large and small whites are about and migrate in greater or lesser numbers from the continent, not only paying attention to our brassicas but quickly decimating nasturtiums. Seakale, stocks and cleomes are other favourite foods.

I wrote last month of *Crocosmia* 'Lucifer', in connection with growing it behind *Lychnis coronaria*. The crocosmia is flowering best in the second half of July and is soon joined, at a lower level, by the bright but pleasing yellow *Coreopsis verticillata*. This has a stiff habit but its stems are thin and wiry and the foliage filigree fine. I prefer it to 'Grandiflora' or to the pale and polite yellow 'Moonbeam', which makes a wretched plant in our too cool climate. I want a sandwich, between the scarlet and the yellow, of soothing blue sea holly, *Eryngium* x *oliverianum*, which is just about the best of its kind with sizeable blue flower heads and incredibly metallic blue stems. So far, it has sulked, probably because it is receiving too much competition from its ebullient neighbours, but I am still hopeful. I enjoyed reading Jekyll on this. 'The whole plant has an admirable structure of a dry and nervous quality, with a metallic colouring and dull lustre that are in strong contrast to softer types of vegetation.'

Strongly structured perennials are at a premium. Among them is *Veratrum album*, a perennial having a tendency (which I also noticed where it was growing wild, in central Europe) to flower freely one year and scarcely at all in another. From a strong basal plinth of rounded, pleated foliage, it sends up 1.5m/5ft branched panicles of white star flowers. Even when the flowers fade to green, its presence is maintained. It hates to be disturbed, but does self-sow a little, which I find a great compliment.

Quite a loner, best seen apart from neighbours, is the wand flower or angel's fishing rods, South African *Dierama pulcherrimum*. It has tough evergreen iris-like leaves, which need cleaning up each spring. The 1.8m/6ft flowering stems are naked for most of their length. They are tough but flexible and arch over into an ever-moving parabola under the weight of chains of pendent racemes of tubular flowers. These are coloured magenta or some shade of pink, sometimes almost white. The seeds are attractive too and the scarious (papery) bracts have an eye-catching way of gleaming when the light is behind them. Dieramas look as though they should be hanging over water but

Big colour contrasts: *Crocosmia* 'Lucifer' with *Lychnis coronaria, Coreopsis verticillata, Eryngium* x *oliverianum* and *Verbena bonariensis*

actually like good drainage. Mine, I think, are most attractive as paving features on our sitting-out terrace. They need to stand above their surroundings. Great self-seeders; control does need to be exercised.

By now, we are right into the prime season for yellow daisies, most notably, at Dixter, with *Inula magnifica*. This grows to 2m/7ft and carries easily branching candelabrums with notably long-rayed daisies, the rays quivering individually when there is a breeze. It makes a good border plant; as it starts late into growth, the widely separated clumps are interplanted with tulips. But it looks even better in one corner of the orchard (formerly a damson grove) where there is a concentration of poet's narcissus. Here we grow a very widely spaced colony of inula clumps which make solo features and are yet members of their community. We leave their skeletons till late winter, though their dead leaves do hang rather like the garments on a scarecrow.

*I. hookeri* is quite different but a favourite in its own way. It has a rhizomatous habit and makes a colony which needs controlling, where there are neighbours. Although only 90cm/3ft high, it does benefit from support. Its buds show the rays twisted in a spiral before they unfold and they are very fine, the yellow soft, as bright yellows go, and this is enormously popular with butterflies. *Telekia speciosa* (*Buphthalmum speciosum*) is in a similar mould, though with broad leaves. It stands 1.5m/5ft high. The involucre of

green bracts is especially noticeable before the flowers are fully open. It contrasts well, in a reserve plot, with the columns of lance leaves of *Helianthus salicifolius*.

*Senecio doria* is a part of the grand display (as it now becomes) at the top of the long border, so I will deal with a lot of that in one big mouthful. It is a self-supporting six-footer with flat heads of small, bright yellow daisies, not unlike a ragwort's but the leaves are smooth, undivided and shiny. It is contrasted behind with a column of purple *Clematis* 'Jackmanii', trained up a long chestnut pole. That is at the back of the border and to one side of it is the white, cherry-like blossom of a New Zealand shrub, *Hoheria glabrata*. On its other side is a hard-pruned bush of *Buddleja* 'Lochinch', which is still a greyish foliage feature, but comes into its own in a few weeks' time (I might as well deal with the situation now), when a group of the fiery *Kniphofia uvaria* 'Nobilis' (2m/7ft) starts performing. And that will be softened by the creamy panicles of *Artemisia lactiflora*, to its right.

But in front of the kniphofia and in violent contrast to it (hence the need for softening agents around) is a large patch of a pink phlox – not a harsh pink and with a paler centre, but bright enough. There is a really harsh pink phlox a little lower down the border and underneath the round-topped, fresh green tree-shrub *Gleditsia triacanthos* 'Elegantissima'. I fell for this when I saw it naked, in January 1954, I should guess, in Jackman's old Woking nursery.

A lot of yellow around here is contributed by the random planting and self-sowing of two verbascum. The perennial *Verbascum chaixii* (1.2m/4ft) has narrow, sparsely branching spikes of small yellow flowers which are surprisingly highlighted by purple stamens. The biennial *V. olympicum* (2m/7ft) we have a great deal of between here and the high garden. It makes a heavy candelabrum (we need to give each plant a stake), which branches generously near the top, making a powerful head of yellow bloom. Some visitors think we have too much of this but Fergus and I think otherwise. In the orchard garden, next above the long border, it looks splendid on a bank with yew hedging for a background and it mixes well (I think) there, with red hollyhocks. All verbascums wilt in hot sunshine, so, if the day is to be sunny, they need to be enjoyed before 11 a.m.

At the front of this top end of the long border I should, perhaps, have mentioned last month an ancient specimen of Jerusalem sage, *Phlomis fruticosa*, with dusty greyish leaves and dusky yellow flowers. I know I've had that since the end of my student days in 1950. It is a sprawling wreck but I love it and its sprawl can be taken advantage of by other plants, like violets and snowdrops, early, and phloxes later on. The violently pink phlox is right next to this and I have to admit that they do not make the best of partners, but the overlap of their flowering is only slight. I can overlook it. I'll deal with the rest of this area in August, because it does run on.

A section of the long border showing contrasting elements

Turning to the bottom of the long border: the large privet *Ligustrum quihoui*, which flowers late in August, is meanwhile making a good support for another 'Jackmanii' clematis. In front of these I like the intermingling of mauve *Phlox paniculata* and the lemon-yellow *Hemerocallis* 'Marion Vaughn', one of the larger-flowered day lilies which has stood the test of time. Near to these is the white version of *Verbascum chaixii*.

Right at the bottom of this, the main section of the long border, there used to be a grove of *Magnolia denudata*. They gradually failed and to provide end-stop solidity, I planted aucubas, but still felt the need of something low, but reasonably solid on the front corner. We chose a summer-flowering hebe (it will flower again quite well if the first crop is dead-headed), *Hebe parviflora* var. *angustifolia*, once known as 'Spender's Seedling'. It doesn't need to grow more than 60cm/2ft high (height is easily controlled by pruning). Presumably descended from *H. salicifolia*, it has linear leaves and open spikelets of white flowers. Through this weaves (in the invaluable way that so many cranesbills have) the pink *Geranium endressii*.

There's another satisfying hebe/cranesbill combination in the high garden, but with the addition of the pale grey stems of *Artemisia ludoviciana* 'Silver Queen'. This grows into a bush (there are two actually, but growing into each other as though one) of *Hebe* 'Watson's Pink'. After a series of mild winters, this is now 1.8m/6ft tall and on its other side the 'blue' *Clematis* 'Prince Charles' (like a more compact and mini-version of 'Perle d'Azur') has a handhold. The hebe is now smothered in short spikes of clear pink blossom. Pink and grey obviously go well together, but additionally I have infiltrating *Geranium* x *riversleaianum* 'Russell Prichard', which is magenta. A splendid performer, it flowers from late May into the autumn. Another strong colour here is the harsh purple *Verbena rigida*. The fact that its flower heads and flowers are small makes the strength of its colouring necessary. The off-white version, 'Polaris', gets you nowhere.

I grow several *Hemerocallis* besides 'Marion Vaughn', which are at their best in July. Two of them, 'Golden Chimes' and 'Corky', raised by the same American breeder, are rather similar, with masses of small trumpets on a freely branching plant. There is nothing coarse about them. 'Golden Chimes' is a somewhat dusky yellow, bronze on the outside. It is less effective than and does not flower for as long as 'Corky', which is a brighter, lighter yellow. That looks pretty growing next to the pale blue double cultivar of meadow cranesbill, *Geranium pratense* 'Plenum Caeruleum'. (I also grow 'Plenum Violaceum', which has deeper-coloured flowers in a tighter, more formal rosette.) A favourite with me, though by no means showy, is *Hemerocallis altissima*, which lives up to its name by growing 1.8m/6ft tall on rather weak stems. It is a night lily. Its mid-yellow flowers are small and they open in the evening, when they are scented. Next morning, the scent has gone and the flowers soon fade.

Delphiniums used to be July flowers but most of the modern cultivars peak in June. A tiresome tendency in them is excessive height. Seven or eight feet is not much use in the average mixed border. Still, if you pick and choose from a trial ground such as the one at Wisley, there's sure to be something to your taste. This is the way I found *Delphinium* 'Mighty Atom', which is of only moderate height and a nice shade of mauve (they don't have to be blue all the time). In the long border, it goes well behind the pale yellow discs of *Achillea* 'Lucky Break' and in front of white *Hydrangea* 'Annabelle'. If you're lucky, delphiniums will live on for many decades and there is one such which I raised from seed, that would certainly win no prizes but is of the faithful retainer type. That flowers in July at the same time that other perennials, including purple

fennel, are looking nice and there are hydrangeas about, notably the small-headed old hortensia with pale pink flowers offset by black stems, *H. macrophylla* 'Nigra'. The delphinium flowers a second time but we need to spray it against mildew. Who doesn't?

July is the big month for carnations, but I do not grow any of the perennial kinds, only seed strains. For bedding purposes, I best like 'Florestan', either in single colours – the red is excellent – or in a mixture. From a spring sowing, we line out the seedlings for the summer and they remain vegetative, making strong plants for bedding out in the autumn. Then, in July, the whole lot flower dramatically and are deliciously scented on the air, as all carnations should be, but the florists' types so seldom are. They grow quite tall and do need discreet (that word again) brushwood support, which is certainly a chore, but for a few weeks the display is stunning – and, I would add, unusual. It completely exhausts the plants, which we discard in early August, and replace with late bedding. This is high-maintenance gardening at its best! There are always tulips among the carnations for a spring display, and we don't rest on our laurels when they have flowered. As a visitor, you will not think that anything looks contrived, I promise.

## Clematis

I have already brought in several clematis, and July does give us the most rewarding kinds in the whole year – those which flower on their young wood and can be so simply

*Geranium* x *riversleaianum* 'Russell Prichard' scrambling through *Artemisia ludoviciana* 'Silver Queen', *Verbena rigida* and mixed verbena hybrids

*Acaena novae-zelandiae* invaded by *Euphorbia stricta* and bird's-foot trefoil, *Lotus corniculatus*, in the floor of the sunk garden

pruned, any time between November and April, by cutting them hard back. Their flowering, unlike those which bloom in spring and early summer, is spread out and not all in one burst.

*Clematis* 'Victoria' is a favourite with me because, although in most ways like 'Jackmanii', it is a much less heavy shade of purple. I prune it rather lightly as I do not want to delay its flowering. It grows behind the pink Hybrid Musk rose 'Felicia' and the two help one another when they coincide. Roses and clematis make ideal companions. I would also point out that I have two plants of 'Victoria' here, which appear as one. This is an old and effective dodge for increasing impact.

*C.* x *triternata* 'Rubromarginata' is small-flowered and a rather wan shade of purple but completely disarms every criticism by its wafted scent over a long period. That grows over the stiff framework of *Mahonia* x *media* 'Buckland'. The clematis is pretty vigorous but its host has raised no objection. It is important in such a situation, however, that the host shrub should be really large, strong and solid before weighting it with a clematis.

Many of our old espalier pears mainly serve as pegs for clematis. I like 'Royal Velours' and I have it close to a path, but it is so dark that Fergus usually has to prompt me to look in its direction at the right moment. After that, of course, I look automatically every time I pass. But it's rather dreadful to think that one can entirely miss the flowering of some plant that has only a short season.

The Texensis hybrid 'Sir Trevor Lawrence' grows over a self-sown cotoneaster, and its prolonged performance has been transformed since we took to spraying it regularly against mildew. Its lily-flowered-tulip-shaped flowers are held upright (like a tulip's) and are as close to red as you'll find in any clematis. In a photograph it will come out pure red, any blue element being eliminated.

'Etoile Violette' was already flowering last month. It is one of the best tempered and most rewarding clematis, not large but large enough, prolific and with a white eye which relieves any heaviness in its purple colouring. I used to grow it over an olearia. When it had killed its support (a common situation), I gave it a stake and it now has the companionship of the vigorous 'Paul McCartney' rose, with large, bright pink flowers, exceptionally fragrant.

The non-climbing old hybrid *C. x eriostemon* is a stayer. Given a most unpropitious siting in turf, at the edge of the orchard, it never complains but trails its indigo bells over a piece of red-flowered *Fuchsia* 'Riccartonii' hedging. I think the point about all clematis is that they should not be considered as isolated units, but be combined with other plants to be a part of a garden's setting.

## Water and meadow

The horse pond area is lively as ever and the main waterlily feature is 'James Brydon', with a season not as long as some of the others but generous while it lasts. Its full, bowl-shaped flowers, between pink and purple, are striking. Yellow continues to be supplied by marginal brooms, mostly of the wild kind, *Cytisus scoparius*, which has an amazingly long season as between plant and plant, all of them self-sown. The weight of blossom brings their branches down to, even into, the water. With the added impact of their reflections, the display is quite something.

The prevalence of dragonflies is noticeable. Being constantly on their territorial beats, their main object is to display themselves. Occasionally, one lands on you. You freeze, trying to prolong the moment.

In the sunk garden pond, I have a pot of *Houttuynia cordata* 'Chameleon'. It is perfectly happy in shallow water and its amazing pink, yellow and green colouring is much heightened in a sunny position and where it is a little starved through root restriction. In a border, it is so rampant as to present something of a problem. We do have it at the top of the long border, but Fergus has had to prevent (or try to prevent) its progress into border neighbours with a vertical strip of metal, sunk into the ground.

There is quite a free-for-all growth of vegetation over much of the sunk garden floor, almost like a meadow, at this stage, before we have attempted to impose order.

The young burrs on *Acaena novae-zelandiae* turn brilliant carmine, in July, and contrast with the yellow of self-introduced bird's-foot trefoil, *Lotus corniculatus*. But I have also introduced a plant of *Spiraea japonica* 'Anthony Waterer', which gives a little height, while its own flowers are the same colour as the acaena's burrs. Very tall, here, and in many parts of the barn garden, above, are self-sown *Oenothera glaziouana*. Its name keeps changing but it is the one with by far the largest yellow flowers. They do not open till well after sunset but continue in good condition the next day, until mid-morning, especially if the weather is dull.

There are plenty of teazels, now flowering. This starts as a narrow band of mauve around the centre of the green cone. It divides and becomes two bands, one moving upwards, one down. It is a strange performance. There were self-sown (nearly everything is self-sown) clumps of spotted orchids flowering here last month. And throughout the summer, the biennial *Euphorbia stricta*, which is a feature in the entire barn garden complex. It is a biennial species with open sprays, about 30cm/1ft tall, of pale green flowers. Where the plants are a little starved, as here in paving cracks, the stems and stalks are contrasting red.

A speciality in this garden, normally seen around us in woodland clearings, is another biennial, *Centaurium minus*, the common centaury. It belongs to Gentianaceae and the rosette of leaves that it makes in its first year is uncommonly reminiscent of the rosettes in *Gentiana acaulis*. In its second, it rises to a foot with an open corymb of bright pink, star-like flowers which only open out in sunshine. A joyful little plant.

The topiary garden is a sea of bleaching grass lapping around the topiary pieces, themselves shaggy with young growth. There are also the two smoke bushes, the green-leaved *Cotinus coggygria*, whose 'smoke', the inflorescence, is pink before ageing grey (wig bush is another name for it), and a light purple-leaved form, with rather duskier 'smoke'. On the wall of the adjoining hovel and climbing on to its roof, the honeysuckle *Lonicera similis* var. *delavayi* is seething with cream-coloured blossom, heavily night-scented. Further along the wall, an ivy, *Hedera helix* 'Buttercup', is bright yellow on its young foliage.

Through the hovel, the exotic garden is gathering its strength. Supporting canes are rather more evident than I should like. The linking thread through this garden is *Verbena bonariensis*, whose heads of light purple are already bright. A great deal brighter are the seedlings, of which we delight to leave some, of the corn marigold, *Chrysanthemum segetum*. You could scarcely imagine a brighter, cleaner yellow. But it gets mildew, in this sheltered site. We actually give a protective spray to this 'weed'. Earliest of the dahlias, from the start of the month, is the small, double, bright red 'Grenadier'.

But to return for a moment to the principal meadow areas: their shaggy appearance does not in the least irk me (it does some), except where wet weather has laid the grass. That only happens where the soil is richer than it should be and in a fiendish season of wind and rain. The wild flower that cheers us up all through the month is the tufted vetch, *Vicia cracca*, which is an excellent shade of blue. In the dampness of the bottom of the upper moat, meadow sweet, *Filipendula ulmaria*, is bearing its creamy flower heads.

## Shrubs

I want to include some shrubs which don't especially fit into my community plantings. For instance, the very first thing you see on arriving at Dixter, in July, is a mature *Genista aetnensis*, the Mount Etna broom. It is growing in meadow turf, whose competitive nature made the broom's early progress extremely slow (and I am trying to establish others, in this area, which are having the same difficulties). But once away, this is the longest-living broom species, giving you thirty years or more. It is almost a tree, at maturity, with very thin, raining branches. They are green and do all, or nearly all, the photosynthesizing; tiny leaves are soon shed. Short flower spikelets occur at the tips of every new shoot, so this becomes a fragrant fountain of yellow, for some three weeks.

By contrast, the other summer-flowering broom, *Spartium junceum*, from the Mediterranean, is stiff and large-flowered, though again on terminal spikes and even more sweetly and heavily scented. It is no elegant beauty but a great performer and its bright, clean shade of yellow is peculiarly satisfying. It doesn't really care for my heavy soil but I get away with it, as with the cistuses, which would also prefer it hot and dry. I grow quite a number, but would specially like to mention *Cistus* x *pulverulentus* 'Sunset'. It is fairly low-growing with sage-green leaves and vivid magenta flowers over an exceptionally long period.

I am a bit snooty about escallonias, considering most of them to be second-class plants but, although its flowering season is short, I do make an exception of *Escallonia virgata*, which makes a moderate-sized, deciduous shrub covered, this month, with white blossom.

*Lonicera similis* var. *delavayi* growing on the hovel

Of the hebes I grow, I have mentioned two. Also of some importance as a corner feature in the high garden are several interlocking plants of *Hebe* 'Pewter Dome'. It is a dense evergreen with greyish foliage, entirely obliterated just now with spikelets of white flowers, whose anthers are contrasting black – always a pedigree point, like the black anthers in some white agapanthus or the black tongue in a chow.

Red is not an easily provided border flower colour, at this season, except in bedding plants – or roses. But the late-flowering *Rhododendron* 'Arthur Osborn' is pure, rich red and is so late as to run on from June well into July. It has a low, spreading habit and rather nice, stiff leaves. I should like it to have the lime-green flowers of *Euphorbia seguieriana* subsp. *niciciana* to keep it company, but that needs renewing very frequently. It flowers non-stop from late May till fall, but exhausts itself after a couple of seasons.

Another lime-green inflorescence is that borne by one of the few shrubby umbellifers, *Bupleurum fruticosum*. It is a cornerpiece in the L-shaped border in front of the house, and has our main bedding-out ideas in front of it. The shrub is a handsome evergreen, but apt to become over-large and unwieldy. Or, if you clip it over in spring, it becomes smugly rotund. However, I find that it can be cut to stumps, in spring, and will joyfully react in the same season with young shoots up to 1.8m/6ft long. It flowers and flowers and flowers and, if you sow its seeds absolutely fresh, can be easily increased that way, though cuttings are, in our experience, difficult.

Yet another lime-greener, grown against a south wall in the wall garden, is *Cestrum parqui*, whose first burst of blossom – panicles of small, tubular flowers opening into stars at the mouth – generally occurs throughout this month if it carried some of last year's wood alive through the winter. If it did not, it has to start again from ground level and will not flower till August. After a July flowering, there will be a second, equally generous crop in autumn. The plant's and flowers' normal smell is rather sour, as in many of the Solanaceae, but at night there is a transformation, with a delicious almond scent on the air. You should bring a sprig indoors to enjoy there.

The summer jasmine that we have always grown is the larger-than-normal-flowered *Jasminum officinale* f. *affine*. This also has extra vigour and if it needs to be pruned to restrict its growth, its flowering will be impaired. But

The foliage of *Catalpa bignonioides* 'Aurea', *Hedera helix* f. *poetarum* 'Poetica Arborea' and *H.h.* 'Buttercup'

at Dixter, where it mixes well with *Clematis montana*, of equal vigour, it can have all the space it wants, with the only pruning necessary the removal of old, flowered wood; hence, it flowers with a will, starting off in early July. White, of course. Being on our sitting-out terrace, its fragrance comes straight through the house when the terrace door is open.

I naturally grow a number of shrubs entirely for their foliage, which is now at its freshest. There is a satisfying group in the high garden. At the back, a golden catalpa, which is far more worthwhile as a hard-pruned shrub, with nice big leaves at or just above eye level, than as a tree. In front of that the arborescent form of ivy, *Hedera helix* f. *poetarum* 'Poetica Arborea'. At 1.8m/6ft, it has grown larger than I expected or wished, but the catalpa still gives it the right background. The ivy is dark green, smothered in blossom in autumn and with orangey fruit in February (soon devoured). By its side, another arborescent ivy, quite low (60cm/2ft) and such a bright yellow that it tends to scorch in hot sunshine. I imagine that to be the arborescent form of 'Buttercup'.

I also, in the wall garden, grow the yellow-leaved form of white poplar, *Populus alba* 'Richardii' (given me by Rosemary Verey), for its foliage, pollarding it hard so as to keep it as a bush. That elicits some disapproval from friends and public, but Fergus and I like it, so that has to suffice – and it does.

## Produce

Good things keep coming in from the garden and need to be dealt with in rather a hurry, sometimes, as with broad beans and green peas. It is so important to freeze them while still young and tender (and before the beans are wearing tough jackets). These two vegetables are the best of any for freezing and so different from the frozen equivalents on sale that I grow large batches. House guests, as well as gardeners and 'volunteers', are impressed to help with the mammoth shucking sessions.

The raspberries, 'Malling Delight', are too large and squishy for preserving, but I make jelly from my four redcurrant bushes and use the blackcurrants in various ways.

Besides the Glyndebourne parties, many friends are in the offing to visit, especially from abroad, which I love and I let it keep me pretty well tied to home. The 10,000 or so paying visitors keep us all at full stretch and there are times, when they are at their most numerous, that I yield to the temptation to keep out of the way. Now and then I come out from the kitchen or some writing in the yeoman's hall of the Benenden house, with the door open into the garden, so that I am well aware of how thickly populated it is – re-emerging properly after 4 p.m., when things are quietening down but there is still plenty of activity. Then there is the slow unwinding, as evening approaches. Perhaps a thunderstorm to freshen things up and keep us on our toes, for there is always the anxiety of hailstones and the damage they can quickly wreak on soft foliage, like the cannas'. Of all the months that flash by, July passes the fastest.

August

The holiday crowds are thick as ever, in August, right up to the Bank Holiday weekend. Yet, in a sense, this is often the moment when time may come to a halt. Given a spell of settled weather, each day is like the last and I can happily con myself into the illusion that summer has come to stay, and that it will float on like this indefinitely.

There are heavy dews at night. The yew hedges have yet to be trimmed (that starts in the last week) and they are hung with dew-laden cobwebs. The countryside around now looks tired and tarnished, the trees, especially the oaks, heavy and brooding. But the garden is an oasis of voluptuous luxuriance. It may pant and go limp in the early afternoon heat (when the public is visiting, I'm afraid), but for most of the time it flaunts, yet in a contented sort of way.

Too many gardens give up in August. Vita Sackville-West hated the month at Sissinghurst – it took Pam Schwerdt and Sibylle Kreutzberger to provide zest for continuing effort. I suppose many families go on holiday; when they return, all seems to be in disarray. Instead of throwing down the gauntlet, they throw in the sponge.

PAGES 150–151  A late-flowering stock bed in the high garden
BELOW  The top of the long border at its peak with abundant phloxes

Fergus and I revel in this season and the many opportunities that it provides. We have been planning for it right through the year and we continue to plan and prepare for September and October. True, the lawns are likely to be brown. They do not come high on our list of priorities and a spot of rain will soon bring them round. In any case, they are neither numerous nor extensive. One has made room for the mosaic, while in the topiary garden we now have meadow areas for half the year, instead of lawn.

## Perennials in season

There has to be a certain falling off in flower power from many perennials, after the middle of the month. From the border phloxes, for instance, but some of these, like *Phlox* 'Duchess of York', in two shades of pink, flower late, while others give us a second flowering, more generous in some years than in others. There are also, if you look for them, plenty of perennials that actually come on in August.

The top third of the long border is an area I am still proud of, so I will take a second look at that. The Jerusalem sage, *Phlomis fruticosa*, has recovered from its dead-heading and has made new, greyish foliage. *Helianthus salicifolius* continues to contribute columns of finely drooping, fresh green leaves. *Buddleja* 'Lochinch' now covers its grey-green foliage with long spikes of lavender flowers. This cultivar is often wrongly named, the misnomer being applied to a clone with much stubbier flower spikes.

The central feature of *Kniphofia uvaria* 'Nobilis' continues to dominate, with its brilliant orange pokers, all through the month, but I would emphasize how important it is, with these pokers, to keep up with the task of removing faded spikes so that they do not mar the continuing display made by those that are later-flowering.

I have also mentioned the cream-coloured panicles of *Artemisia lactiflora*, which loves our heavy soil but still needs heavily watering in time of drought. Six feet tall, it never requires support. I have three patches of it in the long border and two elsewhere in the garden, so valuable a plant do I consider this to be. If you have occasion to split and replant it in the winter, its subsequent display will be a few weeks later. That, too, can be an advantage. *Eupatorium purpureum* subsp. *maculatum* 'Atropurpureum' (also 1.8m/6ft) is another moisture-loving, self-supporting perennial, a little more intensely purple in this clone than in the type-plant and popular with butterflies, should there be tortoiseshells around or, if we're in a lucky year, migrant red admirals or painted ladies.

I have *Hydrangea macrophylla* 'Mariesii', here, a semi-lacecap, with flat heads of (with me) pink flowers having a scattering of large, sterile florets in the centre of the disc as well as around the margins. Another valued shrub is the summer-flowering tamarisk, *Tamarix ramosissima*, with plumes of pink spikelets set among feathery foliage. Leaning over the back of this are the 2.4m/8ft cardoons, which flower all this month. They have rich lavender-blue discs (covered in bees), which always look a muddier shade of mauve in colour photography.

There is a charming, though modest, perennial climber, in this area, *Dicentra scandens*, with little clusters of yellow lockets. That interweaves with an extremely vigorous and showy colony of single white Japanese anemones, 'Honorine Jobert', right at the top of the border. This flowers for two and a half months from July to October.

At the front of this piece of border is an excellent mixer, the popular Polyantha rose 'The Fairy'. A really clear, clean shade of pink, set among glossy foliage. That mixes with self-sown Chinese chives, *Allium tuberosum*, 60cm/2ft tall with umbels of white flowers, the inflorescence retaining its shape all through the winter. Early in the month, I cut the whole group of *Alchemilla mollis* hard back to the ground and it soon refurnishes with a new crop of young leaves.

Lower down the border, *Aster sedifolius* (*A. acris*) comes into its own with a duvet of interlocking mauve daisies. At 90cm/3ft, it needs and deserves the best support with pea-sticks. If I can get a self-sown, scarlet nasturtium to thread through this patch and flower with it, that is ideal, but nasturtiums are cussed and you never know from year to year how they are going to behave.

Midway down the border, I like the combination of a not too tall, purple-leaved canna (interplanted with 'Goliath' poppies, now cut down) in front of the newly ripened clusters of shiny red berries on the guelder rose, *Viburnum opulus* 'Compactum'. The latter needs careful annual winter pruning so that it is always making new wood on which to flower and fruit in the next year. Otherwise it gets into a feast-or-famine routine of biennial bearing.

There are perennials of interest in other parts of the garden. In the high garden, for instance, there is a large area of stock bed which we have planted with a view to its looking nice as well as being useful. There is a garden seat to one side of it and I have tried to ensure that the view from this is particularly pleasing (cheating a little, with some annuals in the foreground). A theme of self-sown purple orach, *Atriplex hortensis*, runs through it but will have to be pulled out at the end of the month before it sheds its seeds incontinently. Fergus is really too indulgent towards this plant, but I have to admit that it does combine extraordinarily well with many perennials, for instance the sunflower, now coming on, *Helianthus* 'Capenoch Star' (1.5m/5ft), bright yellow with an anemone-centred disc. Also with *Phlox paniculata* 'Alba'.

Harmony in pink and yellow: pink Japanese anemones and
*Helianthus* 'Lemon Queen'

Again with atriplex near by, there is a patch of crocosmia which I have called 'Late Lucifer', it being a seedling of 'Lucifer' which usefully flowers a couple of weeks later. A good contrast can be made with that (or with 'Lucifer' itself), and *Aconitum* 'Spark's Variety' (1.2m/4ft). This is deep blue but has the advantage that its laterals are as vigorous and important as the central spike. All appear to flower together, whereas in many monkshoods the central spike, which is dominant, has gone over by the time the laterals are flowering; that looks a bit unbalanced (as also in delphiniums).

The narrow borders that flank the high garden's paths, crossing one another at right angles, provide some satisfying vistas, one of them ending with Lutyens's gate, the other with a yew archway. As you come up the steps from the orchard garden, the angle of the path turns; you are between short, double hedges covered with the red blossom of *Fuchsia* 'Riccartonii', but immediately beyond I have loudly contrasting

Pushiest of the pokers, *Kniphofia uvaria* 'Nobilis', with *Artemisia lactiflora* in front

patches of a bright purple phlox, behind, and bright yellow *Microseris ringens*, in front. This is a composite with clustered yellow daisies above broad, undivided leaves. I'm not saying that it is a plant with a pedigree, but I see no reason for so many gardeners being sniffy about it. Near by, and tastefully toning the loud company down, is the silver-variegated form of *Calamagrostis acutiflora*, called 'Overdam' (1.5m/5ft); an upright feature that contributes helpfully for more than half the year.

Another supportive grass now and for many months to come is *Stipa splendens* (90cm/3ft), with arching plumes that are feathery on first flowering, but close up and become pale beige in colouring. It is an excellent landscape feature. In the barn garden, I have it in front of *Miscanthus floridulus*. I do not generally like putting grasses together, as their similarities tend to cancel each other out, but in this case they are so different as to help one another. The miscanthus has a fountain-like habit, rising within a few months to 3.6m/12ft and having an entirely foliar role. In our climate, if it flowers at all, it is too late and insignificantly.

One more combination of perennials that you might not have thought of! A pink

Japanese anemone – any pink one – with the pale yellow sunflower, *Helianthus* 'Lemon Queen' (1.8m/6ft or more). This has quite small daisies and it gradually builds up a display which reaches its peak next month. But it can be inconveniently tall, so, besides the support which it will undoubtedly require, I recommend lifting and replanting your clumps each winter to reduce their vigour, and pinching out the tips of all the shoots when the colony is no more than 60cm/2ft high. Yet another superb yellow daisy will be at its best, *Rudbeckia* 'Herbstsonne' ('Autumn Sun', 2m/7ft). Curiously, this is less top-heavy in an open, wind-blown site. But we have it housed in with nicely contrasting perennials like eupatorium and *Artemisia lactiflora*, and Fergus manages to keep it upright somehow. Large daisies with a green cone and down-drooping rays of a luminous yellow having just the faintest suggestion of green. Not a brash yellow, at all.

## The exotic garden

I explained in my introduction why we got rid of the roses in the rose garden (all but a few; there are still visitors who make a dive for one or other of these and pretend that there are no other contents). The site, being enclosed and steamy hot in summer, seemed ideal for a little piece of make-believe: that, instead of being at latitude 51 degrees north, for a few weeks the illusion could be maintained that a magic carpet had transported us somewhere like Wagner's magic garden in *Parsifal*, and that we were perhaps in the Mediterranean area and much closer to the centre of things. So we have gathered around us plants that not only enjoy or at least tolerate such conditions, but that themselves, in their flowers or foliage, convey an impression suited to my aims. Quite a number of them are hardy. So much the easier for me, the point being that they should look right.

It quite often happens, for instance, that if a tree is treated as though it were a shrub, by cutting it hard back every year, the resulting growth, albeit restricted, will bear leaves enormously larger than normal – to many visitors, unrecognizably larger. That is rather stimulating, for a start. *Paulownia tomentosa* is the example that attracts most attention. Normally a tree bearing clusters of foxglove-like flowers in spring, it has rounded, furry leaves which arouse no great comment. But if you first establish a young plant (it comes easily both from seed or from root cuttings) and then make a practice of cutting it almost to the ground, each winter, allowing only one or two of the resulting shoots to develop, it will make perhaps 4.2m/14ft of growth in one season and will bear only a few leaves, but these will be of the largest, each upwards of 60cm/2ft across. I tell the curious how easily they could achieve the same effect in their own gardens, but none of them has ever seemed interested in trying. I should add that this treatment is likely to exhaust the plant after six or seven years, but it is easy enough to start again.

PAGES 158–159 In the exotic garden – with plenty of lush foliage setting off the dahlias

Of pinnate-leaved trees that may be treated in this way, the tree of heaven, *Ailanthus altissima*, responds well. Also a charmingly cut-leaved shrub, the sumach, *Rhus glabra* 'Laciniata', as we used to call it, now *R. x pulvinata* Autumn Lace Group (one of the modern, unusable names that we have been saddled with). That suckers madly, but each spring we cut it to the ground and remove all its suckers (they are potted up and sold). During the year, it grows only 1.5m/5ft or so tall, but it is a handsome component.

Effect from foliage is even more important, in this garden, than from flowers. The box elder, *Acer negundo*, has a variegated cultivar, 'Flamingo', in which the young growth includes a lot of pink and white. If you prune this pretty hard each winter, it will be stimulated into making new young growth through most of the summer, instead of merely in one spring burst. You will at the same time be keeping it to a manageable size in a context where you don't want it to grow so large as to compete with fairly close neighbours. There is a canna, called 'Erebus', with glaucous leaves and salmon-pink flowers that looks handsome in front of the acer.

I have quite a scattering of yuccas, which are bold as evergreen plants and more than a little exciting when they carry their candelabrums of waxy, white bells. *Yucca gloriosa* is the largest of these. Then I have two kinds of New Zealand flax, tufted evergreens with strap leaves. One, *Phormium cookianum* 'Tricolor', is absolutely hardy here. It has rather lax, arching leaves, variegated in green, cream and purple. Flowering freely in early summer, it doubles its height to 1.8m/6ft, and although the flowers themselves are smallish, tubular and of muted colouring, the aggregate of many flowering stems makes a strong and exotic impression. The other flax, 'Sundowner' (1.5m/5ft), is more of the upright *P. tenax* habit. There is a lot of pink in its leaf variegation and that looks good near to the pink canna 'Louis Cayeux'. 'Sundowner' can look pretty unhappy at winter's end and may be in need of a good deal of tidying up. But after a mild winter, it sails through without blenching. In any case it will have recovered by midsummer.

Some of the gum trees make handsome specimen bushes. You raise them from seed the previous year – *Eucalyptus gunnii* being one of the most attractive, though *E. globulus* is even more flamboyant and faster-growing – and allow them to grow some 2.4m/8ft tall. The juvenile foliage is small and rounded and a very blue colour (contrasting wonderfully with the leaves of a purple-tinted canna, like the vigorous *Canna indica* 'Purpurea'). *E. gunnii* is generally hardy, so at winter's end, you cut it right back to a stump and it will do the same job again for you. After a few years I find it best to start again with more seedlings. I should point out that the adult leaves are long and lanceolate and not nearly as appealing as the juvenile condition, but the plant will continue to produce juvenile foliage as long as you persist with the hard-prune treatment.

This garden was originally a cattle yard and Lutyens made his formal design around a circular brick cattle drinking tank, which stands about 90cm/3ft above the surrounding paving. Like the other three, elsewhere, I have filled it in with soil, and we here grow the giant reed grass, *Arundo donax*. It is hardy and rises to 3.6m/12ft or so from nothing, with glaucous foliage. A fine, rather bamboo-like central feature. There is another at ground level in one corner. These are thirsty plants.

Bananas add a truly exotic touch, having such large leaves. These do tear into ribbons in a high wind, but in this protected garden they retain their integrity for many weeks. The hardiest is a Japanese species, *Musa basjoo*, and we leave that out all winter, but wrapped up in a jacket of fern fronds. It is extremely liable to poke its nose out with some fresh green leafage, prematurely, even as early as February, only to have it bitten off in the next frost. In a real July heat wave, one new leaf will be produced every ten days – eight days is the record. To see them unfurling is an excitement in itself. Exciting is, indeed, the word that constantly pushes its way forward in writing about this ephemerally luxuriant kind of gardening. *M. basjoo* makes suckers, which we detach in spring and grow as separate plants. When the main stem flowers, that is the end of it. Most bananas of the genus *Ensete* make only the one stem but they are easily and quickly raised from seed, which is on the market. You can sometimes get seed of purple-leaved kinds, which are sumptuous.

There are some hardy euphorbias in the exotic garden but I suppose the only other important permanent feature is *Escallonia bifida*, a large shrub which needs protection and was here before the transformation scene. It seems to have a limited life, however, quite aside from its vulnerability to a hard winter. This is the finest of all escallonias, being smothered, in late August and September, with panicles of starry white flowers. They are incredibly popular with butterflies. Last year (before writing this) I counted eighteen red admirals at one moment.

Another popular butterfly plant is the connecting thread, *Verbena bonariensis*, which I have already mentioned. It grows to 1.8m/6ft and flowers and flowers for nearly four months. We can only allow a few of its myriad seedlings to develop, otherwise we should be engulfed. The plants are short-lived, two or three years being the limit, but they generally survive the winter with a foot or so of their old growth intact, which makes the onset of flowering that much earlier.

Having tidied this garden up and weeded it in March, we planted its tender contents in June and early July, so that now, in August, it really comes into its own. Rapid growth requires generous water availability, so we are constantly having irrigation blitzes.

There is a preponderance of foliage plants among the tender exotics that we plant out from the greenhouses where they spend two thirds of their year. In a hot, sunny bed that we keep on the dry side is a concentration of succulents, with a few cacti among them. We love cacti and would like to have lots of them. When we have built up enough stock, we shall be able to experiment more freely with their hardiness,

especially of the opuntias, some of which endure a tough winter climate in their native American habitats. Of the succulents, aeoniums, both green- and purple-leaved, have stylish rosettes on a woody framework. The glaucous leaves of *Cotyledon orbiculata* (given me by Beth Chatto) are large and rounded, arranged in loose rosettes so as to comprise an admirable group, once settled in.

In a shady bed, on the north side of a yew hedge, I grow shade-loving begonias, with notable success from *Begonia scharfii* (syn. *B. haageana*). It has furry leaves tinged red on the underside, grows to nearly 90cm/3ft and flowers freely, with flesh-pink blossom. I also put my streptocarpus out, here. At the height of summer, when shadows are at their shortest, even this bed is sunny and the streptocarpus don't like that but they come into their own from August on. There are ferns, too, notably *Polypodium aureum*, with deeply cut glaucous fronds, and *Cyrtomium falcatum*, with glossy, pinnate fronds. The latter is more or less hardy but gets going more quickly in the summer if it has overwintered under glass. *Schleffera actinophylla*, an evergreen shrub with compound palmate leaves, is nearly always grown as an indoor plant but loves to have a summer airing. That is now 1.5m/5ft tall. There are others of Araliaceae (the ivy family) like it. In fact we had a whole lot of New Zealand members of this family wished on us by a New Zealander and have had fun with them. Some are really weird.

Another member of this family that turns me weak at the knees is *Tetrapanax papyrifera*. It has large, palmate leaves which are covered in beige felt when young. This is amazingly hardy. We lift and house it in the autumn but the roots that are left behind start a new colony in the following year.

The Egyptian papyrus, *Cyperus papyrus*, is a thrilling plant when it gets going, throwing up 2.4m/8ft, naked stems which are crowned by a mop of thread-fine leaves. We find this harder to overwinter than others in our collection, but manage to secure some of it one way or another, and seed germinates readily. Easier to manage is *Amicia zygomeris*, which is leguminous, with beautiful pinnate foliage that always attracts attention. At dusk, the leaves lose turgidity and collapse. Sizeable yellow pea flowers are produced at unexpected moments, but in no great quantity.

ABOVE Succulents congregated in a dry area of the exotic garden
RIGHT *Colocasia esculenta* 'Black Magic' – highlighted by *Arundo donax* var. *versicolor*

We lift and house our stock, or propagate it from cuttings, which come on quickly, but if you plant amicia against a warm wall, it can be treated as a permanency. Cutting the old stems down to the ground in spring, it will often make 1.8m/6ft or more of growth in one year.

Another notable foliage plant is *Furcraea longaeva*. Superficially it resembles a yucca, but makes a huge crown of glaucous leaves that are not stiff or spine-tipped. Every year it has to be re-housed and I tell Fergus that it will beat him one of these days, but so far he has been its master. When it flowers, it dies, like an operatic diva, but unlike her, it leaves a host of tiny offspring by way of a legacy.

There is a patch of glaucous-leaved *Kniphofia caulescens*, a couple of *Cordyline australis* cultivars, their leaves arranged to look like a conventionally represented explosion, some young members of the palm family, the variegated form of *Agave americana* and a number more of eyecatchers. The garden can be entered by any one of four approaches (two of them through doors in the hovel) and we want to create an immediate visual impact, which bold or colourful foliage plants help you to do and to maintain through the garden's season.

Once in it, you're in the thick of it, but there is a short view through the centre of the garden which I terminate at one end with a splendid foliage plant, *Colocasia esculenta*. This aroid, known in the US as elephant's ears, has fleshy, edible roots and is a feature in Chinese markets. But I grow it for its great shovel-shaped leaves, which are utterly smooth and most beautifully veined, a feature which can best be appreciated when low sunlight provides back-lighting. Dew forms readily on the leaf surfaces, and they even start to drip from the sharp tip as early as 5 o'clock in the afternoon. Once they get going, there's a drip every three seconds or so. I entered the garden with a friend, early

one August morning, and she spotted a toad squatting on the paving under a drip, evidently enjoying a shower. We lowered our voices as though in church and tiptoed away.

There is another colocasia that I have recently been given, called 'Black Magic', with smaller but incredibly dark leaves. I have con-trasted them with a white-variegated plectranthus underneath and *Arundo donax* var. *versicolor* behind; this, a grass with broad white striping. Behind them is a purple cactus dahlia, *Dahlia* 'Hillcrest Royal'.

## Flowers in the exotic garden

There is no flower, at this season, to touch the dahlia for contributing brilliant, clean colour over a long period. The flower shapes, whether single or double, cactus, waterlily-like or so-called decorative, are beautiful, too. I go in for the medium- or small-flowered kinds which flower the most freely. Generally, the dahlia leaf is pretty uninteresting and needs to be kept in the background. The smaller-flowered kinds also have discreet foliage.

*Dahlia* 'David Howard' is my best friend, a neat, smallish decorative of cheerful, apricot-orange colouring and having darkish leaves. It flowers untiringly and eventually reaches a height of 1.8m/6ft. An excellent companion for this is the castor oil bean, *Ricinus communis* 'Carmencita', which has bold, bronze, palmate leaves and, as a bonus, a red inflorescence. Or, for contrast, I like the tall, white-flowered *Cosmos bipinnatus* 'Purity'. Coming down to a more reasonable level at the border's margin, a good mixer, grown from seed as a foliage plant, is *Grevillea robusta*, pinnate and bronze-tinted while young.

Of the red dahlias, the medium semi-cactus 'Wittemans Superba' is a special favourite with Fergus and myself; the hint of purple on the reverse side of its rays being especially subtle. I may say that we chose most of those we grow on the trial ground at Wisley. Try and visit this after they have stopped disbudding, say in late September or early October, as you then get a better idea of their performance as garden plants. Disbudding for choice blooms is an artificial practice which is fun in its way, but does not give the results that most of us are looking for.

Because of its ferny purple foliage, the single (or semi-single) red 'Bishop of Llandaff' is a particular favourite even with those gardeners who disdain the majority of dahlias. That contrasts well with the blue foliage of *Eucalyptus gunnii*. Another single I like is the pale yellow 'Claire de Lune', which also has a pale yellow collar of smaller rays.

On the whole I have a preference for the warm shades – red, orange and bronze – but I do like the clear pink, waterlily-style (with an open-textured arrangement of rounded petals) 'Pearl of Heemstede', and this plays its part in an overall pink gathering with *Salvia involucrata* 'Bethellii' (1.5m/5ft), which is quite a vicious shade of pink with mauve thrown in (I'm not sure why I like it but I do); the self-sowing, mauve-pink *Impatiens balfouri* (90cm/3ft); and the beautiful cherry-pink *Canna iridiflora*, with very large, purple-rimmed green leaves and a gracefully arching inflorescence.

Cannas are the other great contributors to the general excitement of the exotic garden, as much for their leaves as for their bundles of silken flowers. The latter are greatly at the mercy of the weather and you need to go over them frequently, removing dead blooms – they just pull off.

Two of the liveliest for their variegated leaves are *Canna* 'Striata', which is striped in green and yellow; and 'Tropicanna', distributed from Wisley as 'Durban' (the name is still under dispute), which is stripily variegated in rich shades of pink. Both hold their leaves more or less upright and greatly benefit from back-lighting. Both have orange flowers.

The best orange-flowered canna is 'Wyoming' (1.8m/6ft or more), which has purple foliage and goes splendidly with *Dahlia* 'David Howard'. An excellent purple-leaved variety going around as *Canna* 'General Eisenhower' looks like a piece of bronze sculpture, before it flowers (1.2m/4ft), and the flowers are pure red. Its vigour is only moderate, which can be an advantage. My most vigorous and prolific canna is known as *C. indica* 'Purpurea' (1.8m/6ft). It has fairly narrow purplish leaves (quite a dash of green in them) and small orange-red flowers. I like to have a patch of it on the margin of the horse pond. Having the largest (purplish) leaves is the well-named *C. musifolia* (1.8m/6ft) and we grow that entirely for its banana-like foliage, as it has never flowered yet. Even in a Côte d'Azur garden, it remained flowerless. *C. glauca* and cannas derived from it can be grown under water and look well like that. The species has narrow glaucous leaves and small, lemon-yellow flowers.

I like to grow red lobelias in the exotic garden. They peak this month. *Lobelia* 'Queen Victoria' (90cm/3ft) has purple stems and leaves and big spikes of pure, volcanic red flowers. It is a non-branching plant that needs support halfway up its stems. Again, a fine companion for the white-variegated grass *Arundo donax* var. *versicolor*. But seed strains arising from recent developments in the $F_1$ Fan series are a great asset, since the plants branch generously, which greatly extends their flowering season. 'Fan Scarlet' is more effective at a distance than 'Fan Deep Red'. These lobelias make basal rosettes of foliage wherewith to overwinter but should be given protection. Bedding them into a frame is generally sufficient and they can be split to keep them healthy, in the spring.

A general stir is caused by the various angel's trumpets of the genera *Datura* and the larger, woodier *Brugmansia* (which used to be lumped into *Datura*). *D. meteloides* (75cm/2½ft) makes a bushy plant and is generally treated as an annual – by us, anyway. Its white funnel flowers face upwards. They open at dusk and are worth watching as they do it, in a rapid series of jerks. They are heavily fragrant on the first evening.

We cut back and house the brugmansias, in winter, and grow them to 1.5–1.8m/ 5–6ft, so that we can readily admire their large, pendent bells. The white *B. suaveolens* is best known and we also have the rather nice buff-coloured 'Grand Marnier'. Both are heavily fragrant. But in both, the large, coarse leaves are totally undistinguished. I can easily forget and forgive that fault.

The ginger relatives of the genus *Hedychium* find a home here, having good foliage as well as interesting flowers. *H. densiflorum* 'Assam Orange' (75cm/2½ft) has dense spikes of small orange flowers. Its leaves, always borne in two ranks, are less distinguished than most. In *H. forrestii* (90cm/3ft), for instance, they are broad, smooth and bright green. Quite tiny white flowers are nice to have, though not showy. In *H. greenei* (90cm/3ft) the main feature is the shining bronze undersides to the leaves.

The flowers are red, but cannot be relied upon to put in an appearance. This is one of the less hardy species.

We have some favourites at ground level. Tuberous-rooted begonias, for instance, especially the small-flowered scarlet 'Flamboyant'. Also, the yellow-flowered *Oxalis vulcanicola*, a ground-coverer which could become a ferocious weed, were it not frost-tender; as it is, we can sleep easily at nights, when it, too, goes to sleep, its flowers closing. Then, the delightful little prostrate *Impatiens pseudoviola*, which has a long succession of white, violet-like flowers.

There are many more good plants in this garden and it is always in a state of flux, as we are always experimenting. So you will never get bored with it and to us it acts like a magnet, even though there may be no valid excuse for making the detour necessary for a visit. Well, I always emerge with at least a handful of dahlia dead-heads.

## Annuals

One of the best ways to make good the increasing shortfall, in August, of perennials in flower, is to grow plenty of annuals from seed and to make sure that they will be coming on when they are most needed, which will be from mid-month until October. Some, like annual asters, will do this naturally anyway. Others can be manipulated through date of sowing. As many such, like zinnias, are anyway easiest to manage, in our climate, from a late sowing, nature is ready to lend a helping hand. I have already brought in a number of these annuals, but will go on from there. It must be understood that I am writing of plants treated as annuals although, technically, they may be perennials.

Petunias come into that category and some of them, like the small-flowered cascading *Petunia integrifolia*, we keep going from cuttings. However, infection from virus diseases is an increasing danger with a susceptible genus like this, when kept going vegetatively. From seed, it starts with a clean bill of health. The brilliant, almost magenta seed strain 'Purple Wave' is invaluable to me for its prostrate habit. When the colchicums growing in our borders have had their old foliage removed, about the end of June, the bare space left behind allows me to interplant their corms with 'Purple Wave'. The plants soon interlock to form a mat and when the colchicums flower, in early autumn, they rise just above the petunias and make a handsome couple, as we sometimes say of bride and bridegroom.

I (and Fergus too) am passionate about large-flowered zinnias – those with flat (not rolled-back) rays, called dahlia-flowered, double and in an amazing range of colours which you'd think would quarrel violently, but in fact they are immensely stimulating. I think the reason they bring off their daring cacophony is that the flowers are well spaced, not in an indigestible mass, and that in each case the colour is nearly always

*Canna indica* 'Purpurea' by the horse pond

clean and clear, of its kind, whether yellow, red, pink, carmine, white (this one slightly grubby, perhaps) or whatever. A hot summer helps them enormously. You cannot bank on that but if you never take a risk you'll never benefit from that summer when it does come. The chief danger to zinnias is that chilly, wet weather will start up botrytis rot in a part of the plant and it can spread quickly. But if you choose a sunny site, there'll be a good chance of success.

These zinnias grow to 90cm/3ft but I like some of the smaller, bushy types too, notably *Zinnia* 'Chippendale', which is bronze with yellow tips to the rays. We scatter them among mixed plantings, for instance of the *Crocosmia* 'Solfaterre', which has apricot-orange flowers and bronze leaves.

*Tithonia rotundifolia* 'Torch' is obviously first cousin to a zinnia, but grows to 1.5m/5ft at least. The large, hairy heart-leaves are crowned by single zinnia flowers in an amazingly pure, rich shade of orange. In the same mood category are marigolds, *Tagetes*, but the habit of many of these has been spoilt in the dwarfening process, which often results in large flowers on a short plant. What we need is large flowers on large, widely branching plants, but fewer of them will be needed. Small flowers on large plants can be good too and sometimes, as in 'Disco Orange', smallish (but dazzling orange) single flowers on a low plant. I like to grow this with a curly-leaved parsley, 'Bravour', which is as bright a green as you'll find.

One thought leads to another. Bright, untarnished green is precious in late summer, and you find it again in the annual *Kochia* 'Evergreen', which makes a cone-shaped plant of rather formal outline and 90cm/3ft tall if grown well (which we are none too clever at managing, I have to say). We like to make an informal group of these in our mixed borders. Bright green is not necessarily a restful colour but it makes for variety.

I like annuals that make big plants, even if they do require a stake and a tie. Thus, *Cosmos bipinnatus* 'Purity' (already mentioned) at 1.5m/5ft has a lot more to offer in size of bloom and style of plant than the 60cm/2ft white 'Sonata'. A coloured strain that we hold in high regard is 'Dazzler' (1.2m/4ft), which opens intense carmine but fades gracefully to burgundy red (rather old Burgundy that has gone a little over the top). We use that in all sorts of ways. With the purple foliage of *Ricinus communis* 'Carmencita', for instance.

If an annual can look like a shrub, it is doing well, because that means it has structure, which many annuals lack. Notable, then, is the spider flower, *Cleome pungens* (1.5m/5ft). If grown without a check, it makes a widely branching plant, with compound palmate leaves and whorls of interestingly shaped flowers at the tip of every branch. It flowers for two or three months. The colouring can be pink, white or bright mauve or a mixture, which is also compatible. I like this with *Ageratum* 'Blue Horizon' (60cm/2ft) in front. Most ageratums have been dwarfened into stupid little lumps that deserve to be kicked out of the way, but this one, a good shade of blue mauve (bluer than photographs represent it), has a sufficiently loose habit and a tremendously long flowering season without need of dead-heading.

Tall annual rudbeckias are good, mostly derived from *Rudbeckia hirta*, which you see wild as a cornfield weed on the east coast of the USA. I don't like those in which bronze is mixed in with the yellow, as they fuss the bloom up; it is quite sufficiently exciting and a lot smarter with a prominent black disc in the centre of powerfully yellow rays. 'Indian Summer' (90cm/3ft) meets this recipe precisely and we recently went to town with that in our main bedding out, with the lavender bedding verbena (raised from cuttings) 'La France' in front and a permanent planting behind wherein white Japanese anemones and the white-variegated foliage of dogwood, *Cornus alba* 'Elegantissima', predominate.

Of the annual sunflowers that we try out, the most satisfactory has been a strain called *Helianthus* 'Valentine' (only 1.5m/5ft), with pale yellow rays offset by a large, near-black disc. One of the good points about this sunflower is its widely branching habit, which makes for a balanced-looking plant having a longer flowering season than strains with a tendency to go straight up.

A large proportion of the penstemons grown for bedding or in mixed borders, these days, are named cultivars propagated from cuttings. But there is still a lot going for a large-flowered seed strain such as used, appropriately, to be called gloxinia-flowered. We sow these this month for next year, overwinter the seedlings, which are potted individually, under cold (not too unprotected) glass and plant them in their flowering sites in spring. All the colours in a mixture are compatible – red, pink, blush, mauve and purple – and they have a long season, unless hit by a soil-borne fungus.

Another annual that is best sown in August and treated in the same way, to flower from July on, is the sweet scabious, or pin-cushion flower, *Scabiosa atropurpurea* (90cm/3ft). It can have a rather leggy and straggling habit, but not so if well grown and anyway it is admirable for cutting. Flower colouring is usually lavender, pink or white, sometimes rather wishy-washy in a badly selected strain, but the most exciting are the deep maroon-flowered plants with white anthers. These can now be had in a selection called 'Ace of Spades'; I like to mix them into my borders. Sometimes the plants will do a second year.

We keep on with late sowings of annual poppies but among our favourites is the so-called tulip poppy, *Hunnemannia fumariifolia*, which is something between a poppy and an eschscholzia, with purest yellow poppy flowers set off by deeply cut, glaucous foliage. It grows so easily in California, surviving the winters there, but in our climate we have difficulties in establishing the plants, which dislike a change of locale more than most poppies. However, once they get going and if the summer co-operates they are fine and contrast particularly well with bright purple-flowered *Verbena rigida* (45cm/1½ft). Another good companion would be an apron of the prostrate, blue-flowered pimpernel, *Anagallis linifolia*, or whatever the seedsmen are calling it this year. A really intense blue and often mistaken for a gentian. I always grow some of that.

Another of my favourites is *Salvia coccinea* 'Lady in Red' (60cm/2ft), which has a nice habit but plenty of flower power. If the first crop is dead-headed, it usually succeeds in presenting a second. It contrasts well with another annual sage, the blue *S. farinacea* 'Victoria', which is naturally rather late-flowering.

Sorry if annuals went on for rather a long time, but it is a favourite subject.

## Climbers and highlights

A number of clematis will be performing but I really never know from year to year which of them will come out on top and which will suddenly let me down. *Clematis* 'Huldine' is a charmer, with slightly cupped, pearly white flowers only 10cm/4in or 12cm/5in across, and pale mauve on the underside. It is vigorous but also wayward, refusing to flower liberally in some positions. You may need to move it around to find out what suits it.

'Ville de Lyon' usually has a second go on its young wood – such a nice shape and I like the darker red of its sepal rims. It is apt to go bare in its lower regions. This is largely a question of feeding and watering. In any case, if sited among other shrubs or plants, you won't notice what's going on down there. For companionship it has something of a thug, in the herbaceous climber *Thladiantha dubia*, already described. We dig out a quantity of the fleshy tubers by which it perennates.

Sharing the wall behind is the evergreen self-clinging *Pileostegia viburnoides*. It is vigorous and has handsome leaves, but August is its flowering month when (not every year) it becomes smothered in a haze of tiny creamy-white flowers. It is hardy and will thrive on any aspect but must be given a good start. The foot of a wall is often desperately dry. If this is so, plant it forward a bit, then feed and water it well until it has got away. Otherwise you can wait for years and it'll be entirely your fault.

Of the annual climbers that we enjoy growing, *Thunbergia alata* has a rotate flower opening from a tube. Brightest, most contrasty and best is the orange-flowered kind, with a black centre. But there are more wishy-washy shades. Fergus is extremely successful with *Rhodochiton atrosanguineum*, which he sows the previous autumn and brings on under glass in individual pots. It flowers for ages and looks entirely original, with trails of purple flowers at every stage of their development and decay. They never look shabby. The lampshade-shaped calyx persists, but the black, tubular corolla (with white anthers poking out of it) is there for a few days only.

The *Hydrangea macrophylla* 'Ayesha' – that of the polished, incurved, porcelain-like florets – flowers throughout August and has some effective companionship not far away with a pale yellow poker, *Kniphofia* 'Torchbearer', teazels in flower and the foliage, now well developed, of *Melianthus major*, which hold me in good stead for the rest of the year, so I'll come back to it. Not far off, and the garden's best single plant in this, its season, is *Hydrangea aspera* Villosa Group, but you must get the best form. Its lanceolate leaves are furry; the lacecap inflorescences have rich lilac sterile florets around the rim while the central fertile ones are pure blue and rich in pollen, which honey bees collect, and they are so single-minded that the pollen sacs on their legs are also blue, unadulterated by the pollen of any other flower.

Right next to this and flowering at the same time is a tall column of *Eucryphia* x *nymansensis* 'Nymansay'. It never fails to be covered by white blossom, the numerous stamens having red tips. This is scented and rich in nectar, which the bees, especially the wild bees, forage for from dawn on. It sounds like a factory.

To return to hydrangeas, the hardy *Hydrangea paniculata* cultivars, always white, flower this month on their young wood, with cone-shaped inflorescences. I best like those wherein sterile florets are sprinkled through a haze of fertile ones. A favourite, given me by Cherry Ingram and collected by him from the slopes of a Japanese volcano (needle-tailed swifts nested within the rim of its crater, he told me), has been named 'Kyushu'. I have it in the high garden with the pinky-mauve, 1.2m/4ft, Japanese-type *Anemone tomentosa*.

Our myrtle, *Myrtus communis*, planted soon after the garden was made, is right by the terrace door, so that its spicy fragrance is even better placed to waft through the house than the jasmine's. In good years, it covers itself with handsome black fruit. That ripens in November. The other myrtle I grow is *M. luma*, correctly *Luma apiculata*, from Chile. In Ireland and the west country, it makes a tree but it is none too hardy and a hard winter will clobber mine, though it

always recovers and is currently 3.6m/12ft tall. This flowers in flushes – white but no scent. And it self-sows freely.

Perhaps a contender for the award of best August-flowering shrub is *Itea ilicifolia*. It is evergreen with rather thin leaves of a crisp, papery texture, margined in mock prickles. The tiny flowers are borne in pendent, catkin-like racemes up to a foot long, and they

*Kniphofia* 'Torchbearer' growing in front of *Hydrangea macrophylla* 'Ayesha'

are green, heavily night (and early morning) scented of lemons.

The ornamental bramble *Rubus cockburnianus* 'Golden Vale' is luminous with its lime-green foliage and now has poking out from its skirts the chains of blue trumpets from an old clump of willow gentian, *Gentiana asclepiadea*. Once you have the gentian in a place that it enjoys, it self-sows and I have quite a bit of it.

## The meadows

At last we make a start on cutting and composting the meadows. Not all at once, by any means. Some wait till next month, and by the horse pond there is a very worthwhile late display of lesser knapweed, *Centaurea nigra*. In the prairie, which we planted with prairie plants from Minnesota, whose seed I collected and raised some years ago, there is flower from *Silphium perfoliatum*, a tall yellow daisy, and from *Veronicastrum virginicum album*, with clumps of white spikes. Another taker has been *Eryngium yuccifolium*, with greyish foliage and flower heads; it does better here than in the borders. But our successes have been limited. For many of the prairie perennials our turf appears to be too dense.

The first grass-cutting takes place (once I have confirmed that the seeds of *Camassia quamash* have been shed) either side of the front path. We try to do this on a Monday, when we are closed to the public, so that the mess is all cleared up by Tuesday afternoon. A Tracmaster powerscythe makes the first and most difficult long cut. It is far safer than the old Allenscythe, because it stops the moment you let go of the machine. We follow up with closer-cutting tools until we are very low indeed and it looks as though a scorched earth policy is being pursued. In fact, visitors often ask whether we have been over it with weedkiller! But the base of old grass stalks is naturally hay-coloured. Within a week, green

*Itea ilicifolia* by the circular steps

will be appearing and in the second half of the month there will be colchicums in bloom.

Although I love the long grass, there is also something very satisfying in seeing everything clean again. In the orchard, which is our next big area to be tackled, the revealed contours are large ridges and hollows, which is the way land was ploughed in medieval times. The orchard that we inherited came much later.

Now at last we and everyone else can walk or sit or recline wherever we like, without my having to shout at amateur photographers who are treading the long grass flat for the sake of their best shot. It is much harder to cut when flattened, besides looking awful. In fact, we no longer allow photographic groups to come at a discount, since some of their members are so inconsiderate. Many gardens do not allow the use of tripods and I can understand that.

## Produce

Although we always tend to be late with our sowings, there'll be plenty of vegetables coming in by now and I hope that artichokes will keep going. It's always a great challenge with lettuce, to produce them in such a succession that I'm never without my own from June to late October. Perry gets better at this all the time. It's easy enough to remember the first sowings, but less so later, and conditions for the seeds may anyway be difficult in a droughty summer. Vegetables have to come second to flowers, when irrigation facilities are under pressure.

We are into the autumn-fruiting raspberries by the end of the month and, with luck, the birds will no longer be interested. I think 'Autumn Bliss' has as good a flavour as any variety I know. The yellow 'Fallgold' is very sweet (honey bees will besiege it in a droughty spell) but not strong on flavour.

Our one wall-grown morello cherry is a regular cropper and we net it, pitting our wits against the blackbirds. Surely a human should be able to outwit a bird. But our blackbirds are highly intelligent. They'll eat most all of the apricots, if the fruit is left to ripen on the tree, and look most indignant if disturbed in their feasting. I say 'they', but it's usually just the one bird. Peaches are variable in their fortunes. We have never succeeded in netting them and the fruit lies so tight against the stem that it is hardly feasible to fit bags, even if we had the time. Figs, if there is a crop, require a lot of ladder work. It needs to be a heavy crop to make this worthwhile. But a ripe, better still, an overripe fig is food for the gods. Fourth week of August is when the figs can be expected to start ripening.

The only tomatoes we grow are outside, and the first of them should be coming in now. My current favourite for flavour is 'Sungold', but I only wish there were as sweet and tasty varieties among the larger-fruited kinds which are so much more useful to me for culinary purposes.

It is a full and busy month but never less than enjoyable. A hint of autumn creeps in from time to time – one can be sure of that, but it is no cause for lament. I love autumn.

# September

To an extent, we can cruise along in September. The number of visitors drops suddenly by nearly half. This is a pity in a way. The early autumn garden, here, is full of energy and ideas, reflecting our love of the season. The light is no longer so hard in the middle of the day, so the plants look happier. Again, because there are so many fewer visitors, the garden can be enjoyed all the more by those who do come. I, too, can enjoy it more, for the same reasons. There is a general feeling of detente.

Or there would be, if we weren't busy working up to something. To a TV presentation, maybe, and of recent years we have held a week-long seminar for a dozen Americans, mid-month. They are really keen and serious but a lot of fun, too. Our greatest concern is that they should leave, at the end of it, with the feeling that it was all well worth while – both the time and the money as well as the experience. We go in some detail into each of the garden's main aspects: the borders, the bedding, the nursery area and how we propagate, the meadows, aspects of upkeep, of maintaining continuity and much else.

The main burden falls on Fergus but we all take an active part. We have made some wonderful and lasting friendships in this way. When Fergus himself goes lecturing in America, his acclaim is such that he is in danger of being treble-booked.

## Smartening up

The danger in a September garden – you see it everywhere – is sleaze. That is what we least want and we keep going through the borders tidying up. They will not look too tidy, as most plants have grown into each other and that looks as relaxed as it is. But ugly remains need constant removal. It makes all the difference.

The shaggy yew hedges are being assiduously trimmed throughout the month. We start with the eighteen peacocks, so that they shall look smart at the time when the double hedges of *Aster lateriflorus* 'Horizontalis' are building up their flower power. Then we move to the long border and the stretch of hedge running at right angles from that down the side of the orchard. Next, across the orchard to the exotic garden, but here we trim only their outside and top; the inside is left till we have cleared the beds in front of them. On, across to the topiary garden and here we first of all cut the long grass, so formality is at last restored to this area which I have of recent years allowed to take its ease during the summer months.

Grass cutting also continues non-stop – I mean the cutting of long grass. Fergus thoroughly enjoys this, as it entails team work – someone on the machine or machines, others loading the grass on the tractor trailer and then building up the compost heap. We like to get the grass on to this in as damp a condition as possible, otherwise you end up with an unyielding haystack, instead of nicely rotted compost. To this end we include, as the stack is being built, alternate layers of lime and sulphate of ammonia,

PAGES 174–175 A foggy autumn morning in the exotic garden

and we sprinkle the stack, from overhead, with such water as we can muster. It steams in a satisfactory manner and sinks – the faster the better.

While the Tracmaster (mentioned last month), with its front-mounted reciprocating blades, does the initial cutting job – and it does cut quite low – it is followed by the ride-on Countax, which is a rotary mower with sweep attached. I cannot abide mowings left loose on the surface: they shade the living turf beneath them; they have an undesirable manurial effect, whereas poor conditions are required for a rich floral tapestry; they get picked up on your shoes and clothes and brought indoors; they are thoroughly slovenly.

The whining strimmer goes into all those awkward-to-reach spots, like under the medlar and on the steep banks of the upper moat, or around tree trunks, but its trimmings have to be raked up by hand. I loathe the noise of that machine, but it has to be tolerated, intermittently, on five days of each week. Although we renew it pretty frequently, it breaks down even more frequently and my feelings are torn between relief at the comparative peace and agitation that the job is not getting done. Bob Common (whose wife Brenda is our unflappable sales lady in the nursery), is remarkably helpful and quick about repairing breakdowns in our machinery, but I don't believe in being stingy about replacements, if troubles recur. They come cheapest in the long run. We get a new hedge trimmer for the yews, every year, and the old one does duty, for a second year, on rough, tough hedges.

## Bulbs

There is a fairly urgent time factor on cutting some of the meadow areas, before their little season of flowers from colchicums and autumn crocuses gets going. The upper moat's problem is that it was the bottom of a pond for all those years, so turf growth, now that it is drained, is coarser and more vigorous than elsewhere. We usually give it a second cut before the first cuts elsewhere have been completed. This ensures a nice low background for *Crocus nudiflorus* when that gets going. Exactly when it gets going depends very much on how dry the ground is. A heavy shower, and away it goes, but drought will hold it back for several weeks. Mid-month would be average in a moist year. I was interested to see, at Belsay Hall in Northumberland, where this crocus is colonized as at Dixter, that it flowers several weeks earlier, simply because conditions are so much moister. The fact that they are a lot further north, and therefore cooler, makes no difference.

This crocus is a rich purple with yellow stamens, and it stands upright on a strongish stem. It spreads by a stoloniferous habit, so that a single corm will make quite a patch, in time, although I get no self-seeding. The other autumn-flowering crocus that naturalizes well in turf is *C. speciosus*. We have a lot of that in various places (I really don't know how it got into some of them) and the flowering time of these colonies depends on their location, those under the bay tree being the latest, unless I have had the sprinkler on them. *C. speciosus* has a long, weak stalk and is apt to lie on its elbow,

after the first day. I don't find that objectionable. It gives the bluest impression of any crocus, by dint of its heavy veining. The stigmas (or stigmata) are brilliant scarlet and the flowers, if you get down to their level, are deliciously scented. Where you have a big colony of *C. speciosus*, it is noticeable that the spring-flowering crocuses cannot compete.

I have colchicums in the meadows; they stay alive but hardly increase. The pink in their colouring readily distinguishes them from any crocus. My best colonies are in the borders. One of the most prosperous-looking, with substantial, waxy white cups, is the late-September-flowering *Colchicum speciosum* 'Album', and my mat-forming background for that is *Helichrysum petiolare* 'Variegatum', which is less vigorous and therefore less competitive than straight *H. petiolare*. Another good place for a vigorous colchicum is interplanted with *Alchemilla mollis*. From having been cut back six weeks earlier, that is now covered with fresh foliage, which gives the colchicum just the background that suits it.

There are other autumn-flowering bulbs or corms that give you a feeling, if not actually of spring, at least of the year's renewable cycle. Just as some plants are preparing for rest, others are emerging from aestivation and starting to grow by flowering. The hardy *Cyclamen hederifolium* is like that. Its tubers increase in size from year to year, indefinitely. They rest in summer, then carry their galaxies of pinky-mauve or white flowers from late July into November – timing, again, depending largely on the moisture factor. This was another plant that my mother loved to raise from seed; or else she would collect up the seedlings from around old plants, where they were far too thick to do any good. The seeds are tacky and, it is said, attractive to ants, which pick them up and spread them around. I think we must have the wrong ants, as we have to do the spreading.

Some gardeners are clever at establishing cyclamen in turf and we are having a serious stab at that, now. They want turf that is not too dense and competitive, so beneath trees seems right. It is easy enough to mow over them in summer, but if a second cut is on the menu, they must be avoided, as they will already be growing.

*Nerine bowdenii* is a splendid autumn performer. I wish I could say the same of related *Amaryllis belladonna*, which needs a thorough summer baking if it is to flower well, but I haven't given up on that one. It's a question of finding the right place. At the foot of a south-facing, brick-footed greenhouse wall is traditional, but although a cultural success, the colour clash of pink and terracotta is appalling. *N. bowdenii* is as vivid a pink (with a dash of mauve) as you could imagine and an entirely un-autumnal colour, but no less welcome for that. It is a tremendously willing and prolific flowerer, even in shade. Its leaves, in a hot climate, would die away in summer. In ours, they often survive into the flowering period and look rather awful, so I believe in removing them in late August, before flowering stems have shown themselves.

If you plan an association for the nerine, one of the best is with the 60cm/2ft vivid light purple *Aster amellus* 'Veilchenkönigin' – 'Violet Queen' to us. It is of the same height as the nerine and has an upright, self-supporting habit, unlike many of the amellus cultivars. But the nerine is always in danger of starting too late for the aster, so it is worth making a regular practice of giving it a good old drenching, in the second

LEFT ABOVE *Colchicum speciosum* 'Album' among *Helichrysum petiolare* 'Variegatum'
LEFT BELOW *Crocus speciosus*
BELOW Nerines and limonium in the high garden

Good foliage in a shady corner: *Clerodendrum bungei*, x *Fatshedera lizei* and *Hedera colchica* 'Dentata Variegata'

half of August, so as to get growth started. Its new foliage, incidentally, does not come through till January. The bulbs cluster at or above the soil surface, which looks terribly vulnerable, but that's where they want to be and it is no use trying to thwart them.

## Group meetings

It is always fun to think of ways in which to group your plants rather than to treat them as solo items, although that often happens too.

There is a rather feebly growing (though far stronger in California) Virginia creeper, with such variegated leaves that there is little for it to fall back on in the way of green. This is *Ampelopsis glandulosa* var. *brevipedunculata* 'Elegans'. The variegation is pink and white and its stems and tendrils are pink. We find that the best way to grow it is on the flat and we feed it heavily. That goes well with the very similar pink of a bedding verbena called 'Silver Anne', whose rambling habit encourages it to investigate its neighbours. A trio is made up with the shrubby *Ceratostigma willmottianum*, which is a relatively hardy plumbago with deep blue flowers; real blue, not mauvey. If this can bring its old growth through the previous winter intact, it will start flowering in July, but if it has to start again from ground level, it will only now be getting into its stride and its flowering period will be curtailed at the other end by cold nights. Even without a frost, the flowers then become wan. By and large, I get value from my plant, even though it does not have the wall protection that would enable it to grow much larger and more strongly.

In a house-shaded but protected corner of the wall garden, where the sun scarcely penetrates, the suckering shrub *Clerodendrum bungei* is blooming freely throughout the month, with upright, terminal domes of scented pink blossom above darkest green heart-leaves. I love this plant, although it does sucker incontinently; we do our best to contain the situation by digging out and potting up the suckers. This has more good foliage around it, notably of x *Fatshedera lizei*, a hybrid between *Fatsia* and *Hedera*, with large, glossy, bright green leaves. It is a shrub but, its habit being lax, we give it a pretty severe pruning each spring. In another situation, you might prefer to let it trail.

Further along the border and still pretty shaded, I have a colony of the hardy *Begonia grandis* subsp. *evansiana* (38cm/15in), which flowers in autumn but only if the weather suits it (I cannot make out exactly which weather that is). Certainly it likes shade and we feed it well. That has a pink Japanese anemone behind it and the second flowering of white *Hydrangea macrophylla* 'Madame Emile Mouillère' further back still.

In the barn garden, facing north-west and at the back of quite a deep border, I'm really pleased with a combination that starts off with the 1.8m/6ft *Aconitum carmichaelii* 'Kelmscott', which has deep blue monkshoods; and that is next to the white racemes of *Cimicifuga racemosa* (1.8m/6ft), in a purple-leaved form, though the colouring of the leaves counts for little by the end of the season. Beyond these, a favourite annual, whose seeds have only recently come back on the market, the 2m/7ft *Polygonum orientale*, with great sprays of short, deep pink racemes. It is absolutely at its best in September. In sowing its seed in spring, you must be sure not to give them heat, or they won't germinate. Once germination, at a fairly low (but not freezing) temperature, has taken place, you can bring the seedlings on under warmer conditions. Near to this trio, last summer (but who knows if I shall ever repeat it?), I had the rich yellow, black-eyed daisies of *Rudbeckia* 'Indian Summer' (1.2m/4ft), which flowers for more than two months from mid-August. A splendid annual. I also like to use the polygonum at the top of the long border, behind my strongest group of single white Japanese anemones, right next to Lutyens's oak seat. That, as a full-stop, has the rosettes of spiky, grey-green leaves of *Astelia chathamica*, at its orchard end. The astelia shows up from the other end of the border and I only hope that a cold winter won't kill it.

On a more intimate scale and with a good deal of shade, *Arum italicum* 'Pictum', which is currently without foliage, has a crop of scarlet berries, gathered into club-like knobs. That goes well with bright green polypody ferns and with the dwarf hardy *Fuchsia* 'Tom Thumb'. Also small-scale but this time in the sun, the magenta *Geranium riversleaianum* 'Russell Prichard', which has been flowering since May, is still threaded through grey

*Artemisia ludoviciana* 'Silver Queen', but is joined (if I have grown it well) by the stiff, purple-headed *Verbena rigida*. This verbena is not much more than a foot tall, whereas our old friend *V. bonariensis* is 1.8m/6ft and that now has for company *Patrinia scabiosifolia* (1.5m/5ft), whose inflorescence of heads of tiny flowers is very like the verbena's but clear yellow with a touch of green. It is easily raised from seed (if you can get it), but is not too long-lived a perennial and doesn't self-sow, as is the verbena's over-obliging habit.

In the stock bed where there is a seat to one side for contemplative viewing, the plantings are mainly for late summer and autumn. I have a good patch of the recently-become-popular *Plectranthus argentatus* (60cm/2ft) for its large, rounded, silver-grey foliage. Behind it and increasingly abundant throughout the month is the mildew-resistant michaelmas daisy *Aster* 'Little Carlow', lavender verging on blue. We keep it down to 90cm/3ft by frequent replanting. Next to it, the abundantly flowering black-eyed-susan, *Rudbeckia fulgida* var. *deamii*, which is the most cheerful yellow imaginable. There's the white, papery-textured *Anaphalis margaritacea* var. *yedoensis* (90cm/3ft) which is more stylish than others in this genus because of its height. In the background, there is the solidity of shrubs, notably the hard-pruned golden catalpa, *Catalpa bignonioides* 'Aurea'.

As the month progresses, the pampas grasses rouse themselves from their slumbers and I have the 1.8m/6ft 'dwarf' *Cortaderia selloana* 'Pumila', with silken, upright white plumes, highlighting the scarlet hips of sweet briar, *Rosa rubiginosa*. This was accidental in the first place but then became intentional. At what stage am I able to claim some credit? Visitors have an inclination to assume that every good combination arrived by accident and that I am just lucky. Two other roses contribute with their hips, now, in a mixed border setting. In *R. setipoda* they are long and hairy, borne more or less singly. But in *R. glauca* they are in clusters; not a sharp red – quite subdued, really, but they show up well enough. This famous rose has purplish glaucous leaves and goes well with pink Japanese anemones – 'Hadspen Abundance' in this case – and the orangey fruit looks just as good with the anemone. I believe in constantly renewing shrub roses by selective pruning and my policy in these cases is to remove all the flowered and fruited wood, in winter. What's left is the young, unbranched shoots made in the previous season. They will give me the next crop of flowers and fruit, while the next summer's young shoots will have the best foliage colouring, in the case of *R. glauca*, and the most continuously manufactured aroma, in the case of the sweet briar.

So many ornamental grasses are good in autumn, most of them for their flowers, but others more for their foliage. There are many of these through the barn and sunk gardens, fairly well though not indiscriminately scattered around, and they provide a not too dominant theme through the tail end of the year. You get a clear view of them across this garden as well as close to.

## Solo performers

Some plants display themselves most fully if they don't have competition from close neighbours, while others lack companions because I have not yet worked out what these could appropriately be.

My most glamorous *Hedychium, H. coccineum* 'Tara', which Tony Schilling collected in Nepal and named after his daughter, has a corner to itself and has to be a feast in itself, which is not difficult. The foliage is handsome, as in the whole genus, but the terminal racemes of orange flowers are arrestingly showy. This doesn't like competition but

LEFT  *Rudbeckia* 'Indian Summer', *Aconitum carmichaelii* 'Kelmscott', *Cimicifuga racemosa*
'Purpurea' and *Persicaria orientale*

BELOW  *Fuchsia* 'Tom Thumb' with the berries of *Arum italicum* subsp. *italicum* 'Marmoratum'

does respond to the good things in life. We have got the message at last and are pleased with the results. Each flowering spike is fairly short-lived, so perhaps this is a comet rather than a star. I'm not complaining about that. It is definitely hardy, under my conditions.

*Allium senescens* subsp. *montanum*, which was also flowering through most of August, makes a low mat of grey-green foliage with a twist on it, so that the leaves are arranged in swirls. Then a mass of flowering globes, rather like thrift (*Armeria*), and a nice shade of mauve. These are extremely popular with bees and butterflies. What do you put with a plant like that? Really, it would look best near to the margin of a gravel garden planting, perhaps with the little autumn-flowering snowflake, *Leucojum autumnale*, poking through and an inch or two above it.

Another performer attractive to insects because of its mass of sickly-sweet-smelling globes of green flowers, is the bush ivy, *Hedera helix* f. *poetarum* 'Poetica Arborea'. There is a colossal buzzing each time I brush past it, for this overhangs a path. Its foliage is dark and lustrous and it is an excellent solo performer, although I have put it with a suitable neighbour right behind it – the golden catalpa, whose height I keep down to 2m/7ft by winter pruning.

The South American *Eryngium pandanifolium* is a noble evergreen perennial. It has long, narrow, saw-edged leaves, a bit on the glaucous side. The splendidly branching flower candelabrums rise to 2m/7ft or more in autumn and each branchlet terminates in a little globe of discreetly dove-coloured florets. It scarcely appears to be flowering at all, if you look inattentively, but very actively so, if you do. Well, I grew that halfway into

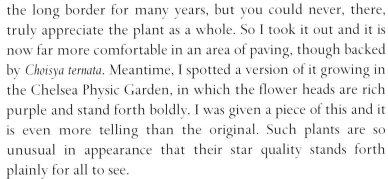

the long border for many years, but you could never, there, truly appreciate the plant as a whole. So I took it out and it is now far more comfortable in an area of paving, though backed by *Choisya ternata*. Meantime, I spotted a version of it growing in the Chelsea Physic Garden, in which the flower heads are rich purple and stand forth boldly. I was given a piece of this and it is even more telling than the original. Such plants are so unusual in appearance that their star quality stands forth plainly for all to see.

In its way, the hawthorn *Crataegus laciniata* (from the east Mediterranean) is another such. If it were only more readily available, I should recommend it as the ideal small tree for the small garden. In shape, it develops quite a presence. The deeply cut leaves are grey, throughout the season. Clusters of white flowers open in June and are followed, in the second half of September, by a glamorous crop of large haws, luminously coloured soft orange (not red). This grows by the front path and is possibly the most noticed plant in my garden.

A more mundane but still handsome hawthorn, by the front path and also in the orchard, is *C. prunifolia*, as generally known; correctly *C. persimilis* 'Prunifolia'. Like all the American thorns, its leaves are oval and undivided. Its white flowers come a few days later than our British thorns' and the heavy crops of fruit, ripening late September and sometimes carried well after leaf fall, are very dark red – so dark that they need

*Plectranthus argentatus, Anaphalis margaritacea* var. *yedoensis,*
*Aster* 'Little Carlow', *Rudbeckia fulgida* var. *deamii* and
*Miscanthus sinensis* 'Strictus' in a late-flowering stock bed

sunshine to warm them up. If this hawthorn is cropping only lightly, its foliage will take on splendid fall tints, but if great effort has been expended in fruit production, the leaves drop without colouring much. It frequently self-sows in my garden, with the help of birds.

Another conventional touch of autumn is provided by a spindle given me by Beth Chatto, from one growing on her boundary. It looks like a form of our native *Euonymus europaeus*, but it is an abundant and, so far as I can tell, regular fruiter. Spindles can be disappointing in this respect. The small plant she gave sulked for the first three years and I wondered if it was going to be a miff. But it then suddenly took off and increased its bulk by a third in one season. The fruit is borne on older wood, not on the young shoots. It is bright pink until the aril, enclosing the seeds, splits, and they are orange. It is one of nature's daring combinations but, of course, it comes off. They always do. One of the many flowering grasses next to this is in pleasing contrast.

## The exotic garden

This is a major feature all through September, though there is little more to be said about it that I didn't say last month. Everything, of course, gets larger and there is more dead-heading to keep up with. The dahlias are sure to be good. The cannas' foliage can be depended upon but their flowers may rot prematurely if the weather is unkind. The streptocarpus improve and the begonias approve of not being beaten upon by too hot a sun. *Cotyledon orbiculata* becomes outrageously lush and there are some enormous rosettes on *Aeonium arboreum*, which looks as though it is receiving signals from outer space. Surprisingly (to me) it sometimes wilts in the sun.

## Produce

There are enough raspberries to supply me liberally, every day, and I can briefly give up my staple breakfast diet of stewed apple. The new season's Bramley's (bought) are anyway harsh and tough to peel, so I'm glad not to need to handle them.

If the old 'Williams' pear tree, inherited from previous owners, is fruiting this year, it will need to be picked in the first week of the month and will be ripe within ten days – a strong, sweet, musky flavour that I love. The skins are tough (and may be scabby); they need to be spat out, or peeled. The season is short.

Early in September, we make salad sowings that have a good chance of surviving the winter. Most important to me is rocket, *Eruca sativa*. Sown now, it will entirely bypass trouble from flea beetle. With luck, I shall be picking it from next month till April.

Many vegetables look their best, being lush with young growth, even if not yet edible. Florence fennel (of the bulbous 'roots') is delightfully feathery. If we thinned it adequately, there will be some really heavy bulbs to harvest. Dill may have run up to flower (it is always running up to flower), but that is beautiful in itself.

The first 'Romanesco' broccoli heads mature; I hate to waste any of that but happily the crop is spread out (unlike cauliflower, which has a tendency to come all at once). If frost holds off, we may be picking it up to the end of the year. Sprouts and purple-sprouting broccoli are full of foliage. We may have to control cabbage white caterpillars. There will also be a swarm of white fly rising like drifting snow, whenever you touch the plants, but they don't seem to matter. I don't want to be eating sprouts yet, so if any mature, I don't look. Time enough for them in winter and early spring.

If I've kept the French beans well picked, I shall be drawing on them and they seem appropriate to the season. I don't grow runners any more. The flavour doesn't greatly appeal to me and I'm sure to be given them if I'm asked out to a meal.

The once-turned compost heap is covered with cucumbers (better last month) and gourds, which are highly ornamental and that is all I want them to be. I enjoy their wayward habits. They are always questing where they have no business to be.

The poets have generally given short shrift to autumn, as do all sorts of folk today. They can only find depression in the shortening days, the falling temperatures and leaves. Not so Keats:

> Where are the songs of spring? Aye, where are they?
> Think not of them, thou hast thy music too

he wrote in his 'Ode to Autumn', about the second week of September 1819, when staying in Winchester. All that I miss, nowadays, from that poem, is the gathering swallows that twittered in the skies – their populations have seriously decreased. They and the house martins used to sun themselves in huge quantities on the long roof of our barn and on the great hall roof, where we could enjoy them while sitting on the terrace, beneath, after lunch. I also miss their mad, glad whirlings and acrobatics, when the mood took them, often over the horse pond.

However, there's little point in nostalgia when the present is also good in its way.

Broccoli 'Romanesco'

October

Very much a favourite month, this. Even writing a capital O at the start of its name is a pleasure. Of course, the weather can be foul; when can't it? It gave us the great 1987 storm. But October does give us spells of the most delectable weather, too, and the golden warmth of its light invests everything with its glow. Nights have a nip in them but by day the air is soft again and we just need to relax in appreciation.

For this reason, we do not busily tear the garden to pieces. There would be far too much to lose. We used to close to the public mid-month but have now extended our accessibility to the end of Summer Time, alias Daylight Saving, which does truly give us an extension to summer. We are selling something of the order of 1400 tickets to garden visitors, which is a worthwhile figure, although it deserves to be a lot higher, if the weather is co-operating sufficiently.

I remember returning on 15 October from lecturing in America, one year, and the scene was unbelievably exciting – so much was looking good. For a start, as I came down the terrace steps (in which there was still a foaming mass of the little pink and white Mexican daisy, *Erigeron karvinskianus*), the big, forty-five-year-old Mexican orange, *Choisya ternata*, was covered in dazzling white, scented blossom for the second time in the year. May is its normal season, but a second crop in October is not unusual and when the shrub brings it off, the blossom is larger and of better quality than in the spring.

The dahlias that we had struck from late spring cuttings and subsequently used to replace early summer displays were now fresh and full of young vigour. In the barn garden, they were making a contrast between ornamental grasses – *Miscanthus* and *Cortaderia* (pampas) in flower and *Calamagrostis* with bleached, upright stems.

A combination that has pleased us, as a replacement for lupins, is the two orange dahlias 'Chiltern Amber' and the quite dwarf 'Ellen Houston'. In front of and mingling with them (for it has a mingling habit) the vivid purple bedding verbena 'Homestead Purple'. No modest little wayside number, it is a swaggering flaunter and just what is needed then and there.

Hardy fuchsias are never so good as when it has become a little cool but not yet frosty. *Fuchsia magellanica* 'Versicolor', which tends to look tired and dusty in high summer, has taken on a new lease of life with fresh young rosy-purple-tinted shoots and dripping clusters of its slender, blood-red flowers. 'Mrs Popple' (90cm/3ft) is in a semi-sulk all summer – partly through capsid damage to its young shoots but I think there's more to it than that. Anyway, its heavy foliage is at last redeemed by a huge late crop of red and purple blossom. 'Genii' (60cm/2ft) is red and purple too, but with the

PAGES 188–189 The flowering of *Aster lateriflorus* 'Horizontalis' reaches its peak this month
RIGHT ABOVE Grasses and late autumn dahlias
RIGHT BELOW *Atriplex hortensis* 'Rubra' (red orach) with *Fuchsia magellanica* 'Versicolor' and *Stipa splendens*

added highlights of yellow-green foliage and red stalks and leaf veins. 'Enfant Prodigue' (90cm/3ft) goes through long barren periods, but that is suddenly a mass of red and purple blossom set among neat little leaves.

## Asters and chrysanthemums

There are lots of lovely asters of the michaelmas daisy type, though I do limit myself fairly strictly to those that remain healthy without our help and to those that do not present a dull and solid block of boring foliage all through the summer. The double hedges of *Aster lateriflorus* 'Horizontalis' that link the topiary peacocks have been building up since their first daisies appeared in early September. They reach their climax on 17 October (I promise) and need no excuse to be visited every few hours – they are in any case conveniently on my way to herbs, salads and green vegetables for last-minute picking. You almost feel that you are swimming between their bands of myriad flowers. Their leaves (scarcely visible by now) are purplish and the prominent daisy discs are purple, while the rays, which are slightly reflexed, are white, though tinted. The plant's habit is by no means solid, but stylishly spreading, with branch tips taking off and doing their own thing. Very firm of texture, however.

In front of them I grow, or try to grow and sometimes succeed in growing well, sometimes rather poorly, low bands of the prostrate, neat-leaved *Persicaria vacciniifolia*. It sometimes misses being drenched by Himalayan mists and loathes drought. But when successful, it is a perfect foil to the asters, having, at the same season, stiffly upright pokers of tiny pink flowers. I shall not say that you must copy my idea, because a good deal of hand-weeding is involved, at one time or another.

I had an amazing little aster from Beth Chatto, *A. ericoides* f. *prostratus* 'Snowflurry'. Its tight little branches hug the ground and now, for a couple of weeks, carry dense white, undulating drifts of tiny, pure white daisies. It is on the edge of the square in the centre of the high garden and I interrupt its flow with the upright spears of bronze evergreen *Libertia peregrinans*. Also supposedly an *A. ericoides* hybrid (though if you visit the east coast states of the USA, where so many of these asters originate, you will hear a completely different story, in which *A. ericoides* plays scarcely any part) is the 60cm/2ft cultivar called 'Esther'. (*Aster* 'Esther' sounds a bit silly, so we don't mind, if there's time in hand, putting *ericoides* between them.) Although not flowering till September–October, 'Esther' has exceptionally bright green foliage, small and neat, so it is not a complete passenger in the summer border. That said, we do often grow it on in a row and then move it into a gap in early autumn.

*A. pringlei* 'Monte Cassino' scarcely merits border space throughout the summer, though its foliage is fresh and neat. Raised from spring cuttings (old plants are rather apt to die out), it's grown on in pots, so it is easy to fill a gap with it at the last moment, in early October, if we're being extremely keen. It is naturally at its best in the last half of the month, pure white, only 75cm/2½ft tall on young plants and with leaves that remain fresh. This is popular in the cut flower market and its season of flowering can be manipulated, as with chrysanthemums.

Of the tall michaelmas, I like to have a few plants of old 'Climax', which makes a widely branching pyramid and carries single, lavender-mauve daisies. *A. turbinellus* (1.5m/5ft) is a winner, with fine, intricately branching growth, all purple-tinted, and spangled purple daisies. Lots of support needed.

It seems natural to progress from asters to chrysanthemums. The smell of chrysanthemum foliage and, to a lesser extent, flowers, is entirely individual, richly autumnal and with a satisfying sharpness. I do not grow any chrysanthemum seriously — they are a little demanding or, if not demanding, a little bit boring. But I love to have them around me. Sometimes, if we have grown a good batch in a row, we move them into the borders just as the first flowers are coming out and are showing us what their colour is. Most of what we have are grown from seed — the $F_1$ Fanfare strain — which are mixed. So, come the autumn, we can pick out those we should like to see again. The double, brownish kinds are often the earliest flowering, which is useful for border display. But the later ones, right into November if frosts hold off, are so good to pick, though you'll need to strip most of their foliage and give them a deep drink, if they are to last in water.

## More and still more later flowers

Sunflowers keep going and the yellow quality in the light suits their colouring to perfection. If you believe that the best is good enough for you, then *Helianthus* 'Monarch' will be hard to beat; it is a large, black-eyed daisy, superb against a blue sky, and this is easily arranged as its own height is around 2.4m/8ft. I am apt to pinch out some (only a small proportion) of the side-shoots, so that the terminal bloom is — I was going to say outsize, but that sounds vulgar. What I do is to leave all the side-shoots on some stems and remove them all from the selected few. In this way, you achieve the ideal of many blooms of varying size.

*Aster lateriflorus* 'Horizontalis' with *Persicaria vacciniifolia*

*H. salicifolius* flowers at last. This is of secondary importance to its foliar contributions, which I have mentioned more than once. But, finally, the terminal 90cm/3ft of a 2.7m/9ft stem branches out and carries quite small but charming black-eyed daisies. You may get them at 2.7m/9ft, and see them against the sky (always blue, of course), or the stem may have been blown sideways at some stage, which doesn't really matter, as the top rights itself to the vertical within hours, but the flowers will then be seen low down and quite a distance from where the plant was sited. In one unpremeditated case I enjoyed them among the rich carmine and red of *Cosmos* 'Dazzler'.

The late-flowering *Salvia uliginosa* (1.8m/6ft) is abundant, at last, with short spikes of light, but pure, blue flowers, each with a white fleck at its centre. That goes with any colour – pale yellow, pink, red – but is a wasted catalyst if segregated altogether. As it is a see-through plant, I often grow it near the border's margin. Its overwintering potential is a bit of a toss-up, so we always have some in reserve under glass.

*Schizostylis coccinea* (45cm/1½ft) is a real autumn flower, but it is hard to predict when its season will start. Early September is ideal, because it then runs on for a couple of months. But it may be a lot later. Sometimes it seems as though clumps that were newly divided in the spring are more precocious than old colonies; at others, not. The spikes of bowl-shaped flowers above iris-like leaves obviously relate it to gladioli and crocosmias. It is an invasive plant and may be difficult

Mixed coleus hybrids with *Eupatorium capillifolium* and *Hedera helix* 'Buttercup'

to get rid of when established in a neighbour. Quite a bit of breeding work has been done to get different colours into this flower, and I have some half-dozen named cultivars, but by far the most effective is *S. coccinea* 'Major', which is strong red and quite large-flowered. Schizostylis love moisture (they will even thrive in shallow water) so my heavy soil suits them.

An autumn-flowerer of which I never have enough is *Saxifraga fortunei* (30cm/1ft), from the Far East. They make a great thing of it in Japan, where it is seen as a pot plant, and there are pink-flowered cultivars as well as the normal white. A deciduous perennial, it has scalloped leaves that are a feature in themselves; then a cloud of white, lop-sided flowers, on which the two lowest petals are long and hang down like Dundreary whiskers. It is happy in cool shade, and I combine it with a prolific autumn-flowering crocus, *Crocus pulchellus* – a clear, light shade of bluey mauve.

The coarsely glamorous *Impatiens tinctoria* (1.2m/4ft) only starts flowering seriously in October, although it should get going in June. Capsid damage to its growing shoots is mainly responsible. The leaves are really ugly, but its flowers, in white and purple, are amazing, and it seems right that they should be heavily night-scented in a slightly excessive and immoral way. The first touch of frost and it is gone, but the tuberous roots can be treated like a dahlia's, and they sometimes survive outside.

I have always preached that kniphofias should, to earn their space, have quite a long flowering season with a succession of flowering spikes. I break this rule with *Kniphofia linearifolia* (1.5m/5ft), which is green all summer, but an unusually bright shade of green. Its flowering stems all rush up together in the first two weeks of October and they flower a good shade of orange, lasting no longer than two weeks. I tell myself that I have room for a few plants like this. *K. rooperi* is also late, though with a slightly more spread-out season. I like that in the barn garden with the 'dwarf' white pampas *Cortaderia selloana* 'Pumila', though that continues for a long time after the poker has been forgotten. The latter also look good in front of *Melianthus major*, while self-sown teazels, albeit dark brown by now, are another strongly designed companion.

When on form, the climbing *Solanum jasminoides* 'Album' against the barn is one of my garden's most striking features through most of the second half of the year. It is generous with its open panicles of pure white flowers and yellow stamens. Once up to the barn's gutter, at 4.5m/15ft, it will continue on to the tiled roof and I can let it do that for a season without any damage to the roofing. But I never know if it will overwinter. Even after quite a mild winter it may be killed to the ground and although it would return from suckers, it is then so late as to make no impression the next year. It is better to start again with a new plant, and we always have stock as we sell it. But that may hang back, too. Then, in another year, away it will go again and I happen to be writing about it at a good moment, when, having made promising growth last year, it looks full of energy in the early spring of this. I know that I have something good to look forward to. There are many interesting nightshades. One that I should love to do well, as you see it in California, is the shrubby *S. rantonnetii*, with sizeable, rotate violet-coloured flowers. They can be so abundant as to smother the entire plant and a shearing back in mid-season is called for. Here, where it is definitely not winter-hardy, we can bring it through easily enough under glass but its subsequent growth is so soft and leafy that such flowers as it has are largely concealed.

Some October flowers are in continuation or a repeat of an earlier performance. Many of the cranesbills, for instance, like *Geranium endressii* and *G. sanguineum*, will come again with fresh foliage and a new crop of flowers if shorn back after their first flush. They may still be flowering, at that time, but have an out at elbows look which can be entirely redressed by firm action.

The first flush of summer-flowering hebes should really be dead-headed – you can often remove the entire terminal shoot with several pairs of flowered spikes. It is rather a tedious job but goes quickly enough if there are two of you. If you are in luck, a willing guest will oblige and it is the sort of job that can hardly end in disaster. The cleaned-up shrub looks vastly improved at once but then forges ahead with new shoots. By October, they will (at least as far south as I garden) be ready to flower again. In fact the RHS Award of Merit won by *Hebe* 'Jewel' was when I showed it at the beginning of November, although its main flowering is in June–July. No hardier than many another showy hebe, if it does survive a few winters it will make a large shrub, 1.8m/6ft high and more across, the flowers being lavender mauve (more intense and less apt to bleach in autumn than in summer) and very sweetly scented on the air. The clear pink 'Watson's Pink' well deserves treatment, though its second flowering is sometimes on the light side. 'Midsummer Beauty', with long, lavender spikes, scented, is a classic for dead-heading and will flower into mid-winter, with a bit of luck. That grows enormous but 'Autumn Glory', which also responds well and has short, purple spikelets, is not much higher than 60cm/2ft and it needs some sort of pruning to prevent its falling apart.

There is one obliging annual that I really must bring in; it is such a stayer. This is generally known as *Cuphea miniata* 'Firefly' (38cm/15in). It makes a little bush and we plant it out where there are alliums – *Allium neapolitanum*, all of whose growth we remove in June before it can seed, and *A. cristophii*, whose dying skeletons we leave and plant around. There will also have been some restrained spring bedding, like a few Siberian wallflowers! (The restraint exercised is not in their colouring but in their numbers and density.) The cuphea has quite deep mauvy pink flowers on a neat bush and it continues without becoming tired or untidy until the frosts arrive.

Two more autumn-flowering bulbs must be mentioned. The flower of the west wind, *Zephyranthes candida* (15cm/6in), has rush-like evergreen leaves; its flowers are like white crocuses. It quickly clumps up and hardiness has never been a problem, here. Flowering may start in late July but builds up, especially if late summer and autumn are

The seedheads of *Allium cristophii* with *Cuphea miniata* 'Firefly'

warm. It responds to the weather. The Mediterranean *Sternbergia lutea* (12cm/5in) remains totally dormant from spring to September, then flowers while putting out fresh, dark green strap leaves. Again its flowers are superficially crocus-like and a brilliant chrome yellow. I have seen mouth-watering colonies on chalky soil in east Kent and my stock came from one of these. But although I grow it in full sun, which is necessary, I never get quite the display that I should like. Still, I enjoy what I do get. I suppose they prefer a lighter soil.

Many grasses are in perfect shape, now, and it always amazes me how many of them choose to flower in autumn. Although my garden is largish, it is divided into compartments and I think that most of these grasses show up best as solo features rather than in groups. They have quite sufficient structure and presence to deserve to stand well above the surrounding plants. This may often be achieved by siting them on a promontory or in a corner, but fairly near to a border's margin. Two of my most effective are 'Windspiel' and 'Transparent', both of which come under *Molinia caerulea* subsp. *arundinacea*. As the name of one of them indicates, they are see-through plants. 'Transparent' starts to look interesting as early as June. Only its basal tuft of foliage is a bit of a let-down; I should really have something lowish in front of it. But I warn that these important-looking grasses do dislike disturbance and will sulk for a full year after being split or moved (which must always be done in spring).

There is currently a mania for ornamental grasses. Don't be either caught up in it or put off by it. Grasses have their place but need to be kept in it.

I often think I grow a lot of different bamboos, but if a bamboo nut visits, I am soon disillusioned. I have scarcely started. But, much as I love them, they cannot just be chucked around. In a mixed border, you need to be careful about their habit, which may be either invasive or given to flopping over the neighbours. A floppy bamboo can look fine in a landscape setting, but there is a limit to my landscape settings. I keep looking for more of them.

I love the elegant *Himalayacalamus falconeri*, now at its best with slender wands that arch over and look wonderful, at the horizontal, when hung with translucent raindrops. But anywhere nearer than 2.4m/8ft to a path, and you'll be in for an involuntary shower-bath on frequent occasions. Some redress can be achieved with stake and string, but there's a limit to that. The last thing you want is for the bamboo to look trussed up. In winter, this bamboo looks threadbare but in spring, the best treatment is to cut out every cane that is more than one season old. The last season's canes will still be without leaves, but they are smooth and olive green and, without the weight of foliage, they stand up and look beautiful in a quite unexpected way, when the pruning has been completed. After twenty-five years or so, mine, which was a seedling given me by a friend whose own plant had flowered and died, itself flowered and died. But it left self-sown offspring, so I am well away with the next generation.

## Autumn features

The sharp smell of October is most attractive and is largely created, I imagine, by drifts of fallen leaves. I never tire of scuffling through them. Unless the leaves are seriously shading plants that need to see the light, we are in no hurry to pick them up and take them, as we eventually do, to spread around rhododendrons as a moisture-retaining mulch. We wait for the wind to blow them into sheltered corners, from where they will the more easily be gathered. Another reason for autumn's smell must surely be the abundance of fruiting fungi. I always hope that there will be worthwhile crops of mushrooms in our meadows. Now that these have been mown, the mushroom caps gleam from a distance. The best chance of a crop is when rains follow drought, but it needs to stay mild, too. Often, rain is followed by cold weather.

Principal leaf-fall starts in the last week and the ash trees are among the earliest to shed. Their leaf stalks make a companionable tapping as they hit the tiles of the potting shed roof. We've still a lot of propagating to get through, including soft cuttings of bedding plants like verbenas and gazanias. There's not much top fruit to pick. The only mature apple tree is that of 'High Canons', a fairly small, light yellow cooker. It keeps till March. We inherited three trees of this and when they seemed near to a state of collapse, I budded one on to young stock and that is our tree.

The handsome espalier pear against the solar chimney breast is a cooker. Unfortunately its name has been lost but it is well worth gathering and will be ripe next month. The dogs adore its fallen fruit and gorge on them and on any other pear. They make the girls extremely overweight and I have no control over their diet until the last of the wild pear's fruit has fallen, in December.

We usually get some sort of a crop from the much-neglected 'Comice' pears, grown as espaliers in the high garden. Each pear is stored in a plastic lettuce bag (with air vents in it) and shrivelling is thereby prevented.

There is an abundance of vegetables, with summer saladings going on well into the month, as well as French beans, if I have kept them well picked. I'm not in a hurry to touch the sprouts or leeks; a November to April season is long enough to be eating them. But the bulbous fennel is often good, now, and in the cooler weather is far less inclined to bolt.

We lift our maincrop 'Pink Fir Apple' potatoes, hoping for dry weather in which to do the job so that the tubers can be stored (in a bin, made for the purpose) with little mud attached. Sometimes, if we have been unable to ward off the dreaded blight with our protective sprays, we have to lift in September. 'Pink Fir Apple' is an old variety of waxy texture, excellent for general purposes as well as in salads, but no use for mashing. I buy King Edward's for that – I don't grow them because floury potatoes are the norm; waxy types are hard to find in the shops. Our potatoes last us well into spring. They are a weird sausage shape, often with knobs on them, and most easily peeled immediately after cooking.

The autumn raspberries will go on cropping for most of the month, until gales blow all the berries off.

With luck and a steady man on the job, we shall complete the yew hedge clipping, and that will enable them to retain their sharp, architectural outlines for the next seven months, before they start growing again.

Pear 'Doyenné du Comice'

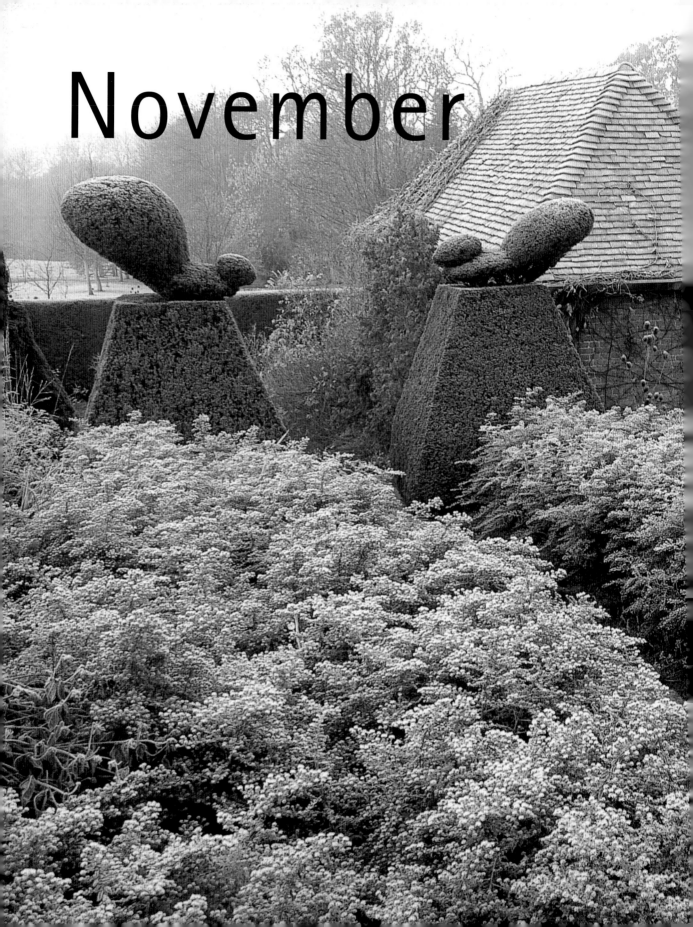

November

The month of November, in my part of the world, is widely reviled. The clocks have gone back, the days are rapidly shortening, it rains (wettest month of the year), it blows or else it settles down into gloomy fogs.

Why is it that people so often remember only the weather's worst features? It seems to be a kind of self-pity. 'This is the life I am expected to endure,' they seem to be saying. The brighter days are totally ignored and forgotten. November can be a month of largely beautiful weather. I remember the one when we were having our huge barn roof re-tiled. The task had had to await our being closed to the public; hence the choice of this unpropitious moment. I took photographs of work in progress and they were invariably backed by blue skies. There wasn't a hitch. Good weather in November is not as rare as you think. Start making daily notes on it and you will see that I am right.

## Work and more work

But it is apt to be a month of panic stations. Now that we at last have the place to ourselves, there is a tremendous amount of garden work to catch up on. Threat of frost is imminent (sometimes, to be honest, frost comes as something of a relief; absence of frost may make you feel that you'd be a brute to tear the summer bedding to pieces just yet). In respect of some of the contents of the exotic garden, we were already becoming twitchy before the end of October. Crises have a way of arriving at weekends, when there is least help around to rush plants into protection ahead of a frost warning.

So, already, we will have housed the tender succulents and the evergreen begonias – varieties that are not normally let out of glass protection anyway. Streptocarpus will have been taken in, too. Now it is the turn of all the other winter-tender plants. We are not in a hurry with cannas and dahlias, which are actually easier to deal with once limp and black. Their roots will be safe enough, kept waiting. But they will have been housed in the cellar by the end of the month, or soon after.

The exotic garden takes on the appearance of a shell-scarred battlefield, full of unfilled holes where plants were removed and Fergus, or whoever, didn't look back over his shoulder to assess the scene he had created and level it off a bit. No time for such niceties (until I protest).

We cut down male fern fronds before they have withered, because we need them as protection to plants that will not be housed, notably the bananas, *Musa basjoo*. They are wrapped into a thick fern overcoat. It will sink a little, after a few weeks, and need to be topped up so that the banana's snout continues to be protected.

Cannas and dahlias are boxed up into old potting soil, so that their tubers or rhizomes are the better able to remain plump, not drying right out. Now and again, through the winter, they are visited and given a watering. Their cellar does have a little

PAGES 200–201 Frost in the peacock garden, with topiary, grasses and hedges of
*Aster lateriflorus* 'Horizontalis'

heating running through it, I am glad to say, since I have to live above it and there are airy cracks between the oak floorboards.

There is all the spring bedding to do, and spring bedding also includes early summer bedding with lupins, aquilegias, verbascums, foxgloves, sweet rocket, anchusas, sweet williams and perennial dianthus grown as biennials. There are carpeters like double daisies, doronicums and various types of wallflowers, as well as the self-sown forget-me-nots which we move around.

I have to admit that the weather, as well as the day length, can be most unco-operative, but Fergus has a system of laying out boards to stand on when planting, so that the planter's weight is distributed and does not hopelessly poach the ground where he has stood. The ideal is to clear away the summer bedding and replant all in one swoop, if not in one day. You will find that the ground under the old bedding is always friable and reasonably dry, until this cover is removed. If you can immediately fork it over and plant, conditions will be ideal. But woe betide if you fork over and have no daylight left to do the planting. Sure as fate, it will rain overnight and all those air spaces that have been created will fill with water like a sponge. If it was a frost that threatened, you could at least cover the ground, overnight, with hessian or tarpaulin, so as not to have to wait for a thaw the next morning before planting can be resumed.

Some of next year's bedding can be moved in very simply. Things like sweet williams and foxgloves have fibrous roots and are easily handled. But members of the Cruciferae family have rather sparse, thick roots, off which their surrounding soil is only too ready to drop, leaving the roots exposed and liable to dry – even in November. This is notably the case with wallflowers, moved from their rows in the open ground, and we may have to water them in. The month embraces the possibility of every sort of weather.

Ice in November to carry a duck,
Rest of the winter all sludder and muck.

You simply cannot judge what weather the winter is likely to have in store from anything experienced in November.

## Bulbs

Immense numbers of bulbs need to be planted – the majority, tulips. We sorted our own tulips over during the summer, separating those that looked large enough to flower next spring from those that didn't. The latter get rowed out to grow on, but often have to wait till December. Tulips are forgiving; you can keep them waiting and as long as they've been in a cool place and haven't sprouted unduly, no harm results.

We shall have ordered and received a whole lot more tulips, the larger quantities for our bedding projects. First the carpeters are planted; then the tulips are all set out in their positions for planting (the bulbs having first been rolled in a fungicidal powder to protect them from botrytis). The actual planting is very quick, using a narrow trowel. We only plant a couple of inches or so deep. There's no point in going deeper. The best soil is near the surface. So we just lever the soil to one side, pop the bulb in and there you are, one every five seconds or so, which allows for moving your own position.

We also think of places where we can plant tulips among perennials. And then there are the ones that will be grown for display in large containers. Michael sets the containers out for me and the bulbs are handy in the packing/selling shed, so I place each bag (he can gauge how many bulbs to use out of it) in the container that I should like to have them in.

There are narcissi, hyacinths and crocuses, too. The narcissi should really be planted first, ideally in September, as they become active early, but they still have to wait. Shoots on the Paperwhites are often quite long before we get around to them, but the problem with them is to hold them back till Christmas or later, not how to bring them on. Once they are potted, I keep them cool as I dare, short of allowing them to be frosted.

Most of these bulbs, in their display pots, go into a cold frame and all we need to do is to cover them with glass, if the weather is wet or frosty, but to remember not to leave them covered for so long that they dry out. Although not forced, this slight protection tends to bring them into flower noticeably earlier than those planted outside.

Some bulbs we'll use for naturalizing. At last, but often not till November, the ground is soft enough to enable us to use the bulb planter easily and quickly. This wonderful old tool, which we have had since before World War I, has a long shaft so that fifty or a hundred plugs of turf can be extracted at a time, before the hands-and-knees operation of actual planting. I am careful to remove plugs in a random fashion, with different intervals between each hole made. Otherwise you find that you have planted in straight lines. Neither do you want to plant in circles.

Our clay soil has virtually no stones in it, so there is no undue resistance to operating the planter, nor undue wear on it. I have a large trugful of old potting soil and put some of that into the bottom of each hole before planting the bulb, after which the top half of a plug, which includes the best soil, is pushed on top of the bulb. It all goes pretty quickly. Unused divots are collected up and used to fill unwanted holes and hollows.

## Other tasks

The prairie, whose American contents flower and set seed late, may not be cut until November and that is the only cut it will receive, so we like to make it tight and thorough. Really wet weather can make this a difficult task. I have known Fergus do it with a scythe, which he loves to use, but on the whole he has to admit that machinery does the job more quickly.

We give the front path area, the upper moat and the orchard final cuts, which

Autumn colour by the lower moat

encourages fine turf and provides an almost lawn-like background for the short-stemmed snowdrops and crocuses that will be flowering early next year. Daffodils will already be showing through this month, so we want to cut the orchard, in particular, before that happens. As usual, all the grass that's cut is gathered up and removed for composting.

We can start the winter digging as soon as plots where we grew on the bedding or where there were summer vegetable crops have been vacated. Some awkward vegetables, like beetroot, which I don't want to lift, have to be dug around if they are in the middle of an otherwise vacated plot. There is an art, which we have yet

*Mahonia* x *media* 'Lionel Fortescue'

fully to learn, about growing our vegetables so that those that will be cleared at the end of summer are separated from ground-keepers, which will remain till the next spring. Beetroot is principally a summer crop, but I like to leave the uneaten roots till the spring, using their young, sprouting shoots as spring greens. In a hard winter, they get killed, and I might as well not have bothered, but you can't tell about that in advance.

We dig rough, turning over large clods which frost breaks down, but first we dress the ground liberally with our own compost, most of which was made from grass taken off the meadow areas. Gourds (and cucumbers, long since finished) will have been grown on the old heaps. When their foliage has been wind-blasted, you can the better see what your crop is and it'll not now be too late to collect and use it (for ornament), so long as there's not been a frost.

In the house, I'm back in my winter quarters and can enjoy fires again. The wood cut last winter will have been fetched out in September, before the ground got soft and slimy. A huge stack of it is made close to where it'll be sawn and stored, under cover. There isn't always time to store it all, in which case I receive some pretty wet stuff in my fireplaces, but it is only externally wet. The sap will mostly have dried out during the summer, which is the main thing. My first fires will be using wood left over from two winters ago. That burns like tinder. It is extravagant but gives out terrific heat with the minimum of effort in.

## Autumnal autumn

Most talk of the autumn garden centres on the notion that there should be conflagrations of foliage and, to a lesser extent, berry colour, such as brings hordes of visitors to Sheffield Park gardens (thirty-five miles from me) and other semi-woodland gardens, several of which are located in Sussex.

Such has never been my aim at Dixter which, with its formal design, was not intended to flaunt the arboreal treasures of Japan and the USA. However, if a plant, shrub or tree colours, as well as giving me other kinds of pleasure, that is a bonus. In any case, even on the basis of the sort of gentle colours that our native flora puts on, autumn cannot help being colourful in its own way.

Oaks take on their russet hues well into the month. They overhang the lower moat and on quiet days you hear the plop of their ripe acorns as they drop into the water. Field maples turn bright yellow. When my thoughts are unfocused, I have often mistaken such a maple for a flowering broom. I grow two Japanese maples and they seem to like me well enough. *Acer palmatum* 'Senkaki' is the freshest imaginable green in spring. It now changes to clear yellow and then, as its leaves fall, reveals the pink colouring of its young twigs. That pays its rent several times over. Then, the compact and upright *A.p.* 'Shishigashira'. I fell for that seeing it over many years in Alan Roger's garden at Dundonnell, in Wester Ross. Its jagged leaves are crimped, almost parsley-like and dark green, but they colour up quite late in autumn. I grow it in the barn garden and it doesn't seem out of place.

I have never got on well with rowans. I do grow some but they are pretty stiff in habit, not a bit like those you see in the north. 'Joseph Rock', for instance: its leaves flare up to perfection, for a week or so, and it sometimes carries crops (soon eaten) of its deep yellow berries, but the tree as a tree has none of the voluptuous freedom of habit that I have admired in Perthshire. But there are other pleasures.

Our mulberry turns yellow. Its leaf-fall can be a tame affair, spread over quite a period, but if a frosty night occurs at the right moment, all its leaves fall within half an hour the next morning, lying as a thick carpet underneath the tree. The medlar never fails. Such a prettily shaped small tree, for a start; its foliage turns warm brown while its fruits, although themselves quite a dark brown, are fascinatingly shaped.

I have the hermaphrodite form of *Celastrus orbiculatus*, a deciduous climber whose weight is taken by a couple of stout chestnut poles as substitutes for the now defunct old pear, which was the first host. Celastrus leaves turn luminous yellow. When fallen, they reveal garlands of ochre-yellow, spherical fruit, which then split, themselves, to reveal scarlet seeds. Pick them quickly at this stage, before the weather spoils them.

They make admirable winter decoration.

Another hermaphrodite in my garden, self-pollinating and requiring no deliberate mating, is a butcher's broom, *Ruscus aculeatus*. This is quite a low, mildly suckering evergreen shrub with dark green, sharply pointed foliage. Its large, crimson berries are freely borne in most years. They look amazing when struck by winter sunshine and last through to late spring the next year.

The wild pear loses most of its leaves around 10 November. If there have not been strong winds, it will now, on bare, loaded branches, be hung with bright yellow fruit. This fruit is quite small and often not recognized as a pear's, because almost globular and without the usual pyriform neck.

*Ilex* x *altaclerensis* 'Golden King', a virtually prickle-free holly with foliage broadly margined in yellow, makes a column at the top of the long border. It is a great feature at every season, but even more so than usual now that it has ripened its red berries. For, despite its masculine name, this is a female clone. Birds usually set about it just before I want to pick some for the Christmas pudding, although in another year, the berries will remain untouched, well into spring.

There are self-sown *Cotoneaster horizontalis* all through the garden. This shrub has a wonderful structure, stiff, yet full of curves. It is the perfect support for minor climbers, like the annual *Rhodochiton atrosanguineum*. But it is much more than that. There is usually a plentiful crop of its crimson red-berries and, if the birds have spared these, they contrast with the near magenta colouring that the foliage takes on late in the month. Dormancy is brief; new foliage is already expanding in February.

A grouping that I particularly enjoy at this season is on the lower terrace. I can sit to admire it on the low retaining wall that is raised at this point to just the right height for sitting and contemplating and purring at the feel of low sunshine on your back. There is the oak-leaved *Hydrangea quercifolia*, whose purplish autumn colouring takes ages to mature. On its left and behind, a great rounded bush ivy, the adult manifestation of variegated *Hedera canariensis* 'Gloire de Marengo'. It flowers very late and is now smothered in globular umbels of ivy blossom. Sometimes frost will interrupt the display; usually not. At the back, 1.8m/6ft *Miscanthus sinensis* 'Strictus', my favourite zebra grass, is still lively with striped foliage.

Another member of the ivy family that flowers in November is *Fatsia japonica*, now presented, as it were, in the wall garden by the dachshund mosaic in front. The fatsia is a very large, bold evergreen shrub, made almost frivolous by its panicles of white flower umbels. Near by is its hybrid with ivy, x *Fatshedera lizei*, whose main point is its lustrous foliage but that too is having a go at flowering.

A surprising number of evergreens change colour at this season. My most conspicuous example is the softly textured conifer *Chamaecyparis thyoides* 'Ericoides'

*Fatsia japonica*

(1.5m/5ft), of which I have planted two together. They are naturally cone-shaped and coloured sea green in summer. But they now rapidly change to deep purple, which looks dramatic behind a planting of pale ever-grey *Helichrysum splendidum*, whose upright spikes form an apron in front. The conifer starts to lose this colouring and to return to green as early as January, whatever the weather, which seems strange. To its right, *Thuja occidentalis* 'Rheingold' takes on richer, burnished golden hues than usual, sometimes so deep as to look in danger of dying. But all is well.

## Mahonias and company

The mahonia that I grow which turns purple in winter is *Mahonia* 'Undulata'. The leaf surface is polished but curved as well, so it catches the light at different angles. The one that I should really like to succeed with is the American *M. nervosa*, which is low-

growing and suckers, when happy. Its leaves are long and narrow — beautiful at all seasons but amazing when richly bronzed in winter. It is apt to be tricky in cultivation and I have failed once, but with Fergus at the helm shall try again. An open, leafy woodland soil and part shade is the prescription for success. A pity I haven't woodland, nor a woodland soil, but then all gardening is a simulation. We deceive the plants and we beguile ourselves.

Some of the flowering mahonias make their mark just now, putting on a surprisingly colourful display in friendly yellows. Best for its foliage is *M. lomariifolia* — a long leaf with numerous in-curving leaflets. None of its hybrids can match it in this respect, but it is distinctly tender and I have it in front of the apricot and its south-west-facing wall. The clustered flower strands are upright and so is the shrub's habit. I prune it back quite often and quite hard in spring, as I do the others. Beside it is *M. japonica*, which is a not very striking shrub but has lemon-yellow flowers over a long season, only just starting, and with a powerful lily-of-the-valley fragrance. The crosses between these two species are classified as *M. x media*. They are all showier than their parents, hardier than *M. lomariifolia*, having good foliage but little or none of the lily-of-the-valley scent. I have three of them. 'Lionel Fortescue' is the first to flower and at its best this month. It makes a large shrub and its upright flower bunches look great if you can see them against a blue sky. Honey bees love to visit them; there's little other forage for them, by now. 'Buckland' comes on a little later and its flower strands are borne more horizontally. 'Winter Sun' is a newcomer, already in bloom.

Another predominantly autumn-flowering shrub is the endearing, if insignificant, *Buddleja auriculata*, with panicles of tiny, buff-white flowers and wafting as generously as did *B. davidii* in summer. *B. auriculata* is evergreen and its foliage has none of the generally accepted buddleia coarseness. It will grow to 3.6m/12ft on a warm wall and does require wall protection. Its habit is mildly suckering; even if a harsh winter cuts it to the ground, it will return from suckers, once truly established.

Flowering grasses are very good in November, although the cultivars, already mentioned, of *Molinia caerulea* suddenly disintegrate. One of the best is the late but regularly flowering *Panicum virgatum* 'Rubrum' (1.2m/4ft), with open-textured panicles and a reddish tinge. That lasts a long while.

Of almost spring-like freshness is the foliage, produced quite late in the season, of the polypody fern, *Polypodium interjectum* 'Cornubiense', of which I wrote in January, and that is seen beside the very newest leaves of another long-season performer, *Arum italicum* 'Pictum'. Yet we can expect our first hoar frost, too, and that makes the aster hedges look as though they are flowering a second time. November is a month of all seasons and a reminder that the year is a cycle, without beginning or end.

The horse pond in autumn

December

All the peoples of the temperate northern hemisphere celebrate the turning of the year and the passing of its shortest day, in December. Our excuses for celebration may be Christian or pagan or associated with some other religion, but whatever they are the break is welcome. Hope palpably lies ahead as the evenings begin to lengthen. True, we are only in the first month of winter and its worst discomforts and worries lie ahead, but winter has its saving graces and the gardener is well aware of them.

I refer to early December as the phoney winter, as the season seldom shows its teeth till later on. In fact, there are often a whole lot of reminders of summer flowers, which can be included in bunches to bring indoors.

We shall still be desperately catching up, in these early weeks, with many tulip bulbs to find places for. The last of them get lined out in a spare plot. These are usually the smallest, for growing on to use in the borders a year later, but some are of flowering size and come in for handy picking, to include in mixed bunches.

*Cotoneaster horizontalis* continues its dazzling display for the first ten days, while *Spiraea thunbergii* puts on a final act. The female *Skimmia japonica* has clusters of large crimson berries which will last through the winter, untouched by birds. My plant is self-sown and cramped between paving stones. It is also in full sun, which doesn't really suit its best health, so its foliage is yellowish. But, as its growth is now slow, the berries show up all the better, not being much concealed by the young shoots of the previous season.

Anything that flowers outdoors now is sure to be extensively written about in the gardening press. There is so little competition. Two of the main shrub protagonists, this month, are the Chinese witch hazel, *Hamamelis mollis*, and wintersweet, *Chimonanthus praecox*. As shrubs, both are pretty boring in the summer and that goes for a number of others of these winter-flowerers, so they are scattered around the garden, where they can be absorbed by their neighbours in the summer. This would not be possible if they were all gathered together in a winter garden, visible from the sitting room or the kitchen, as is frequently recommended. If I want to enjoy them at close quarters (and I do), I pick them and bring them in.

Our oldest wintersweet must date back to 1920, or thereabouts. It was given to my mother by our neighbours. Not knowing its ways, she thought it a dead loss as it did not flower for the first six years or so. This is normal, in seedlings, but once they do start they never fail. However, they do need plenty of sun heat to ripen their wood and coax them into setting flower buds. We have several plants, now, one of them a brighter, cleaner shade of yellow than the others, which are dingily coloured, but the scent's the thing – a wonderful spicy aroma on the air. First blooms

PAGES 212–213  *Mahonia* x *media* 'Buckland'
in front of Big Dick
LEFT  Some grasses hold us in good stead in winter:
*Calamagrostis* x *acutiflora* 'Karl Foerster', *Cortaderia selloana*
'Pumila' and a *Miscanthus sinensis* cultivar

normally open late November, a peak being reached at the turn of the year.

By the end of January, nothing is normally left and it is the same with the witch hazel. This, too, has a delicious, spicy fragrance, best enjoyed indoors. The flowers (unlike wintersweet) are amazingly frost-hardy. Our two specimens were given us in the 1930s, considering which they are by no means enormous, partly, maybe, because I raid them for flowering branches so heavily. Their rounded, hazel-like leaves are liable to a marginal leaf scorch, in summer, but we correct this with wood ash applied to them from my winter fires. I also have a young plant (too young to pick from, alas) of *H.* x *intermedia* 'Pallida', which is a lighter, brighter shade of yellow and has longer petals. It is much the showiest of the witch hazels. I know the red-flowered kinds have their advocates, but it is a pretty muted sort of red with little garden impact and I don't really see the point, unless you're making a collection.

Branches of wintersweet are especially welcome for bringing indoors, though their spicy fragrance is soon lost if kept in a warm room. Witch hazel needs to be coaxed a little, but only a little, to have it in flower for Christmas. Picking it ten days beforehand will certainly do the trick. I would far rather have that than silver or gold glitter on teazel heads. Wands of winter jasmine buds, *Jasminum nudiflorum*, are at their readiest to open, this month; such a cheerful shade of yellow.

*Prunus* x *subhirtella* 'Autumnalis Rosea' has a long and broken season, greatly affected by weather. If the winter is prolonged and cold, it may not be at its best till March, but in most years it reaches its peak in mid-December. That, of course, is a must for picking. My specimen, dating back to 1940 or thereabouts, has only just been dismissed and I made sure, before that happened, that I had a strong youngster, struck from a cutting off the old tree, with which to replace it. The original was a standard, which is normal, but makes it unnecessarily difficult to plunder for branches to bring indoors. Most of them are within the reach only of a long-arm pruner. The replacement will be a bush and therefore far more accessible. It may make a multi-stemmed tree in course of time. I don't want every tree to be on a leg.

Frosts become more frequent as the month progresses, but there are far longer periods when the horse pond is unfrozen and can reflect the plants around it, notably the dogwoods. Now that the old waterlily pads are vanishing, we can enjoy a far larger surface area of water and the pond seems twice itself, especially as it is full to its

ABOVE Wintersweet, *Chimonanthus praecox*
RIGHT *Cotoneaster horizontalis* with a female *Skimmia japonica*

overflow. This is a very large pipe, installed by my father, which takes excess water underground right across the garden and down to the lower moat, on our boundary.

Skeletons of ornamental grasses play a large role in the December garden, especially the various cultivars of *Miscanthus sinensis*. Best and most persistent of the lot, however, are the clustered stair-rods of *Calamagrostis* x *acutiflora* 'Karl Foerster'. Pale and luminous even in the darkest weather.

December could be as dreary a month as January, but the festive season prevents this and provides a much-needed break. Even the weeds understand the rules; their growth has almost come to a standstill. But the forward pulse of the year is evident from week to week, if not from day to day. The much-loved garden, all that's new in it and all that's old, is barely marking time and we are ready to steer it forward into another year.

Whatever happens after me, I should like to record my hope that no one, for lack of personal creativity, will fall back on the old cliché of recreating this, that or the other with the same plants that Christopher Lloyd used and in the same way. We have too many fossilized gardens around already. I realize that there are not so very many inspired gardeners in the world, but they do exist and I should like to think of one or other of them having a good time at Dixter for many years to come.

# Index

Page numbers in *italic* refer to captions.

All plants without hardiness zone – 'Z' – ratings are annuals or tender perennials that are treated as annuals, or they appear only in a photograph.

# Acknowledgments

## Author's Acknowledgments

In dealing with proofs, captions, the order of photographs and all matters pertaining to putting this bed to bed, my closest friend and head gardener, Fergus Garrett, has been my greatest ally. It was he whom the publishers approached when in a state of panic, not me.

Jonathan Buckley has been a wonderful photographer, visiting every month for the past six years. As a result, there were at least twice the number of photographs we should have liked to include, had not the price of doing so been prohibitive.

The publishers have been sympathetic to my demands and have always been pleasant to work with, albeit themselves demanding.

## Publisher's Acknowledgments

The publishers would like to thank Marie Lorimer for the index and Sophie Lynch for her help.

*Project Editor* Jo Christian
*Text Editor* Sarah Mitchell
*Managing Art Editor* Jo Grey
*Art Editor* Prue Bucknall
*Editorial Assistance* Tom Windross
*Production* Hazel Kirkman

*Picture Editor* Anne Fraser
*Editorial Director* Kate Cave
*Art Director* Caroline Hillier

Achive photographs on pages 7 and 10 courtesy of Christopher Lloyd

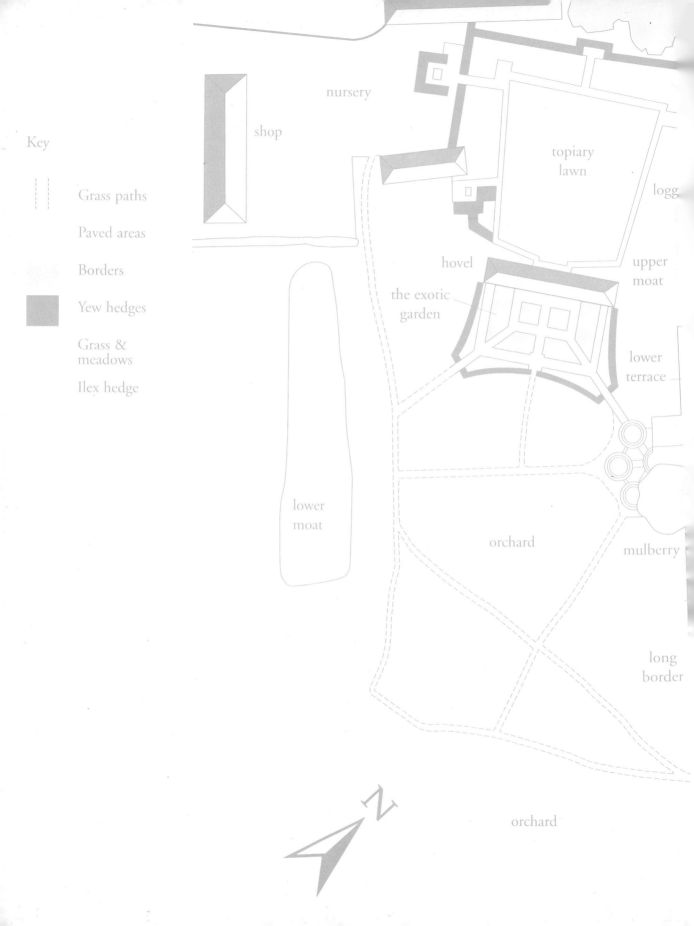

Key

Grass paths

Paved areas

Borders

Yew hedges

Grass & meadows

Ilex hedge

nursery

shop

topiary lawn

logg

hovel

the exotic garden

upper moat

lower terrace

lower moat

orchard

mulberry

long border

orchard

N